1993

Social analysis of edi

Critical Social Thought

Series editor: Michael W. Apple
Professor of Curriculum and Instruction and of Educational Policy
Studies, University of Wisconsin-Madison

Already published

Social analysis of education

After the new sociology

Philip Wexler

Routledge
New York and London

For permission to reprint extracts from the following copyrighted material, grateful acknowledgment is made to: Bergin & Garvey, for Wexler, Martusewicz and Kern, 'Popular Educational Politics'; Routledge & Kegan Paul, for Wexler, 'Structure, Text and Subject'; to Croom Helm and Len Barton for Wexler, 'Organizing the Unconscious' and 'Movement, Class and Education'; to *Interchange* for Wexler, 'Ideology and Education'; to Philip Altbach, for Wexler, 'Social Change and Education'; to Rachel Sharp for Wexler and Grabiner, 'The Education Question'; and to Sage, for Wexler, 'Ideology and Utopia in American Sociology of Education.'

First published in 1987

Paperback published in 1990 by
Routledge, an imprint of
Routledge, Chapman and Hall, Inc.
29 West 35th Street, New York, NY 10001

Published in Great Britain by
Routledge
11 New Fetter Lane
London EC4P 4EE

Library of Congress Cataloging in Publication Data

Wexler, Philip.
  Social analysis of education.

  (Critical social thought)
  Bibliography: p.
  Includes index.
  1. Educational sociology. 2. Sociology.
I. Title. II. Series.
LC191.W499 1987 370.19   87-9554

ISBN 0-7100-9964-9 (HB)
ISBN 0-415-90340-8 (PB)
British Library CIP Data also available

Contents

Series editor's introduction

Over the past two decades, radical traditions in both the sociology of education and curriculum studies have drawn upon each other to build a critical analysis of education. They have focused increasingly on the complicated relationship between curriculum, teaching, and evaluation in schools and the structures of inequality in the larger society. What has come to be called the 'new sociology of education' – a term that serves as an umbrella for a wide array of political, conceptual, and research tendencies – has made considerable progress in moving primarily from an emphasis on the connections between schooling and the reproduction of such inequalities to a recognition of the contradictory roles education plays in a social formation.[1] Even with such important changes in perspective, however, a guiding thread behind this work continues to be a concern with culture and ideology. At first, this meant that critical scholars in these traditions attempted to link the knowledge that was taught in schools to the relations of power and control in society. School knowledge was ideological knowledge.

The interest in ideology critique can be seen in a statement by Michael F.D. Young in his well-known volume, *Knowledge and Control*, 'Those in positions of power will attempt to define what is taken as knowledge, how accessible to different groups any knowledge is, and what are accepted relationships between different knowledge areas and between those who have access to them and make them available.'[2] Thus, school knowledge is not neutral and its role in education is bound up in relations of domination. This is obviously what might be called a relativizing program, a program that has provided the roots upon which even the increasingly sophisticated new work on the relationship between culture, economy, the state and education rests.

Historically, this program of analysis has been critically important in enabling us to examine the place of our formal institutions of education – and the curricular and teaching policies and practices within them – in the cultural and economic reproduction of class, gender and race relations. It has also been very productive in illuminating the ways in which concrete groups of people contest such relations of inequality. However, on both a conceptual and a political level, a relativizing program is paradoxical. For if knowledge is related to one's social position, to power and control, doesn't that hold true for one's own position as well? While the 'new sociologists of education' have often successfully shown many of the connections between ideology and school life, shouldn't their own position be subjected to the same rigorous criticism? This is where *Social Analysis of Education* begins.

In essence, Wexler relativizes the relativizers, by showing the social locations from which their own positions emerged. This has been attempted before, but never in such great detail.[3] His aim is not to dismiss the contributions that have arisen from the critical community within sociology of education. After all, he has had a place in building this community. Rather, he wants to point out the limits of its conceptual apparatus, limits that must be transcended if such critical work is to make a real difference.

Wexler argues that, even with all its insight, the new sociology of education did not understand itself. It did not recognize its own expression as part of a cultural and class movement. While having a positive moment, in, for example, freeing educators from the misguided faith that education always leads to increased equality, the new sociology needs to be seen in another, less positive way. It is part of 'the cultural formation of an identifiable social group which is engaged in socio-cultural action on its own behalf.' That is, the new sociology of education was in part an ideological form of the new middle class and was filled with the contradictory tensions of that class fraction. It represented an ambivalent professionalism, one that had contradictory and ambivalent attitudes toward leftist social movements and toward academic and professional status. In the process, it displaced its politics from the struggles of social movements in the larger society to the domain of theoretical debates in the academy. While fortifying its academic position by focusing on theories of reproduction and resistance, it was unable to deal with specific historical transformations such as the new right.

This inability to deal adequately with such new social movements actually prevents our understanding of the role education can play in social transformation. The main currents in the new sociology of education, in Wexler's words, function as a *discursive blockage*, not allowing new ways of thinking about knowledge and power to evolve.

What has happened because of this? 'Left professional middle class institutional intellectuals became a socially residual remnant, rather than the institutional vanguard of an ascendant social class segment.' The residual quality of their position is no more visible than in their attempts to move beyond simple reproduction theories to theories of contradiction and resistance. Progress has been made, to be sure, but at the expense of misrecognizing many of the emergent social and ideological tendencies in our society.

The view of education as largely reproducing societal structures of inequality, to be sure in a relatively autonomous and contradictory way, is not always inaccurate. In times of relative social stability it has more than a small measure of truth about the relationship between class and education. However, in times of social crisis it is simply insufficient. Metaphors of cultural and economic reproduction are too static, too limited, to capture the dynamics of restructuring that are currently emerging.

> If . . . the maintenance of ruling classes is accomplished not by the transmission of deep false consciousness – cultural reproduction – but instead by redefining the very meaning of schooling and restructuring the institutional relation between schools and other aspects of the social formation, then the theoretical and political questions are different. Efforts of ruling classes are aimed toward accomplishing their hegemony not only by the imposition of their culture as fact. Rather, classes rule through the work of accomplishing social reorganizations. During social crisis, these efforts at reorganization are intensified and become more apparent. It becomes easier during such times to begin instead with the assumption that the accomplishment of class hegemony requires not simply economic and cultural domination, but constant social reorganization and restructuring.

What are these reorganizing and restructuring tendencies? The extension of the commodification process into nearly all areas of social life and the growth of corporatist structures are among the forces now acting to reorganize education.[4] This is most obvious in the pressures on education generated by the rightist conservative restoration.

The attempt by the right to become hegemonic is seen culturally and economically in the 'restoration of "traditional" values and social relations' and the intense pressure to reorganize public institutions around the interests of market capital and the logic of commodification. These do not stand alone. They are embodied in and are the concrete expressions of large-scale social movements, social movements that first look to undercut and dismantle what has been taken both as the common culture and as the accepted public means of school finance and then seek to reintegrate school curricula and school finance within these movements' own principles of 'cultural restoration' and the reassertion of capital.[5] What Wexler calls the *marketization of education* is one result. The public is evil; the private and the market are now virtuous. An idealized family and fundamentalist religious ideologies act to legitimate this marketization and partly humanize it.

Wexler's analysis of such commodifying tendencies, especially his discussion of marketization, extends and then goes considerably beyond my own analysis of this process in *Education and Power*.[6] His ability to link these rightist social movements to other movements that sponsor the growth of procedures for rationalizing curricula, teaching, and evaluation and then to connect both sets of movements to the larger restructuring of education around the commodity exchange process makes his points even more insightful.

Social Analysis of Education devotes a good deal of space to tracing out the growth and effects of these commodifying tendencies and processes of reorganization. In so doing, it is also called upon to examine some of the other major aspects of the critical tradition in education that have sought to deal with these effects. For example, Wexler criticizes the logic behind much of the critical or Marxist-oriented ethnographic research in education. In many ways, such research simply reproduces in transfigured form the qualitative correlational approaches of conventional sociological studies. A new 'variable,' school knowledge, is simply plotted against a series of differences in social attributes such as social class. However, in employing this logic, these ethnographies tacitly provide ideological support on another level for the commodification of education, even when they may be overtly opposed to such a process. They too remain caught in the dominant cultural ideals and practices.

The same critical scrutiny is given to the emerging theoretical literature on 'critical pedagogy.' The social effects of these abstract theories are also hidden from their practitioners; but these effects can be just as damaging as those tacitly within the logic of critical ethnographies. These effects include the continued distancing of new sociologists from residual and emergent social movements, replacing the specifics of a genuinely political education with generalities that only serve academic purposes, and the steady demise of any more complete social understanding that would inhibit the flight from the real history and real politics of concrete groups of people.

What should replace the theories of reproduction and resistance, the models of objectivist research that are hidden so deeply even in qualitative inquiry, and such decontexualized critical pedagogies? We must first reconnect theory, research, and practice to historical movements in society and education. Drawing upon Wolin's work, Wexler makes the point that 'Many of the great theories of the past arose in response to a crisis in the world, not in the community of theorists.' This would require seeing society as a whole as the *product* of historical collective action. But this is not all. Knowledge itself must be seen as a process of transformation. It is the result of concrete human activity which is socially patterned. Thus, both society and knowledge are de-reified, in essence de-commodified. Only in this way can we relate education and school knowledge to a more thoroughgoing analysis of class consciousness and class formation and only in this way can we overcome the limitations of what has been taken for granted by the new sociologists of education and by curriculum scholars.

Specifically, Wexler turns to life history, the new politics of knowledge and identity of French feminism, literary criticism, semiotics, and structuralist theories to demonstrate how struggles over identity, discourse, language, meaning, and knowledge can herald broader social movements that could be emancipatory in intent and practice. The study of these areas and a recognition of how the formation of class and subjectivity works through 'symbolic movements for knowledge and identity' can lead to a rearticulation of the connection between educational politics and social analysis.

This is one of the most significant claims of the book. It argues for a major overturning of the conceptual underpinnings of any culturally interesting sociology of education. In brief, this position implies that symbolic and literary theories – *not* necessarily the previous social theories the field has relied upon – constitute the basis for a new critical social theory of education, in large part because their very aim is to uncover the social practice of significance. They are responses to the question of how meaning is produced, a question that must be central to the study of education. This is a crucial point according to Wexler, since in this society significatory or knowledge practices have become of prime import.[7] Furthermore, unlike the traditions which guided the new sociology of education, literary and symbolic theories are not backward-looking but forward-looking, not residual but emergent themselves. *They already anticipate new forms of social symbolic practice.*

As with a good deal of this volume, this is a claim that is certain to generate controversy. Yet *Social Analysis of Education* directs a significant portion of its energies to demonstrating the potential of theories drawn from these literary traditions. It attempts to show how such approaches (post-structuralism is one example) anticipate in their very form a new politics in society, one in which 'the struggle over the means of producing discourse, over language and the practice of forming discourse, becomes the major locus of social life.' In order to accomplish this, the volume reviews the contributions of Derrida, Barthes, Foucault, Baudrillard, and others. It shows how their theories can help us think more seriously about the practice of collective criticism and collective cultural creation, with education having a critical role to play in such collective action.

Social Analysis of Education is a considerable theoretic achievement. It goes to the very heart of the analytic and political foundations upon which an adequate sociology of education might be based. There are times when Wexler's arguments are meta-theoretical and very abstract, but such foundational work is one of the things so necessary today when critical educational scholarship seems to be increasingly fragmented and to have lost some of its conceptual moorings. Those educational scholars and sociologists who may not see the relevance of such theoretical labor could be reminded of the statement by the noted economist who once remarked that those people who dislike theory, or who claim that they can easily get along without it, are simply in the grip of an older theory.[8]

A number of interesting studies are already showing the power feminist and critical literary theories can have in illuminating the construction of meaning and subjectivity in education.[9] What remains to be done is a synthetic work that provides the conceptual underpinnings for a future sociology of education that places knowledge and identity at its very heart. Philip Wexler has brought us much closer to that goal.

Michael W. Apple
The University of Wisconsin, Madison

NOTES

1 This change can be seen in the conceptual progress made from earlier to later work in this tradition. See, for example, Samuel Bowles and Herbert Gintis, *Schooling in Capitalist America* (New York: Basic Books, 1976), Philip Wexler, *The Sociology of Education: Beyond Equality* (Indianapolis: Bobbs-Merrill, 1976), Michael W. Apple, *Ideology and Curriculum* (Boston and London: Routledge & Kegan Paul, 1979), and Michael W. Apple, *Education and Power* (Boston and London: Routledge & Kegan Paul, Ark Edition, 1985).

2 Michael F.D. Young, 'An Approach to the Study of Curricula as Socially Organized Knowledge,' in *Knowledge and Control*, ed. Michael F.D. Young (London: Collier-Macmillan, 1971), p.32.

3 See Gerald Bernbaum, *Knowledge and Ideology in the Sociology of Education* (London: Macmillan, 1977).

4 Compare this to his provocative analysis of similar tendencies in Philip Wexler, *Critical Social Psychology* (Boston and London: Routledge & Kegan Paul, 1983).

5 I have discussed the implications of these tendencies not only in class but in race and especially gender terms in Michael W. Apple, *Teachers and Texts: A Political Economy of Class and Gender Relations in Education* (Boston and London: Routledge & Kegan Paul, 1987).

6 See Apple, *Education and Power*, especially Chapter 4.

7 For further discussion of this, see Mark Poster, *Foucault, Marxism and History: Mode of Production versus Mode of Information* (Cambridge:

Polity Press, 1984) and the discussion of the role of technical/ administrative knowledge in culture, the state, and the economy in Apple, *Education and Power*.

8 Terry Eagleton, *Literary Theory* (Minneapolis: University of Minnesota Press, 1983), p. vii.

9 See, for example, Linda Christian, 'Becoming a Woman Through Romance,' unpublished Ph.D. thesis, University of Wisconsin, Madison, 1984.

Preface

What I have tried to do in this book is to work through the new sociology of education, in order to help free myself, and hopefully others, from the constraints of its understanding. My aim is to articulate the terms of a 'post' new sociology of education beyond both conventional and radical sociologies. To accomplish that, I interweave intellectual and social history and theoretical re-reading.

Despite the historicist tenor of my analysis, the aim is not to abandon traditions or to insist on an automatic and constant overturning of academic paradigms, but to historicize in order to expand the range of the tools of understanding that are now culturally available to provide a social analysis of education. Rather than sacrifice historical understanding to a wrongly claimed loyalty to present politics and paradigms, I aim toward the ideal of an historically and culturally embedded social analysis.

I work through the sociology of education, historically, culturally and conceptually, only in part to be able to look toward a greater range for the social analysis of education. My other interest is to share my own path in this field; from a critique of the specialized academic discourse of sociology of education, to an engagement with questions of educational practice and research, and then, to a broader rethinking of the social analysis of education, which points toward a new politics.

Acknowledgments

I want to thank my long-time friend and colleague Michael Apple for his continuing professional support and editor's patience. I also thank my doctoral students at the University of Rochester for their teaching and their help. Thanks especially to: Tony Whitson, Emily Moskowitz, Warren Crichlow, Deborah Bart, Rebecca Martusewicz, June Kern, Jeff Lashbrook, Elaine Dannefer, Hyung-yeel Koh, Douglas Noble, and Rubina Saigol. For their invaluable assistance in the production of the manuscript, thanks to Kathryn Murray, Dirk Wilmoth, Hyung-yeel Koh, Susan Ponticello, Margaret Davidson, and Margaret Zaccone.

The University of Rochester has provided me with excellent conditions for work, underlined by an unwavering commitment to academic freedom. For that I thank Robert Sproull, Walter Garms, and more recently, Dennis O'Brien, Brian Thompson and Guilbert Hentschke. Among my stimulating and supportive colleagues in Rochester, I especially want to thank Christopher Lasch and William S. Green, although they rightfully would not wish to be held accountable for my views.

Ilene, Michael and Ari Wexler created the right balance, by expressing both their generous understanding for the special circumstances of writing and their expectations that I carry my part in household labor.

I am grateful to all of them.

Urge and urge and urge
Always the procreant urge of the world.

Walt Whitman

. . . . we want to draw the lesson that nothing is gained by
yearning and tarrying alone, and we shall act differently. We
shall set to work to meet the 'demands of the day', in human
relations as well as in our vocation.

Max Weber

PART ONE
Social analysis and sociology of education

1
Revision

Introduction

The cultural revolution that was expressed early in the student movement and that later appeared in paradigmatic critiques of academic social science has been contained. The form this containment takes is self-congratulatory. The existence of so-called critiques and alternatives gives the aura of transformation and progress within society. In fact, these alternatives operate as blockages to the exploration and realization of deeper differences and changes. The new sociology of education is an asserted example of this dynamic containment. Progressive change and its difference from the 'old' is advertized. But, there are no questions asked that challenge the mode of doing new sociology of education, or that lead to an understanding of it as a particular kind of historical cultural practice. Do we ask: Of what historic movement was new sociology of education a part? Do alternatives work to block reclamation of the larger social aims that first inspired them? Does the legitimacy of alternative paradigms and status of radical academic professionals block perception of new social movements?

The starting point of the social analysis of education that I offer in this book is to criticize the academic alternative of new sociology of education. My criticism is that the new sociology of education is not reflexively historical. It is not understood as part of a cultural and class movement. Without this basic reflexive social understanding, it becomes easy to extract concepts and theories from collective historical movements. I think that has happened in the new sociology of education. My purpose is not simply to perform an ideology critique of the new sociology of education, although that is a valuable devaluation of objectivist pretensions. Ideology critique, however, can become the carping historicism that stops questioning at one's own front door. My aim, rather, is recollective and redemptive: to redeem understanding of the social and historical character of knowledge. With an historical, social grasp, university knowledge can be understood as a collective product. It can become a useful cultural resource for encountering and transforming the social present.

The new sociology of education has a history. I review that history, to loosen the grip of historically reified knowledge that poses as 'new' or 'radical.' I aim to show how the new sociology of education is limited by the horizons, hopes and defenses of earlier times and previous social conflicts. I want to press forward the still unrealized critical analysis that I think was promised by the new sociology of education and remains contained, rather than fully realized in theory and in practice.

New sociology of education

The main tendency in new sociology of education's recent past has been to attack the institutions and culture of liberalism, to criticize its educational concepts and practices. We can see, I think, how the new sociology of education attack on liberalism was part of a broader historical movement which included: conflict of class factions and social groups; cultural boundary shifts; reformulation of professional identities within the academy; and reorganization of educational institutions more generally. The new sociology of education, like other types of university knowledge, belongs to an historically identifiable social group engaged in cultural action on its own behalf. The dilemma that group now faces is whether to continue refining and rationalizing cultural residues of its past that are now institutionalized as legitimate knowledge, or whether instead to look ahead to an uncertain and increasingly polarized future.

My criticism of the new sociology of education is that while it asserted the interested social basis of the old sociology of education, it neglected its own historicity. The new sociologists failed to explore the practical and intellectual relation of their work to the historic developments to which it belonged. New sociology shared with conventional academic knowledge an illusion of sociocultural autonomy. That illusion of autonomy is integral to, and protective of, the academic norm which codes conceptual change only as theoretical advance, rather than as also rationalization of cultural change. This does not mean that there were not important conceptual changes in the social study of education indicated by the rubric 'new sociology of education.'

The new sociologists of education made a particular effective claim to analyze the social construction of meaning and to apply the social theory of knowledge neglected by their predecessors in the old sociology (Young, 1971; Brown, 1974). Symbolic inter-reactionism and various versions of Marxism replaced the liberal old sociology of education's commitment to its central theme of estimating the value of education for social mobility. 'Correspond-ence' (Bowles and Gintis, 1976) and 'reproduction' (Bourdieu and Passeron, 1977; Apple, 1979a) became organizing concepts that proclaimed a less hopeful mood about the social possibilities of education. New sociology of education asserted instead a socially less sanguine theory of the relation between education and society. Drawing on the work of educationists as well as sociologists, gleaning encouragement from a more theoretical mood, new sociology brought into play the Marxism and phenomenology which had been generally excluded from American academic social science. Yet, even in that paradigmatically radical achieve-ment, it already slighted explication of the deeper cultural sources of the critique of liberalism, in Romanticism, and even in historical materialism.

It is a deeper criticism of liberalism that now presses the new sociology of education to awake from the recent respectability it discovered in its role as alternative within the apparatus of social science. But unlike the earlier post-sixties academic radicalism which drove new sociology of education, the deeper criticism, while it has a long social history, has now a different and less direct origin. It seems to arrive at sociology of education from afar, as a result of a kind of discursive status consumerism and academic fashion consciousness. Critique is now applied to sociology of education by borrowing from modern social and cultural theory. But the high status discursive resources that are borrowed as ideas to be applied, are themselves part of a much larger cultural and social transformation that includes the transformation of educa-tional practice.

Incipient changes in educational practice hint at a wider redefinition of, generally, social movements and social theory. The new sociology of education is poised to articulate education's pivotal position in the social transformation and in the redefinition of the relation between social practice, social movement, and social theory. A central motive for my critique of the new sociology of education is to impair its current academic cultural use. For like other social science 'alternatives,' it operates as a blockage to the articulation of the present social transformation.

The new sociology of education achieves this *discursive blockage* by occupying the space allocated to negation and critique. Is the 'old,' 'mainstream' sociology of education liberal and meliorist? Then the 'new' sociology of education announces the pervasiveness of domination. Is the sociology of education obsessed with mobility and status attainment? Then the new sociology discovers as its topic educational knowledge and the reproduction of social classes. Occupying the culturally legitimate space of negation, the alternative academic discourse garners discursive power to itself at the cost of elevating its counter-concepts to the same transhistorical static level as those ideas that it opposes. While it claims to be 'new,' as I will show, new sociology of education actually recoups and repeats the logic and concepts of an earlier time, the time of its origin in opposition. It has the effect of blocking the articulation of a contemporary critical analysis. It does that by assimilating the voices of opposition to its central concepts, but remaining silent about the social and cultural transformation now occurring which changes the very meaning and terms of opposition. The new sociology shares with the old the same *formal* ideology, the same way of thinking and talking about knowledge and about its own utterances. In Foucault's (1970) term, it is part of the same *episteme*. In its cultural form, despite the critique of liberalism, it expresses the same representational realism as old, conventional or mainstream sociology. It antedates current transformations in technology, culture, and social knowledge. Going beyond the formal cultural limitations of the new sociology of education, and its socially conservative uses requires, I think, a challenge to that larger episteme, to the form of sociology.

Social analysis

I want to suggest that sociology is being replaced by social analysis. While social analysis is not a direct representation of changes in social life, it is part of a broad set of historical changes in social production and organization, in the content and forms of cultural expression, and in the aims and linguistic means of analytic social work. What are these broad changes and what do they imply for social understanding?

There are many attempts to describe a current broad set of changes at the global level: Toffler (1971) indicates a third wave; Bell (1979) describes a post-industrial society; Luke (1983) develops the theme of an ecological society. At an equally global level, a cultural transformation is described when: Baudrillard (1981) describes and criticizes the semiological reduction and the arrival of the speechless, consumer society; Foucault (1979; 1982) writes of a disciplinary, discursive society; MacCannell and MacCannell (1982) announce that it is 'the time of the sign.'

At this general level, changes are being described in the language and form of systematic social understanding as well as in the productive system, social organization and cultural forms of society. Geertz (1980) has described a 'refiguration' of social thought, by which he means that the metaphors which structure social analysis are increasingly drawn from the humanities rather than the so-called natural sciences. The shift in the kinds of metaphors used in social theorizing represents the current weight granted to the words and images of symbolic action and cultural performance, and indicates also a redirection in the goal of social science toward 'interpretation.' Processes of significance, of making meaning, and the traditional locus of their study, become the focus of an interpretive social science. More and more of shared social meaning and the activity of social understanding is encompassed by the now auratic term: text.

'The rise of the text' (Rorty, 1982) in social analytic language is more than just a shift in the locus of metaphors, or the disciplinary bases of social science. It is also a modern occasion for the renewal of Romanticism as a social movement, and despite its own ethos of dispersion, also becomes the center of a contemporary critique and metaphysics. The imagery and methodology of textualism goes beyond a disciplinary realignment. Rather, as Barthes

7

(1981:43) puts it, '. . . textual analysis impugns the idea of a final signified.'

Derrida's (1982:3–27) concept of 'differance' is another assertion against the philosophical foundations of objectivism. The insistent deferral of some thing itself, in favor of the relational dynamism of the representational system makes not 'the text,' but the chain of signification into the crucial active process. The oppositional system which anthropological structuralism first generalized from linguistics is put into movement by further extending the relational difference model to the sign itself. If structuralism abrogated the view of a natural tie between object and language as its representation, post-structuralism severs the necessity of a relation between representing concept and symbolic expression, between signified and signifier (Young, 1981:15). The free-play of the structure (Derrida, 1970) decenters, defers (the signified, the referent, the subject, the center, the transcendental being), and introduces linguistic playful movement, 'jouissance,' as the activity antithetical to any understanding of process as an emanation from a center or subject. Not the text, but textuality, signifying movement, is the key term for the deeper analytic alteration that Geertz taps by the term of 'refiguration.' This movement is broadly called 'post-structuralism' (Young, 1981; Lentricchia, 1980; Rorty, 1982). Like the text metaphor which is its more assimilable, though essentialized, trace, this movement is seeping into institutionalized channels of social analysis.

The transformation includes then post-industrialism in social life and post-structuralism in social analysis. However, like every condensation of succinct insight, the global descriptions oversimplify and leave out too much. Talk of post-industrialism as the general social change that reflects a tremendous growth in information technology and the communications apparatus should not obscure the extent to which social life continues the exploitative patterns that have typified industrial social relations. Recognition of the increased importance of new mass cultural forms of symbolic communication does not erase the still-engaging power that organic attachments and interactional rituals have to determine social commitments and to form social identities. Any post-industrial society that is now surging forward is also carrying with it encasing and determinative elements from earlier patterns of industrial and preindustrial forms of organized social life. Likewise, a refiguration of cultural performance, either in the high culture of the academic discourses of the social sciences, or in the symbolic action that occurs in every other sector of social life, is also limited by extant cultural forms and commitments. For example, the social organization of discourse production in the academy has not been altered by the renaissance and spread of interpretive paradigms, or by provocative declarations about 'the end of metaphysics' (Derrida, 1982), 'humanism', and 'man' (Foucault, 1972). Also, centralization of the mass culture industry has become more complex, but it has not been arrested by the rise of computers and telecommunications (Schiller, 1981; Mosco, 1982). Mass cultural forms of speech and entertainment have not been evidently shattered by the revolution in technological production. Descriptions of global transformations in productive energy, social organization, cultural form, and academic discourse, have all, I think, to be tempered, though not dismissed, by recognizing the continuing influence of the past.

There is a second type of qualification to attach to discussions of a global transformation and of an historic emergent new age in forms of life and discourse; the more specific social changes that occur within larger cycles, and affect everyday existence. For example, there has been a lot less talk about historic restorations than about revolutions and refigurations. Yet, in the United States, there is every sign that we have been going through precisely the kind of classic restoration that Marx described in the *Eighteenth Brumaire of Louis Bonaparte* (1959):

> An entire people, which had imagined that by means of a revolution it had imparted to itself an accelerated power of motion, suddenly finds itself set back into a defunct epoch and, in order that no doubt as to the relapse may be possible, the old dates arise again, the old chronology, the old names, the old edicts . . . Society now seems to have fallen back behind its point of departure.

This cultural restoration, which has revived earlier images, rhetoric, and cultural content, is also related to particular and specifiable processes of institutional reorganization. In the past decade, a deliberate effort to dismantle social welfare aspects of the state has occurred. Simultaneously, there has been an economic crisis more severe than any since the great depression. Within that cultural atmosphere and institutional strategy, new forms of social organization have emerged, notably a move toward a corporatist model of social life.

In these social and cultural conditions, which clearly include a change in the analytic languages and prevailing mood of the academy, it is no longer a question of substituting Marxist categories for functionalist ones, or field methods for multivariate research. In this current movement, *the activity of social knowledge* is being dispersed and diffused back into collective history and into the process of making meaning. That is the key to the formal change from sociology to social analysis. The battle lines are now drawn differently: no longer between positivist and anti-positivist, or liberal and Marxist sociology, history and hermeneutics, or even humanities and social sciences. Rather, the oppositions within the domain of knowledge are between: symbolic practice against conceptual magic; points on a moving grid against secured foundational edifices; and, of social analysis as a symbolic movement against the disciplinary sociology that has operated as a rigidified, and culturally compartmentalized scientistic self-denial of practical activity.

The legitimating bar of scientism that separates social analysis from other forms of cultural expression currently has the effect of blocking any view of a deeper and more pervasive alteration that social science now shares with a wider cultural movement.

The idealist character of American social science is not that it asserts the causal primacy of ideas in its explanations of the course of events. It is that it denies that social science is a practical symbolic activity. From this vantage point, Marxist social science in America has generally been no less idealist. There too, social analysis as an historical cultural activity has been obscured in favor of a quest for apparently more accurate facts and truer theories. An alternative view is to see social analysis as historical action. In this view, its meaning is only historical, social, and practical. It counts only as a consequential cultural moment within the flow of specific historical movements. I know that such an alternative can send a chill of anti-scientific relativism to the heart of orthodox and liberal alike.

Sociology entertained this possibility, but only briefly and then only on the periphery. It politely took into account social, symbolic, practical, historical, and collective factors which externally influence sociology. An ahistorical, unsocial, and static core of knowledge remains as the canonical, mainstream, 'real' sociology. The result has been that the insight that social analysis is symbolic collective historical action remains marginalized as a separate sociology of knowledge or science.

The alternative form of understanding suggested by the term 'social analysis' is to take seriously the current movement of society and culture. This movement makes it less possible to reify, to essentialize, and to compartmentalize historical, collective symbolic movements into things, concepts, or persons. It is an historical movement that is redundantly announced in many analytical languages: post-structuralism, semiotics, anti-humanism, textualism, post-industrialism, the information society, the micro-electronic revolution, the video-age, anti-logocentrism, deconstruction, and decentering. It is a movement that has historically been denied in the name of the superiority of science, individualism, and truth, but has now burst through a constraining cultural grid at many points. The constraints themselves are defined differently: as speech rather than writing (Derrida, 1970); as the language of the law of the father which represses the primary incestuous, semiotic evil of the language of the mother (Kristeva, 1980); as industrial production and thought which blocks understanding of the newer productive forces of ecological informationalism (Luke, 1983); as the literal, official encratic codes which devalue poetic, figurative language (Barthes, 1981; Bloom, 1982).

As social analysis, this negative and creative moment goes beyond the critique of liberalism that typified the first, late-1960s renaissance of social theory in this generation. Social analysis beyond sociological liberalism, in both its 'old' affirmative and 'new' negative aspects, does not simply express the historical movement or changes. It emerges along with them, and even at that, not as an open, equal partner. The symbolic process of analysis is neither one of autonomous scientific development nor superstructural representation. Rather, the analysis performed is a composition that includes: symbolic residues of historical movements that have passed; inscriptions of seepages of shared but symbolically inchoate and unsystematized practices; wishes that have begun to cross boundaries of conventional stigma to become anticipations of the future. The social analysis that emerges within the current transformation is crystallized momentarily and for particular purposes. It is a rational and collective *'bricolage'*, whose performance is unintentionally being made possible by contemporary de-reification of the symbolic environment. We can of course, suppress the voice of this historic movement, in the name of more established kinds of oppositions like 'old' and 'new' sociologies of education, or liberalism and Marxism, and continue to work on the basis of more lucid and secure epistemological foundations. What I wish to do, however, is to inscribe the transformation, culturally and socially, and to work through and past its formulation in high cultural theory. I want then to place that expression at the point of the social configuration that I think is the most powerful in the transformation: education.

Despite the salience of education in this linked series of broad multiform transformations, the education/movement relation is being almost entirely missed and unrecorded by sociology of education. New sociologists of education are instead preoccupied with qualifying their earlier insight that education may operate to accomplish the reproduction of social and cultural formations. All the current academic debates about reproduction and resistance (Giroux, 1983), or at a higher level of abstraction, about structure and agency (Giddens, 1979), are taking place very far from the actual historic changes which are occurring. From an historical, cultural vantage point, the reason for that is that they are engaged in an ordinary academic process of paradigmatic cultural rationalization. The unintended result, however, is that much greater and broader changes in social and cultural forms, and in the relation between social practice and social theory, which bring the education question to the fore, remain largely unanalyzed and unspoken.

After the new sociology of education

I want to offer a social analysis of education that works by taking account of these transformations of post-industrialism and of post-structuralism. An historical social analysis of education also takes account of historically specific 'local' institutional reorganizations, and of the class and identity politics of social movements. My aim is to reverse the current ahistoricism of the new sociology of education. Like the 'new contextualism' (Shapin, 1980) in the history of science, I see even paradigmatically basic concepts in the context of their historic social uses, as the cultural performance of collective historical actors.

I am going to risk relativism in order to be able to understand education within the changing social media in which it is practiced and signified. I am going to risk trendiness by taking modern literary theory seriously. I see this aspect of cultural theory as the displaced site of a contemporary critical social theory which is now in hiding, suppressed and distorted. I aim to draw the changing relation between literary theory, social theory and social change, to explore the relation between post-structuralism and post-industrialism, and then to assert that what is central in that relation is education.

'Education' ordinarily signifies a wide range of social practices that we think of organizationally as schools. The school, as we know it, is a concrete historical social institution. However, rather than see it in new sociology of education terms as the place where social reproduction of class structure, along with elements of popular resistance, occurs, I suggest that the school be thought of as the place where cultural distortion occurs. What is distorted is unrealized but knowable, socially shared, though only partly articulated historically appropriate processes of knowing and of transforming knowledge (Bernstein, 1982). In this view, everyday school education is a practice of *suppressed speech*. That doesn't mean that there isn't ordinary talk in schools, or elaborate forms of cultural expression, or class domination. What I mean by education as distortion is that the contradiction of education (like that of the sociology of education) is that it is at once a discursive blockage against realizing and articulating knowledge, and also 'contains' – both includes and constrains – the most powerful, though diffused and fragmented, cultural resources of historical knowledge. That is one reason, I think, that contemporary social conflicts, movements, and cultural expressions, while dispersed and decentered, continue to carry forward and elevate education as a central social question.

In an analysis that begins with a re-historicizing of the new sociology of education, the promise – that it once dared speak over the numerically mystifying chatter of the education/mobility relation – to study knowledge as a transformative practice is reconsidered. The study of social knowledge, and an understanding of education as the historical activity of knowledge, is revised in the terms of modern cultural theory generally, and in the language of post-structuralism in particular. But, I do not accept post-structuralism at its own self-presentation as historically and culturally transcendent, anymore than I take comfort in the claims of the new sociology of education. I place that discourse too in an historical context, and try to re-connect post-structuralism to post-industrialism. At a very general level, I believe that the culture of late modernism, to which post-structuralism belongs, is bound to the historical social organization of a late modern productive apparatus. My hypothesis is that the disruptive diffusion and decentering current in which social and literary modernism flow is one of a new stage in the history of the commodity. If you need a causal hero or villain, then hold the dialectic of the commodity responsible for the contemporary ethos of decomposition.

Where once it was the sign of congealed and hidden human labor, a mystifying abstraction and capitalism's kernel social form (Lukács, 1971), commodity logic is now the social determinant of a deconstructive mood. In modern terms, I would describe commodity fetishism (Marx, 1971) as a process of blocking or obscuring social energy crystallization in the composition of transformative activity by transcendental, effective social abstractions; money is the classic example. In a modern, critical commodity analysis, one important tendency of post-industrialism is that the connective processes that formerly worked as abstract cultural mystifying processes are themselves now being uncovered unintentionally in the ordinary course of social production.

According to this hypothesis, de-reifying demystification occurs because the full exploitation of dispersed energies requires articulation of all the abstract linkages of production that formerly operated as mystifiers. The deconstructive decomposition of the sociocultural relations of production is now both a requirement of advanced production, and secondarily, in the capitalization of information, an additional means of profit. In this process, knowledge of social composition, of the processes of social relation, becomes rationalized and prepared for sale. In this virtually 'post-commodity society,' the network becomes the core image – indicating the need to make processes of relation rational rather than mystified. Networks, which were once what hid the creative force and exploitation of human labor, are made transparent, in part for sale and profit.

In these social circumstances, knowledge is not simply a dead resource for accumulative production. It is the political medium for collective organization. Post-structuralism's flickering signifier is not playful; it is instead a sign of invitation for the expressive entry of human energy. Post-structuralism is the discourse of movement inside the increasingly transparent, but emplaced, network of informational production. The more dynamic symbolic system that is post-structuralism is, I think, a form of cultural life as internal exile. As Handelman (1982) argues, it is ultimately a discourse of exile. Yet, in its apparent disrespect for truth, this discourse still affirms the Enlightenment faith: the power of human knowledge is reinterpreted as a process of symbolic movement. From these diverse levels of historical movement: global transformations; institutional reorganizations; the re-figuration of the metaphors and language of social science and its unexpected confluence with modern literary theory; and new turns in the dialectical road of the commodity, the *'post-commodity hypothesis'*, I begin to construct the organizing points of a social analysis of education.

Instead of using the new sociology of education concepts 'reproduction'and 'resistance,' I analyze educational change in the historical terms of institutional reorganization and social movement. In place of the ordinarily central theoretical role assigned to either so-called structural or cultural/critical Marxism, I substitute a critical and reflexive synthesis of post-industrialism and post-structuralism, that I am calling social analysis. I try to specify this analysis not only in historical analyses of educational change, but also by studying knowledge. I view school knowledge in light of processes of decomposition and dereification, rather than the more familiar causal sociology of knowledge. Against the ordinary concept of 'socialization,' I begin to historicize the social psychology of education, and then hint at the empirical work we are doing in developing an analysis of the symbolic economy of identity production. I bypass individualist voluntarist models of resistance, to emphasize instead the politics of collective symbolic movement, as the practically refigurative and motivating interest in education. I suggest that the current distorting suppression of education – in school practice, in academic hierarchies of discourse, and in the sociologies of education – is part of the larger repression of a conscious, rational, and collective regulation of the relation between social theory, social movement, and social practice. I embark on the road that begins beyond this repression, to specify the current historical practice of eduction.

In the remainder of part one, I combine a conceptual and contextual analysis of the academic discourse of the new sociology of education; I want to make good on the promise of reflexivity. In the second part of the book, I use as an analytical method a critique of the basic assumptions of the new sociology of education. By that method, I try to develop the central concepts, commitments and methods of a social analysis of education. In that analysis, institutional reorganization, social movement and a de-reified practical knowledge are markers of the new field of work. In the last part of the book, I try to show how a social reading of post-structuralism and a critical reading of post-industrialism can combine toward an historically appropriate theory and practice of education. I want to suggest that the path I follow in the book, through and beyond the new sociology of education, leads to a new politics in which education is understood as a collective discursive practice. This view, rather than the contemporary combination of functionalist structuralism and romantic individualism ('reproduction' and 'resistance') that typifies the new sociology of education, is one that I hope will be enabling: both for a more complete revision of our analysis of education; and, for the kind of politics required to revise the conditions and practices of our everyday ineluctably social lives.

2
The rise and fall of the new sociology of education

Recollection

From this historical and practical view of social knowledge, the new sociology of education is one expression of a much larger historical movement. It represents, in academic language, the changing ideology of a generational and class social faction. It represents – by desublimating – this ideology particularly well in the language of education. For education falls low in the hierarchy of academic discourses, and can perform the cultural function of obliquely and harmlessly underlining social truths, just as do marginals, deviants and other low-status characters in social life generally. At the same time, knowledge practices that are now suppressed and distorted are also socially powerful; educational discourse contains transformative potential. In a symbolic society, under conditions of symbolic movement, the power to form and direct speech is the heart of political power. Education is that formative capacity. Sociology of education is its contextual representation, an articulation of the historically specific social meaning of education. In order to be able to rationally recollect that meaning, to make it usable, sociology of education's earlier historical social roles, which become its ideologies, have always to be identified, so that they can be continually surpassed.

The new sociology of education was produced in the course of collective cultural action by a segment of that social group which Ehrenreich and Ehrenreich (1977a and b) have called the 'professional-managerial class.' The origins and sociocultural path of this group have not simply determined the changing course of the new sociology of education, but have also its basic terms and mood. The social history of this class segment is written within the

17

culture of professionalism, and, like this general culture, is now at a point of bifurcating contradiction. Beyond a combined bureaucratically incorporative surface of professional success for some and occupational underemployment for other members of this stratum (see for example, Burris, 1983; Abel, 1984), two alternative paths of action now emerge.

One path is the effort to think and work past the larger structured socioeconomic crisis, and to place the study of education within a new vision of collective mobilization and action. The other path acknowledges the current condition of political defeat and lives the kind of internal social exile that follows it. Rather than articulate a new coherent vision, this course of action disdains coherence as a totalizing activity, and prefers to claim as its own badge of accomplishment historically newer forms of dispersed and fractionated speech. These divided paths of cultural action bring to light ideological limitations of the new sociology of education, and press toward a rational recollection of the discourse that will surpass new sociology's current operation as a discursive blockage. In this chapter, I am going to trace the social and conceptual paths that have led to this contemporary crossroads of either mobilization or exile in the new sociology of education.

The sociocultural, contradictory history of an academic professional group is, however, an incomplete guide to the conceptual content of an academic field. The theoretical and research content of the field is more than the academic display of the cultural performance of a class segment. The new sociology of education is also defined by particular historical internal professional boundary disputes. The concepts and language of the field are shaped by specific cultural resources that have been brought to bear in the course of class cultural action, in professional discourse and conflicts, and in a process of collective self-definition. These particular resources and disputes have included: a consistently ambiguous, but changing, relation between education and sociology; importation of models of educational analysis from British sociology; a belated impact of German critical theory; and French Marxism.

To understand the rise and fall of the new sociology of education, I try in this chapter to take account of several determinative moments – the social history of the carriers (the 'tragers' is Weber's (1963) term) of this specialized academic subdiscipline, the professional alignments within it, and the changing concepts that constitute the field. First, I describe at a general level the contextual approach to social knowledge that informs this brief history. Second, I set the stage for the new sociology of education by indicating the social movement of its carriers and reviewing the conceptual pre-history of the new sociology, the 'old' sociology of education. Third, I attempt to trace the development of the new sociology paradigm. I bring the historical description up to the bifurcating contradiction of the present, and to the beginnings of still another path toward understanding education.

Social knowledge: a contextual approach

A contextual approach to knowledge is neither conventionally materialist nor idealist. Textbook sociological custom is to collapse Marx and Weber into the convenient polarity of materialist reduction and idealist elevation. Yet, neither Marxist nor Weberian traditions are antithetical to approaching knowledge as an historical, collective symbolic practice. Discourse, while it can be autonomously described, is understood as always and integrally historical and social. Here, ideas or concepts are not viewed as reified, determined objects, or as transcendental supra-historical subjects. Neither object nor subject, social knowledge is a process of contextually meaningful symbolic action.

Marx describes the relationship of the intellectuals of a particular social class and of materiality and thought in contingent, dynamic, contextual terms. (Marx, in Bottomore and Rubel, 1956:82, emphasis added):

> What makes them representatives of the petty bourgoisie is the
> fact that *in their minds* they do not get beyond the limits
> which the latter do not get beyond in life, that they are
> consequentially driven, *theoretically*, to the same problems and
> solutions to which material interest and social position drive the
> latter practically.

> Unless material production itself is understood in *its specific
> historical form*, it is impossible to grasp the characteristics of the

intellectual production which corresponds to it or the *reciprocal action* between the two.

Weber's descriptions of religious intellectuals express the same historically specific differentiated, contextual view of the relation between material and intellectual interests. (Weber, 1963:131–2, emphasis added):

> If one wishes to characterize succinctly, in a formula so to speak, the types of representatives of the various classes that were the primary carriers or propagators of the so-called world religions, they would be the following: in Confucianism, the world-organizing bureaucrat; in Hinduism, the world-ordering magician; in Buddhism, the mendicant monk wandering through the world; in Judaism, the wandering trader – and in Christianity, the itinerant journeyman. To be sure, all these types must not be taken as exponents of their own occupational or material class interests, but rather as the *ideological carriers* of the kind of ethical or salvation doctrine which most readily conformed to their social position.

Despite these theoretical origins, classical sociology of knowledge encourages such an historical and dynamic contextual study of knowledge less well than does recent empirical work in the history of science. A good example of a modern contextualist approach to social knowledge is Shapin's (1980) synthesis of historiographic research in eighteenth-century science. Shapin writes of this research (1980: 96, emphasis added):

> This corpus rejects currently dominant notions of the social uses of science. Instead, it explains the career of Newtonian natural philosophy entirely in terms of *its uses in specific contexts.*

'Context' here does not mean the impact of external social factors as variables. Rather, it means that scientific activity is directly cultural action. In this view, '. . . one cannot understand scientific judgments without attending to the context wherein scientific accounts were *deployed*' (Shapin, 1980:98, emphasis added). An understanding of concepts as cultural action is exemplified by such specific historical interpretation as Margaret Jacobs' reassessment of Newtonianism. According to Shapin (1980:98–9):

> She vigorously rejects Pope's 'illumination' model of the diffusion of the new natural philosophy and replaces it with the notion that conceptions of nature are *tools*, instruments which historical actors in contingent settings pick up and deploy in order to further a variety of interests, social as well as technical.

The social use meaning of a contextual approach to knowledge goes beyond acknowledging the role of scientific cultural meanings in social processes such as group conflict. It attends rather first and immediately to the activity, the doing (Shapin, 1980:133) of scientific cultural representation. Shapin calls this a 'new contextualist tradition', which he juxtaposes to the traditional contemplative view of scientific knowledge (Shapin, 1980:132):

> Empirical work by the Jacobs, Wilde, Brown, Lawrence and others has demonstrated that considerations of social use were intimately associated with the production, judgment and institutionalization of science in the late seventeenth and eighteenth century.

Brown's (1974:179–216) research on changing concepts in eighteenth-century English physiology is a good example of the contextualist approach to social knowledge that is being developed in the history of science. For Brown, professional status dynamics are an example of how key social uses have affected changes in the paradigmatic conceptual content of physiology. He argues that changes in the physiological paradigm were a part of '. . . broader, more closely connected and subtly influential changes in the nature of English medicine' (Brown, 1974:193–4, emphasis added):

> And, as I have contended elsewhere, one important motivation for the adoption of iatromechanism as English medicine's new official orthodoxy seems clearly to have been the desire 'to raise. . . (the profession's) *prestige* again, thereby improving. . . (its) political position. The collegiate physicians had been condemned in public, persecuted in Parliament, and ridiculed in print. By turning to 'mechanical' ideas like

21

(Thomas) Willis' they could – or at least they wished to –
forestall further charges of ignorance, intellectual
backwardness, or conceptual confusion . . . For as
iatromechanists they would look more like responsible
contemporary scientists, while they avoided further
professional embarrassment. . .

Brown concludes his study with the observation:

We are now in a position to notice just how closely variations in
eighteenth-century English medical theory correlated with
social and institutional changes, specifically in *the professional
position* and attitude of the London College of Physicians.

This relation between the social dynamics of organized professional activity and changes in the content of scientific ideas has
been argued also in the sociological work of Ben-David and
Collins (1966:451–65). Their hypotheses about the contextual
determination of the content of scientific concepts are framed
more within the metaphors of genetics than in the linguistically
oriented terms of the new contextualists. But they share in the
attempt to explain conceptual changes as integral aspects of
historical social movements, particularly the movement of segments of professionals. The change they wish to explain is the
origin of the academic discipline of psychology. Professional status
needs are placed within the wider context of academic organizational and market conditions. The origin of psychology is seen as a
case study in the 'growth' of ideas. Following the genetic metaphor,
the selective mechanism which influences ideational fertility:

occurs where and when persons become interested in the new
idea, *not only as intellectual content but also as a potential means
of establishing a new intellectual identity and particularly a new
occupational role* (Ben-David and Collins, 1966:452, emphasis
added).

They see the origins of experimental psychology in late
nineteenth-century Germany as a professional movement of
higher-status physiologists, under limiting market conditions, into
philosophy and its questions, but who bring with them the

empirical methods of physiology. Ideas are at least in part developed and disseminated through the creation of new scientific roles, which in this case was the outcome of academic-organizational professional mobility dynamics. Cross-field mobility can create those roles through the 'mechanism of role-hybridization.'

Role-hybridization, organizational mobility, group conflict, and intra-professional struggles for legitimation and prestige are examples of specific contextual dynamics in which various cultural resources are worked-up into scientific, academic ideas. Concepts are developed in the course of collective cultural action; not outside of specialized knowledge traditions, but simultaneously integral to the needs, practices and aspirations of the producing, 'trager' groups. The character and direction of the symbolic action and the knowledge, traditions and broad cultural surroundings used as resources may be different in each domain of academic knowledge.

The social knowledge of education, no less than that of physical, biological or psychological knowledge, is also produced at the confluence of social movement, broad cultural resources and specialized conceptual traditions. Yet the new sociology of education, perhaps protected by its claim as a critique of established knowledge, has so far appeared as acontextual, placed above and beyond social history.

Context of the new sociology

Social movement: PMC and the New Left

While there is no systematic data available about the social origins of the producers of the new sociology of education in particular, their common social location was identifiably that of university 'intellectuals.' It is a matter of no small dispute how to characterize university intellectuals in class, or even general stratification, terms (Walker, 1979). There is, however, agreement that there has been a change in the distribution of the labor force, with an increase of intellectual and scientific or 'mental workers.' The dispute is whether the change represents a redefinition of skills within a 'new working class,' or whether it indicates the rise of a separate and historically novel social class. Ehrenreich and Ehrenreich (1977a and b) argue that these mental workers have a specific historic function within the social division of labor; they

23

are neither capital nor labor. They are a professional-managerial class (1977a:13–14, emphasis added):

> We define the Professional-Managerial Class as consisting of salaried mental workers who do not own the means of production and whose major function in the social division of labor may be described broadly as the *reproduction of capitalist culture and capitalist class relations*.

In their account, this historic class begins its ascent in America during the Progressive period, between 1890 and 1920. Its social role is to mediate the sharpened class conflict between capital and labor, by rationalizing and reforming the older forms of capitalism toward a socially defended, expert-regulated, modernized corporate capitalism. 'The characteristic form of self-organization of the PMC was the *profession*' (1977a, I, 26, emphasis added). This professionally organized class of rationalizers and regulators of capital, which 'exists as a mass grouping only by virtue of the expropriation of the skills and culture once indigenous to the working class' (1977b, II, 7), is the social basis for the rise of the American New Left Movement during the 1960s. The political economy of the 1960s was so extraordinarily favorable to university expansion (Altbach and Berdahl, 1981), that some working-class youths were indeed recruited to fill student and, ultimately, faculty positions. The evidence, however (Flacks, 1971), suggests that academic radicalism during the 1960s was nurtured by a subjective sense of plenty and a class-confident assertion of professional middle-class autonomy. Despite the recruitment of working-class youths to the university, the leadership of the New Left movement was drawn from the professional middle class (Flacks, 1971). This interpretation supports the Ehrenreichs' general hypothesis that New Left radicalism was not the expression of an historical proletarianization, nor the voice of a new working class. Rather, the academic social radicalism of the period was an expression of the increasing social power of the professional managerial class.

It is clear that the social movement within the university occurred at a time of virtually unprecedented expansion in American higher education. By some estimates (Kerr and Gade, 1981:112), enrollments doubled between 1960 and 1970. The expansion of the period was expressed in the first report of the Carnegie Commission on Higher Education, in 1968 (cited in Stadtman, 1981:102):

Today's enrollment is almost 6 million students on a full time equivalent (FTE) basis. More than one-half of this growth took place in the decade from 1958–1967. Estimates indicate that enrollment will pass 8 million if Carnegie Commission or other proposals are adopted to remove financial barriers for students from low-income families.

Less certain is what were the effects of this expansion. For university leaders like Clark Kerr, the expansion of the university was central to national economic development (quoted in Breines, 1982: 99–100):

What the railroad did for the second half of the last century and the automobile did for the first half of this century may be done for the second half of this century by the knowledge industry: that is, to serve as the focal point of national growth. And the university is the center of the knowledge process.

But to student radicals, the university meant 'academic super-markets' (Altbach et al., 1971) and bureaucratic alienation. Student leader Carl Davidson wrote (in Breines, 1982:103):

The teaching and learning workers . . . are alienated from each other, isolated and divided . . . What should be an active creation and re-creation of culture is nothing more than forced and coercive consumption and distribution of data and technique.

There are a variety of hypotheses that try to explain the rise of the New Left. For Breines (1982), it was a prefigurative politics of community; for Keniston (1968), the expression of an inter-generational psychodynamic conflict; for Rothman and Lichter (1982), a Jewish politics, bolstered by authoritarian tendencies among a minority of Christian students. But if we follow and elaborate the class, professional and organizational argument of

25

the Ehrenreichs, the New Left movement is inherently contradictory.

Driven on the one side by the optimism of an expanding class, when they encountered a working class and black presence in the alienating boom multiversity, middle-class student radicals were increasingly driven also by the class guilt they experienced. Prominent among the several paths toward the social resolution of this guilt, which the Ehrenreichs describe, was one where the simultaneous expression of class self-confidence and class self-rejection could be resolved within the familiar medium of professionalism. The result of a class-inspired, historically conditioned self-ambivalence was *an ambivalent professionalism.* By the late 1960s and early 1970s, acting as professionals, one segment of the New Left inspired a culture and organizational infrastructure of a democratizing anti-professionalism. They proclaimed a demystifying use of professional knowledge, against the hierarchical pretensions of credentialled expertise (Ehrenreich and Ehrenreich, 1977a, II, 16). The contradiction of class optimism and class guilt was institutionally channeled as a contradictory professionalism that claimed professional legitimation in order to criticize professionalism.

The ideology-critique with which the new sociology of education begins makes sense within such a contradictory professionalism. It academically criticizes and tries to demystify legitimate knowledge by identifying it as a representation of limited and historically transient social interests. As Mannheim (1936) showed, the critique of knowledge is a tool in the struggle for status and power. The cultural dynamic within which the new sociology develops goes beyond a contradictory professionalism which included ideology-critique on the agenda of its political struggle.

The new sociologists of education were not, I hypothesize, centrally participant in university radicalism. They were instead *latecomers* to the student movements of the 1960s. Unlike the Ehrenreichs' interpretation, my view is that their belated radicalism is not simply a direct continuation of the student movement. Rather, it is a displaced imitation of it, an attempt culturally to recapitulate the practical historical course of the movement mentally, *in theory.* In this view, the new sociology of education does not become an ideology. It is ideological from the outset. It aims to relive the ideal and culture of the radical social movement within the university *after* its time had already passed. In this view, new sociology of education is a rationalized cultural representation of identity politics: it is part of a *post*-'movement' effort to create a meaningful professionalism that is consonant with the ideal of a defeated social movement. Like other academic expressions of 'western Marxism,' it is a discourse that is formed in the aftermath of a political defeat (Anderson, 1976). The symbolic action which *is* the new sociology of education recapitulates that defeat, restating it abstractly and obsessively. It is an academic representation that not only recapitulates, but simultaneously struggles also to transcend in theory the collective action that became historically blocked in practice (see Gouldner, 1970, for an early general statement of this view).

Conceptual pre-history

If the new sociology of education is historical, contextual symbolic action, it is also an academic field of specialization that has a history which predates the 1960s. Although this history of the 'old' sociology of education is little known or discussed in new sociology of education, it belongs to the same historical social movement of the professional middle class that I hypothesize has produced the newer discourse. The new sociology begins during a time of university expansion and general societal increase of professional middle-class power; the 'old' sociology begins in Progressivism, with the initial surge of professional middle-class power. Yet, despite the social continuity, this past is so little noticed or mentioned by so-called new sociologists of education that it has taken on the aura of a 'pre-history.'

In an earlier effort to grasp this past (Wexler, 1976) I saw pre-1960s sociology of education as conceptually integrated. Indeed, there is a conceptual consensus on the surface that can be sensibly related to the wider culture of the Progressive movement. But the conceptual surface hides an institutional and professional history which is conflictual. Among academic social analysts of education, there is a central historic conflict, between the educationists and the sociologists. Reminiscent of Ben-David and Collins' analysis (1966), educationists have played a definitive role in a hybridized field of educational sociology, but from a position of professional status inferiority – a role later replayed in the new sociology of education.

In Richards' account of the history of the field, internal paradigmatic differences are broadly catalogued as the general sociology group, the normative theory and social foundations groups, and the social technology group (Richards, 1970:10, 180). The history of conflicts among these groups, which is supported by Card's (1959) encyclopedic account of 'educational sociology,' shows that an enduring point of division has been between the social reform and policy interest of the educationist educational sociologists and the 'scientific,' objective aspirations of sociologist educational sociologists.

The sociologists had more of the several academic prestige currencies. But the educationists had more influence in the associations and journals specializing in the social study of education. Szreter's content analysis (1980:179) of the first five years of publication of the *Journal of Educational Sociology*, from 1927–1932, indicates the distribution of contributors by professional affiliation.

> . . . we are left with 137 educationists and 20 'straight' sociologists, a ratio of approximately 7:1. Small wonder that Editor Payne spoke in Vol.2/3, 1928 of 'the development of educational sociology . . . very largely separated from sociology'.

This finding supports Card's earlier research (1959:140), where he asserted that for the early period of the field: 'The majority of leaders were trained more in education than in sociology or educational sociology.' An historical review of the organization which sponsored the journal, the National Society for the Study of Educational Sociology, reflects the educationists' strength, and confirms the educationist professional origins of organization office-holders (Card, 1959:134). The organization was dissolved in 1931, but the sociologist Waller still complained about the influence of those 'self-styled educational sociologists' (cited in Richards, 1970:133). Even later, however, educationists continued to maintain some hold on the field, particularly at Teachers College, Columbia, where the earliest courses in educational sociology had been taught by Henry Suzallo in the first decade of the century. There, the central reformist interest in education continued under the heading 'social foundations of education.' By the time the field's journal's name was changed to *Sociology of Education* in 1963, the split between a 'scientific' sociology of education and a 'reformist' and interdisciplinary social foundations of education was already institutionally well established.

'Legitimate' sociology of education at the time that the university radical movement began in the 1960s was the so-called 'objective' analysis of the sociologists, rather than reform-minded educational sociology of the educationists. Social activism had apparently given way to science. Yet, the paradigmatic assumptions of this objective sociology of education were deeply engaged with the social regulative interests and ideology of the Progressive movement (Wexler, 1976). Research was typified by an implicit commitment to the ideal of fair individual competition for unequal reward, in the context of social institutions believed to be fundamentally politically neutral or neutralizable.

A central research theme, of the established, 'old' sociology of education, was to show how true individual competition in schools could be sullied by external, interfering factors. An exemplary application of this interest, which continued well into the 1940s, was to demonstrate how students' parents status differences could alter the informal social relationships, and ultimately the academic futures of youths (Hollingshead, 1949). By the 1950s, the field's central focus on inequality and education was expanded to include studies of the relation between inequalities of school resources and student achievements. The apparent no-difference finding of Coleman's (1966) national study was a surprising upset to this mode of scientized Progressive sociology of education research. But, neither positive nor negative findings led out of the meritocratic individualist model to any sustained alternative attempts to connect distributional inequities to societal structural dynamics, or to seeing internal school processes as constitutively political or economic. On the contrary, inequalities were thought of as fundamentally external, brought from outside to an occasionally inefficient, but essentially socially neutral, school system. The failures of poor and minority group students were treated as corrigible expressions of family-determined 'cultural deprivations.' High achievement was traced to family-conditioned 'achievement values' and motives (Rosen, 1961).

By the 1960s, the Progressive research traditions had culminated in a consistent educational policy: equalize school financing and provide 'compensatory education' for cultural deprivation (Bloom et al., 1965). But, as one of the leading latter-day Progressive, 'objective' sociologists of education observes (Sewell, 1971:803): 'Unfortunately, current large-scale efforts to improve the cognitive development of socially-disadvantaged children have not thus far had promising results.' Yet neither the practical nor the scientific failure of its hypothesis blocked extension of scientific sociology's translation of Progressive commitment into *the* taken-for-granted paradigm of the field.

By the 1970s, the 'status attainment' (Featherman and Hauser, 1978) model had become the pervasive research currency of American sociology of education. This model directly, and unintentionally, maps an historical cultural redefinition of American educational ideals. Rush Welter's (1962) historical hypothesis is that the popular belief in education as a political institution of democracy has become a legitimation for accepting inequality, as long as there is free competition through education. The status attainment model shared this revised understanding of the relation between inequality and education. It retreats from the historic American view of education as a means of popular political efficacy, toward the modern competitive faith that education is the key to success within a taken-for-granted, socially organized inequality (Fatherman and Hauser, 1978:9) '. . . a central assumption . . . is that the hierarchies of socioeconomic statuses that differentiate the life chances of adults in American society are predetermined.' 'Mobility,' in status attainment research, means '. . . the persistence and change in socioeconomic status through work and schooling, whether gauged by reference to parents and their offspring (intergenerational mobility) or by reference to career changes (intragenerational mobility).' What this meant operationally was ordinarily charting the occupational positions of fathers and sons of different age cohorts on a grid of ranked occupations. Mobility was simply the amount of 'movement,' and the results of national surveys indicated that there certainly was that. The question remained, however, of what sense to make of the movement. In part, difference in position can be explained as a result of changes in the occupational structure (decline of farmers, for example), demographic influences on replacement rates, or generally what were called 'structural' factors. Additional mobility, so-called 'circulatory mobility', was taken as more direct evidence for the 'permeability' or openness of the system. The empirical findings were quite generally that a substantial part of the mobility is structural, but that there was continuing 'permeability' in the system.

A second research area of the 'old' sociology – though less central than the assumption of education as the continuing medium of competitive individualism – 'objectively' represented the Progressive commitment of efficiency, cooperation and professionalism in education. The efficiency movement phase of Progressivism in education (Callahan, 1962) later appears in research that follows the industrial efficiency model of educational practice. In research, this meant studying the school as a series of abstracted organizational variables which were correlated with dimensions of individual student attribute outcomes, particularly attitudes (Feldman, 1971) and achievements (Boocock, 1972). Correlations of these abstracted variables substituted for analyses of the flow of everyday social life in schools, as well as the wider social reasons that might have shaped the cultural definitions of those individual attribute outcomes. Consistent with this abstracted and scientized approach, 'politics' was seen as an intrusion on 'professional control' in education. The claim that professionalism was apolitical operated not simply as the practical ideology of school management, but also appeared to influence the definition of suitable research questions. As one researcher wrote in a moment of partisan honesty (Kerr, 1964:59): 'the system is threatened with loss of professional control. Our attention has therefore focused upon one set of organizational mechanisms which tend to restore security and maintain this control.'

In the 'old' sociology of education, one tendency within the American Progressive movement was expressed in research based on competitive individualist images of equality and on decontextualized organizational models of professionally managed efficiency. This more 'conservative' strand of Progressivism also affected sociological study of school knowledge. School knowledge was studied either as an occasion for academic stratification or as a medium through which to create a moral societal consensus. Among early sociologists of education, Finney (1922), Peters (1924) and others argued that schools ought to create moral conformity and impart differential knowledge appropriate to the social origins and probable destinations of students. Less openly prescriptive, but substantively similar, views later appear in Parsons' (1959) 'theoretical' sociology of the school. There, he takes as his central task a speculative reconstruction of how conformity to the role-orientations of American schoolrooms produces value learning for social consensus. Dreeben (1968) generalized and disseminated this moral consensus understanding of school knowledge, through a description of schooling as socialization to the ideals and practices of the Parsonian pattern variables of independence, achievement, universalism and specificity. The 'new' sociology, despite similarities in class locations, is not the direct successor of this 'old,' scientific, liberal, and Progressivist American sociology of education. The producers of the new discourse confront a different historical and cultural context.

The rise and fall of the new sociology of education

Rise

The specialized academic discourse that I am calling, and that calls itself, 'new sociology of education' does not replace the 'old' sociology of education. Nor is the new sociology a continuation of New Left movement radicalism. The movement *did* have a social analysis of education. It centered on a critique of the social organization and relations of the university (see, for example, Altbach et al., 1971; Miles, 1971). It aimed also to theorize an educational practice outside the 'sphere of state education in various 'free school' educational movements (Graubard, 1974). At the same time, the effect of new sociology on academic, so-called 'mainstream' sociology of education was surprisingly minimal, even at the theoretical level. Indeed, in a content analysis of the theoretical orientations of papers published in *Sociology of Education*, Picou found (1979; Wells and Picou, 1981) that there was actually a decline between 1975 and 1978 in the number of papers in the 'radical-critical theory' category. Significantly, that category was consistently the lowest of all theory groups represented in the journal between 1963 and 1978.

The new sociology of education did, however, have a describable form and content. It did occupy an academically public place; the place of the 'new' and 'critical' in the social analysis of education. It showed itself different from both 'the movement' and 'the mainstream' in its form. The discourse of new sociology of education indicates its sociocultural meaning by the language that it uses. The language of new sociology is academic, if not academicist and scholastic, in its abstractness and insistent pretension to being 'theoretical.' But its content is drawn from general radical theory that is self-consciously *distanced* from education. Sharp (1980:10), for example, urged:

> Those who wish to understand education should, if necessary, forget about it for a number of years and concentrate their attention instead on more significant issues concerning the nature and dynamics of capitalist societies.

Radical, though abstract, academicist language performs the work of distancing not only from the talk and practice of the low-status domain of education, but also from the memory and fear of political defeat and the possibility of professional stigma and exclusion. If the discourse 'new sociology of education' is a cultural action, staking out a professional academic identity by a revision of an anti-professional and anti-academic social movement, then both belated identification with the movement and legitimate status within the academy can be satisfied by the linguistic hybrid, 'radical/academic theory.' (For a discussion of methods of revision, though in a literary context, see Bloom, 1975.)

The contradiction between professionalism and anti-professionalism among the professional middle-class strata described by Ehrenreich and Ehrenreich (1977a) is accentuated if the discourse's producers are only vicarious participants in the defeated anti-academic and anti-professional movement. What can be read through the narrative history, the conceptual content, of new sociology is a simultaneous abstract or displaced replication of the movement's course *and* efforts at theoretical inventions to avoid its eventual demise. The same ambivalence both toward the movement and toward academic professional status is what fuels the expression of two paths that lead past the contradiction: either to continue the goals of the movement through a renewed social mobilization; or to express the consequences of political defeat and marginal academic incorporation in an appropriate theory and language – a language of exile. Radical/academic theory is the cultural form which helps contain that contradiction, and so blocks the realization of either path.

Within this general cultural process, it was a fusion of several specific conceptual traditions and sociocultural dynamics that constituted the rise of the new sociology of education. In the post-movement, ambiguous condition of academic social science, three distinct pathways merged to fuse the new discursive articulation. First, as during the earlier transformative historical moment of American Progressivism, educationists asserted their legitimate claim to a social analysis of education, independently and against the academic sociologists of education. Second, sociologists generally, and sociologists of education particularly, were more attentive to the theoretical interests of European sociology than they had been since before the Parsonian synthesis. In the wake of a period of academic cultural turbulence, 'European theory' again signified external social status as well as intrinsic interest. Third, academic disciplinary boundaries had been somewhat relaxed, so that history and economics seemed less alien fields to some sociologists than they had appeared during the post-war years of the peak of professionalization in sociology.

There are evident, though obviously not exhaustive, examples of each trajectory. Among the educationists, Michael Apple, a philosophically oriented curricularist, emerged by the mid-1970s as the leader of the political-social wing of the radical 'reconceptualist' movement in the educational field of curriculum (Huber, 1981:14–87). By the end of the decade, in a review of two British books, Apple (1978) was using the term 'new sociology of education' to include also his own radical social analysis of schooling; an analysis that had begun with an ideology-critique of the curriculum field (Apple, 1979a). In sociology, Jerome Karabel, an American sociologist working in England, used the same term in a 1976 paper, and identified it as a British, rather than American, sociology of education. He wrote (Karabel and Halsey, 1976:533):

Perhaps the most striking feature of the 'new' sociology of education is that it is almost entirely a British creation; it has, as yet, made few inroads into American educational research.

My work during this period (Wexler, 1976:77) was one example of a third dynamic. While I was institutionally located in sociology, the early ideology-critique of sociology of education drew heavily not from sociology, but from the so-called 'revisionist history' of education of Katz (1968, 1971), Spring (1972), Lazerson (1971) and Karier et al. (1973). Yet, I described the emergent discourse as 'a set of new research emphases' (1976:55), and as an 'alternative sociology of education' (1977:44).

The clearest announcement of a 'new sociology of education' was, as Karabel had correctly reported, in England. In 1972, an article reviewing the field was already entitled 'The New Sociology of Education' (Gorbutt, 1972). In this paper, Gorbutt asserted that the new sociology of education was an aspect of a broader new 'interpretive' paradigm of social constructionism. At the same time, he acknowledged Michael Young's now classic statement (1971:3): 'sociology of education is no longer conceived as the area of inquiry distinct from the sociology of knowledge.' In his attempt to explain the British development, Karabel (and Halsey, 1976:535) had attributed the successful application of the interpretive paradigm in education in part to the hospitality of the British to the sociology of knowledge tradition represented by Karl Mannheim. He observes also that the institutional locus of this new British sociology of education was largely in the education colleges, and particularly at the London Institute of Education. While Young's statement may now appear as an exaggerated expression of the new direction of interest, he accurately assesses that the 'new' sociology of education was focused on the question of school knowledge. This theoretical centering on the knowledge question brought together the sociology of knowledge tradition and the more classroom-based, pedagogical interest of the curricularists in both classroom interaction and school knowledge.

Although Young provided the programmatic statement for the British new sociology (see, for example, Brown, 1974), the combined interest in sociology of knowledge and pedagogical and curriculum practice had been brought together earlier, in the work of Basil Bernstein. It was Bernstein who, rather than issue a general call for a redirection of interest away from the research of Halsey et al. (1961), and others that much resembled the

American social mobility interest and mode of research, accomplished a combinatory innovation in his research on social class differences in youths', families' and schools' languages (Bernstein, 1958). Importantly, not only did Bernstein direct the training of the new sociologists at the London Institute, but the theoretical combination which he performed, in an empirical way, was far from any of the theoretical tributaries of the American New Left. Bernstein's early sociology of knowledge did not represent the sociology of knowledge of either Mannheim or Marx. Rather, it was an application to educational knowledge of Durkheim, a sociologist of knowledge derided by the American academic left.

The early British 'new' sociology of education was not the direct expression of a British Left movement. Marxism, or 'neo-Marxism', in the customary term of the British sociologists of education, entered this discourse later, in the mid-1970s, and appeared as a critique of the subjectivism and ahistorical structuralism of the first, 'new' sociology of education. The later work (for an overview, see Banks, 1982) included self-criticism by the early new sociologists (Young and Whitty, 1977), and finally an explicit attempt to reformulate the entire problematic into a Marxist framework (Sharp, 1980).

By then, the 'new' sociology of education had become a part of the wider international academic movement of critical social theory. The social dilemmas and cultural action of the academic latecomers, the fused articulation of educationists, British new sociology and American revisionist history, and general critical social theory combined then to shape the early course of new sociology of education.

New sociology of education

This new sociology is a direct counter-point to the assumptions of the old, mainstream, conventional sociology of education. Against the scientific pretensions of objective knowledge, work in both the educational and social science fields that gravitates toward the label new sociology of education aims to analyze social knowledge in schooling and social knowledge about schooling as relative, socially determined and ideological. (For examples, see: Young, 1971; Brown, 1974; Bernstein, 1975; Young and Whitty, 1977; Wexler, 1976; Karabel and Halsey, 1977; Apple, 1979a, 1982a,

1982b; Sharp, 1980; Giroux, 1981, 1983). Against the study of school as the channel of individual mobility that validates a permeable, meritocratic social order, new 'sociologists' in economics (Bowles and Gintis, 1976), history (Spring, 1972), education (Olsen, 1981), and sociology (Bourdieu and Passeron, 1977) redefined the social function of schooling as the social and cultural reproduction of regimes of inequality. Against the view of schooling as morally consensual and socially integrative, new sociology sees conflict, opposition, and resistance (Willis, 1977; Giroux, 1983; Apple, 1982a; Wexler, 1985a).

Ideology, reproduction and resistance are simultaneously organizing themes of the new sociology discourse and markers on a path of cultural action. They are expressions of a history in which a segment of a socially marginal professional stratum revises, in the medium of academic theory, the course of an antecedent social movement as part of its practice of establishing a legitimate identity. Efforts to articulate this identity draw from revised memories of the 1960s university movement, education-distanced general critical social theory, and the internal contradictions of 'PMC' professional culture. The focused articulation that results is a radical academic theory which reads and displaces into education the conditions and contradictions of its carriers' history.

'Ideology' was both the first key conceptual term and social moment in this history. The demystification of professional knowledge among movement 'radical' professionals described by Ehrenreich and Ehrenreich (1977) also appears later as the core activity of the new sociologists of education – in the language of ideology-critique. Ideology-critique, which in its simplest form is debunking, is a practical struggle against solidity, against the successful displacement of historically specific social relations into transcendent and naturalized 'knowledge'. This historical abstraction and displacement, that Marcuse (1968: 88–133) called the 'affirmative character of culture,' is a cultural practice accessible to ascendant and subordinate as well as to ruling groups (Mannheim, 1936:40).

The specific discourse of ideology/education, which is the cultural work of a particular group of university intellectuals with a concrete history, can also become ideological. I have argued that 'carriers' of this discourse, the sociologists of education, expressed both an oppositional and legitimating ideology of a group trying to make a culture and professional place for itself within an established institution. In debunking the established knowledge in the academic specializations of education and sociology, the first ideology-critique was an authentic critical cultural practice. It was an aspect of the critics' own collective efforts for emancipation and mobility.

In the expanding academy there was a foothold for carriers of the ideology critique. With marginally successful academic inclusion, they were able to draw upon a large and previously academically suppressed tradition of critical and Marxist theories of ideology. Almost directly, with the application of ideology-critique to education, the new sociologists, especially the educationists, borrowed a term from Bourdieu that renamed their academic practice as the study of 'cultural reproduction.' This later 'theory' in the new sociology of education retained, however, the same assumptions of the earlier ideology-critique. Beneath the language of newly discovered continental cultural theory, remained the logic of ideology-critique: the concept of ideology as distorted knowledge and emphasis on its role in societal maintenance and stability. But, by then, the critique of knowledge was no longer directed against blockages in the work situations of its proponents or undertaken in the name of collective self-emancipation. The object of critique was not university knowledge, but school knowledge. At stake was not the oppression of the theorist, but the role of the school in the oppression of others, notably, 'the working class' (Willis, 1977; Anyon, 1979).

Economic and cultural versions of the hypothesis that education is a means of class and societal reproduction appears to replace ideology-critique as the central issue of the radical social analysis of education almost as the academic movement metonymically replaces the social movement. During the late 1970s, a time of a decrease in political movement activity and an increase in the academic discursive movement, there was a diffusion of terms of the reproduction discourse. 'Reproduction' operated as a magnetic center for the various movements, particularly among the educationists, that were coalescing into an American new sociology of education (Apple, 1982b). Yet, the 'theory' of cultural reproduction was, despite introduction of terms like 'hegemony' and 'cultural practices', still deeply that of ideology-critique: imposition of the ideas of the powerful on the powerless, against their own objective interest, and the cover-up of this activity by the claims to the neutrality and timelessness of knowledge. As Sharp (1980:84) acknowledged, 'The key substantive issue (is) . . . . that of the role of ideology in social reproduction.' There was a certain irony in the shift of terms from critique to reproduction. It almost appears as if the analytic terms were socially self-indexing; as if the demystifying activity of a group's successful institutional entry stage were abstracted to an historically appropriate change in the character of its professionalizing labor. Did reproduction really refer to the Carrier Group's own cultural reproduction through the accumulation of 'cultural capital' (Bourdieu, 1977)?

During this broadly political quiescent and narrowly academically discursively active phase, traditions of radical scholarship little known in the American academy generally, but certainly excluded from educational discourse, were collected and catalogued. The most popular division was between structural and cultural theories of reproduction. Althusser was viewed as the leading structuralist, while despite Bourdieu's coinage of the term, ultimately it was the Frankfurt school that was used to represent culturalism. Within a structuralist framework, Althusser offered a theory of ideology (1971:127–86) that was appropriated to both generalize and legitimate ideology critique (and its users) as a theory of cultural reproduction. According to his own succinct summary:

1 'Ideology represents the imaginary relationship of individuals to their real conditions of existence.'
2 'Ideology has a material existence.'
3 'Ideology interpellates individuals as subjects.'

Althusser's contribution provided new sociology with a view of ideology as a material practice, rather than as 'ideas': ideology as interactive significatory practical activity (Coward and Ellis, 1977). The cultural mining of Marxist structuralism for the discourse of reproduction unexpectedly opened what later becomes an analytic way to a linguistic and practical approach to ideology. Althusser's second contribution to a theory of the role of ideology in social reproduction is no less important: ideology works by positioning the subject. Ideology 'interpellates,' positions or produces the subject. This, according to Althusser (1971:172), is the 'elementary ideological effect'. His description of ideology leads away from the imposition of ideas to an analysis of the discursive practices which prevent anything but an imaginary relation to the real. This is accomplished by the linguistic production of the false individuality of the 'subject' whose subjectivity contributes to her/his subjection.

The Frankfurt school (Frankfurt Institute, 1956) analysis of culture was also used to establish the view of education as a site for reproduction. As with Althusser, when the Frankfurt school work is appropriated in the accumulative phase of the new sociology discourse, it unintentionally points away from a 'theory' of cultural reproduction as ideological transmission. It leads instead from 'ideas' to the study of socially organized apparatuses through which culture is produced. Yet, in the process of appropriating the analysis to the language of cultural reproduction, ideology-critique is still represented as the signal contribution (Giroux, 1983). While they were indeed masters of the art of ideology critique (for reviews, see Held, 1980; Wexler, 1983), the Frankfurt school's effort is rather directed toward the forms and content of cultural mass deception in the 'culture industry' (Horkheimer and Adorno, 1972). The study of mass deception through cultural production returns them to a central social relational concept in Marxist theory: commodity fetishism. Their analysis is an attempt to show how commodity production in the labor process is replayed in the cultural form and content that creates the psychology of the dominated subject.

The structural and cultural redeployments of these several traditions were also supplemented by more specifically educational statements. Bowles and Gintis (1976) explained the reproductive role of schooling in capitalist society through a 'correspondence principle.' The 'correspondence principle' asserted that schooling meets the needs of capital by mirroring within schools the class-differentiated, alienated social relations of the workplace. Another model emphasized the importance of class-cultural educational reproduction as part of general societal maintenance (Bourdieu and Passeron, 1977; Apple, 1979a). Cultural reproduction theory argued that the class culture of dominant social groups is transmitted in schools as universal, legitimate knowledge, stratifying both knowledge and students, in order to reproduce a class society.

Fall

The move from the language of ideology to the language of reproduction represented an acknowledgment of the systemic character of social domination and of education's role in it. By the early 1980s, however, social reproduction through schooling was viewed as incomplete, contradictory, and contested (Apple, 1982a). The symbolic identity, the culturally performative role of the new sociology of education, is revealed by the reasons given for the shift toward a qualified reproductionism. Willis (1977), in his small case study, from which the term 'resistance' was appropriated, had argued that subcultural opposition among white working-class high school boys was an essential moment in the process of class reproduction through schooling. New sociologists were later urged, however, to champion the concept of resistance as a statement of their 'optimism' and as a demonstration of their loyalty to the political goal of emancipation (Anyon, 1981a; Giroux, 1983). The symbolic use of new sociology in a process of collective identity formation and professional legitimation among the post-movement academic latecomers was underlined by the view that failure to echo the theme of resistance in education was not so much scientifically wrong as socially disloyal and politically incorrect (Giroux, 1983).

Within this cultural action of elaborating a discourse as an assertion of professional and political identity, the central concepts of a structural political economy model of schooling and its complementary view of class cultural rule through the transmission of ideology as educational knowledge, were, however, modified. The concept of totality was replaced by an awareness of relative institutional autonomy. Structural integration gave way to the description of internal contradictions. The reproduction of social domination was conceptually mitigated by the study of conflict. Sources of social change were found in an unfolding set of structural contradictions of the capitalist economy, and in the cultural autonomy and resistance of the working class. The reproduction theme fell into disrepute even among its original proponents (Apple and Weis, 1983).

The sublimated conceptual articulation of a radical-professional identity among low-status (educationists and sociologists of education), post-New Left academics did replicate the movement's obsessive critique of liberalism and the romantic individualism of its understanding of political opposition and change. The term 'hegemony' could also be read as a collective self-index: the psychology and language of movement activists remained caught inside the discursive grid of the regime's ascendant class culture (Wexler and Whitson, 1982). The effort to avoid defeat, in the discursive action of the new sociology, like the direct action of movement predecessors, led to a negative, though fully-contained oppositional expression of the dominant American ideology:individualism. The rhetoric of educational resistance replayed the hegemonic, though negative, individualism of the larger culture (Anyon, 1981a; Giroux, 1983). As with the radical university movement, the new sociology began to founder because its social analysis was so incorporated in the prevailing culture that it could not grasp the historically specific conditions that made possible its own forms of speech.

During the last few years, it has become evident that at least two of the conditions that had made new sociology possible were disappearing. The first was that the culture of liberalism had been overtaken not by its friendly, even filial opposition, but instead by a powerful American New Right. Within a cultural restoration on a broad social front, liberalism retreated in university social science too, responding to state-sponsored demands for a more commodified, market-oriented explanatory language (*Wall Street Journal*, 3:27, 1981:54). New sociology was late reacting to this deep cultural alteration. As late as the early 1980s, the discourse was directed against the liberal public schooling that was being attacked and dismantled from the political right. The 'radical' educational discourse that had been fueled as an historical negation of liberalism was unprepared to find liberalism on the run, under attack from a powerful New Right. Without that 'primal scene,' commitments and terms of the social educational discourse which had remained in the mood and the language of the New Left were disoriented. The rhetoric of resistance had been preempted by the New Right's public language of reaction and restoration (Johnson, 1985).

Second, the university expansion that had nurtured the ambivalent professionalism of the professional middle-class academics was completely reversed. Already by the mid 1970s the rate of academic salary gains, which had risen to an average of 40 percent during the expansionist decade, had receded, and in fact reversed course. An academic labor market, that in the previous decade expanded the class-basis of training and recruitment to fill positions, was being described in terms ranging from zero-growth, to drastic decline to simply 'collapse' (Kerr and Gade, 1981: 126,124). While it may have been possible earlier to ignore or underestimate the New Right's educational campaigns, by the 1980s, the unemployment, and political dismissals of radical professional academics were evident (Burris, 1983; Parenti, 1980, Abel, 1984). The analytical heritage of the new sociology of education left its producers relatively disarmed in the face of rightist social movement. The conceptual path from ideology to reproduction to resistance had operated to block analysis of processes of historic movements of class cultural action. In retrospect, the reproduction-resistance or structure-agency binaries now seem remarkably similar to the traditional bourgeois antinomy 'individual-society' that has a cultural autonomy linked to obscure the possibility of a collective historical understanding of social life. The same kind of bifurcation operated in research. So-called ethnographies reduced traditional 'thick description' (Geertz, 1973), to ordinary positivist, correlational logic, between class and curriculum (see, for example, Anyon, 1981a). 'Subjectivity' was posed as the alternative to positivist research. 'Reflexivity' in research (Ruby, 1982) meant personal, individual remembrance. Division of research logic between positivism and reflexivity limited the possibility of research as a practical action.

The ascendance of the New Right and the underemployment of younger academics generally, and particularly radicals and educationists, made the solution of an individual, though culturally based resistance appear increasingly unrealistic. While the new sociologists could deny their own professional class situation to glorify a resistant culture of working-class youths (Willis and Corrigan, 1983), the rightist educational movements were increasingly undeniable. This historical reality of rightist collective action and social movement pressed the new sociology discourse from ideology reproduction and resistance toward an articulation of education in relation to social movements.

An early indication of a redirection from concepts of resistance to collective action, social movement and mobilization was that interest in the concept of ideology was redefined. Ideology as cultural domination came to be seen as only one moment in a more general process (Wexler, 1982: Apple and Weis, 1983). The discourse moved toward theorizing social change through the familiar terms of ideology. The ideology/education relation was reinterpreted from the perspective of social and collective action rather than reproduction. There was interest in 'a positive moment,' of ideology as an element in historical instances of social mobilization. One sign of the shift was the rethinking of Gramsci (1971). Gramsci was an important political activist and writer, whose work had been 'rediscovered' by the American New Left and incorporated in the reproduction discourse model of cultural domination as 'hegemony' (Wexler and Whitson, 1982). Now, Gramsci's historical, formative understanding of ideology was 'rediscovered' (Gramsci, 1971:376–7):

Ideology itself must be analyzed historically . . . to the extent that ideologies are historically necessary they have a validity which is 'psychological'; they 'organize' human masses, and create the terrain on which men move, acquire consciousness of their position, struggle, etc.

In reinterpretations of Gramsci, and appropriations of the work of historians like Williams (1969), Rude (1980) and Kelley (1982) to educational discourse, ideology was increasingly seen not only as cultural domination, but as a socially formative aspect of educational processes of social change (Wexler, 1982). During this time, there began talk of the 'sites' of collective action and social movement. Historical knowledge about the role of education in collective action and search for 'new' movements were analytic paths for new sociologists of education trying to see beyond reproduction and resistance. Interest in the new movements (Habermas, 1981) and in the history of collective revolt turned most of the new sociologists away again from analyzing their own social lives, and perhaps for good reason. For what was the social situation of the radical academic professional middle class?

On the one hand, underemployment and the success of rightist social movements propelled new sociology toward a renewed, though idealized, interest in collective mobilization and social change. But this interest was expressed as a working-class interest, not a professional middle-class interest. Its 'site' of projected operation was in public schooling, and not in the academy. On the other hand, the academically incorporated, 'successful' PMC had not won the secure institutional base for social change that it had once anticipated. Instead, like other bureaucratic professonals, it was subject to what Derber described as a (1983: 318): 'growing dependency on administrative coordination and a growing ideological proletarianization reflecting loss of control over the selection and allocation of tasks. . .' Once professional knowledge was seen as power, the 'cultural capital' of a new middle/working/ professional class. Now, professional workers were seen as defending themselves by 'ideological desensitization,' denying the importance of asserting their own social values or goals (Derber, 1983:327). Instead, surveys revealed, they turned to 'intrinsic' work satisfaction. As Derber put it, they look for '. . . cognitive, rather than moral, development' (1983:326). Subordinate to administrative coordinators, professionals channel ambitions to technical, 'cognitive' work autonomy. This contraction of the social power of professionals, while inside a powerful social institutional apparatus, is an historically different and new sort of exclusion for the class faction from which the sociologists of education were ostensibly drawn. It is a kind of internal exclusion, an internal social exile, ironic for those first driven to ideology-critique by the aims of professional, institutional inclusion. Yet, for some PMC occupations, the narrow 'technical' to which a new form of professional proletarianization pushes them, is language use itself (Gouldner, 1979). Here, discourse can become the last refuge of social power. The decomposition of discourse indicates a new cultural politics: a desperate effort to exercise power through decomposition as a new form of internally exiled power.

The new sociology of education discourse follows, though in an abstract, rationalized language, the social path of its producers: from ideology-critique to awareness of systemic reproduction through the accumulation of cultural capital; and then from idealized and socially displaced individual cultural resistance to the dissonant bifurcation between an idealized social mobilization and an unconscious politics of internally exiled speech.

I think that it is the effort to surpass this inchoate contradiction that finally pushes new sociology out of the Progressive liberal paradigm, with which it is bound in negation, and beyond an abstract appropriation of Marxist theory in new sociology, toward a social analysis of education. Historically, social change itself has made it unrealistic to understand education simply as mobility or as reproduction.The everyday social life of radical educationists and sociologists of education, wherever it refuses institutionally blinding routinization or ritualizing paradigmatic rationalization, insists on an historical awareness and on a continuous revision of social analysis. The new sociology of education can now be recollected by replacing it into the historical process from which cultural performances of legitimation have abstracted it, and so blocked its realization. As Marx wrote of the Utopian social theorists (Bottomore and Rubel, 1956: 65):

. . . these theorists remain Utopians who, in order to remedy the distress of the oppressed classes, improvise systems and pursue a regenerative science. But as history continues . . . they have no further need to look for a science in their own minds; they have only to observe what is happening before their eyes, and to make themselves its vehicle of expression. . . . But from this moment, the science produced by the historical movement and which consciously associates itself with this movement, has ceased to be doctrinaire and has become revolutionary.

PART TWO

After the new sociology
of education

3
Reorganization

From reproduction to change

The new sociologists of education articulated the loss of liberal faith in the socially reformative power of education. They focused academic attention away from models of educationally facilitated individual mobility, toward the study of schooling's role in perpetuating social inequality and class domination. As Persell (1977) asserted in her book on the sociology of education and inequality, the reproduction of inequality is the main effect of education: 'In today's America, the institution of education is called upon to maintain, reproduce, and legitimate the inequalities of society.' By inculcating the belief in reward for merit, through education, when in fact there is little 'circulatory mobility' for those either at the bottom or the top of the social hierarchy, schooling helps reproduce the class structure. The status attainment model positioned educational against family variables as a measure of achievement vs. ascriptive determination of status. But they neglected study of the process of schooling, which the new sociologists had shown is not limited to objective, neutral, and so-called technical skills. It includes also a 'hidden curriculum,' a pattern of class relations and beliefs (Apple, 1979a). In this view what this social education accomplishes, behind the shield of teaching technical skills and enabling meritocratic achievement, is the reproduction of socialized labor power for society's relatively fixed social classes. In education, social power operates behind the ideological shield of an appearance of meritocratic and education-ally mediated individual social advancement. In its distrust of individual mobility claims, universal conceptual models of society, functionalist social theory and normative consensus, the reproductionist critique was a revolt against the prevailing liberalism.

The earliest and boldest expression of this rejection of liberalism in social misunderstandings of education was the correspondence view of Bowles and Gintis (1976:131):

> The educational system helps integrate youth into the economic system . . . through a structural correspondence between its social relations and those of production . . . the social relationships of education . . . replicate the hierarchical division of (alienated) labor.

Their analysis was criticized and complemented by a variety of reproduction theories, especially the 'cultural capital' theories that emphasized the class character not only of the social relations of schooling, but tried also to show that social class reproduction was accomplished through the partial and stratified character of school knowledge. Curriculum as well as classroom was seen as an element of education's complicity in the reproduction of an hierarchical society. School knowledge that is presented as asocial and politically neutral is shown to be class-specific knowledge that operates to legitimate differential socially reproductive sorting as meritocratic achievement (Bourdieu, 1973; Bernstein, 1975; Apple, 1979a).

Later, new sociologists of education disclaimed this earlier work as mechanical or simple-minded. Instead they argued that reproduction through education, even when successful, is always achieved through processes of resistance, contradiction and contestation. During a time when the liberal ideological hegemony was being replaced by a complex technocratic-conservatism, the new sociology, formed in and against the liberal period, nevertheless remained a critique of liberalism. Its critique of liberalism continued to focus on the socially reproductive power of common state schooling, at the time that the educational sector was moving toward marketization and privatization. The culture of liberalism, both in the academy and in the wider social world, was giving way to an altered structure of perception and meaning.

While everyday cultural meaning was being restored to traditional ideological themes such as work as careerism, solidarity as family, and historical hope as religious fundamentalism, new sociology also took flight from an unexpected reassertion of the politics and culture of capital.

New sociology discourse was particularly displaced to an idealization of working-class resistance, although it was increasingly also drawn to modernist cultural theories' emphasis on discourse and its decomposition. Continuing efforts at paradigmatic rationalization and collective professional identity legitimation through 'theorizing' were accomplished at the cost of historical, institutional analysis of social change, and particularly of educational change. Reproductionist theory, however qualified by concepts of contestation, contradiction and resistance, appealed to an abstract rather than historically specific critical analysis of education. But historical social change pushes toward the interruption of comforting routinizations. Socioeconomic crises disrupt the apparent validity of both historical identities and, when they are not successfully denied, academic theories. As Wolin (1980:182) observed: 'Many of the great theories of the past arose in response to a crisis in the world, not in the community of theorists,' and, further (1980:186), '. . . most of the major theories have been produced during times of crisis, rarely during periods of normalcy.' It is a social crisis that is shaking loose the blockage of the new sociology, and slowly returning the critical social analysis of education to specific historical social processes and context.

When class rule of the social context is seen as fairly stable, then it does make sense to analyze how, beneath the ideology of meritocratic achievement, unequally distributed and produced cultural capital, not recognized as such, but viewed instead as individual differences, plays a role in the reproductive maintenance of a class society. In these conditions, the social relations of the school are seen as a semi-autonomous, contradictory, but largely reproductive mediation between the family and the individual on the one hand, and, on the other, the societal structure of inequality in which system needs such as accumulation and legitimation are met. The reproduction view is apparently most accurate as a representation of class rule for such periods of relative social stability. If, however, the maintenance of ruling classes is accomplished not by the transmission of deep false consciousness – cultural reproduction – but instead by redefining the very meaning of schooling and restructuring the institutional relation between schools and other aspects of the social formation, then the theoretical and political questions are different. Efforts of ruling classes are aimed toward accomplishing their hegemony not only by the imposition of their culture as fact. Rather, classes rule through the work of accomplishing social reorganizations. During a social crisis, these efforts at reorganization are intensified and become more apparent. It becomes easier during such times to begin instead with the assumption that the accomplishment of class hegemony requires not simple economic and cultural domination, but constant social reorganization and restructuring. I want to point toward aspects of social processes of education which emphasize not only the social relations within the school, but also the social relation of the school, to the social formation.

By focusing on how schools produce and distribute unequal cultural capital, and so contribute to social reproduction, the importance of the processes of educational change and reorganization are slighted. The issue that the historically specific conjuncture forces upon us is less a matter of the internal transmission of educational cultural capital than of the institutional reorganization and change of education. Hall (1981: 113–37) described this changed situation as a 'recomposition of the educational state apparatuses and redirection of resources and programs . . .' In this historical situation, forms of class rule involve destruction of whole ranges of activities and organizations. By continuing to emphasize cultural inequality and reproduction, which is, of course, a method of class rule, historically specific institutional analyses of educational changes are ignored.

In the aftermath of the cultural and institutional 'crisis' of the 1960s, the reproduction view helped supplant the decontextual, input-output individualism of the old sociology with an emphasis on systematic class reproduction through schooling. The crisis of the 1980s, in turn, placed in question basic assumptions of the new sociology. It was as if the concepts of ideological domination, class system reproduction and individual cultural resistance in education that had defensively congealed, like brittle insignia of legitimation, now diffused to display constituent social processes. The dynamic historical creation of social life through processes of institutional change and reorganization, class conflict, collective action and movement, and cultural and knowledge transformation was brought to the surface of awareness by historical crisis processes themselves. Taken together – institutional and class analysis of change, study of collective action and movement, social knowledge and cultural change – these processes form an approach to social and educational change that was neglected by both old and new sociology.

In this chapter, I begin to analyze socioeducational change by providing an institutional view: analysis of the historical change and recomposition of the organization and operation of social institutions as part of the collective action of historically significant groups of social actors. The socio-economic crisis that began in the early 1980s offers a particular historical context and example of an institutional reorganization in education.

Education and crisis

Social crisis and academic discourse

The crisis which now makes processes of educational reorganization and historically specific forms of class conflict more apparent has its own historically specific character. In the United States, it is a crisis which incites a prophetic voice even among technocratic, cautious and dull bureaucratic ideologists. There are now public prognosticators of every sort. A few years ago, social diviners found iconic meaning in the fashion of disaster films. Now, mass panic occurs in real life. The imagery of structural collapse is replaced by fear of anonymous poisoning. At the same time, more literal fears grow; by the early 1980s, television news was posting rising unemployment rates as it once did the Vietnam body-counts.

The social crisis is so sharp and it has brought to the surface so many social possibilities that even academic sociologists could be roused to a social analysis, but they fearfully continue to insist that sociology has no active role in social life. They forgo the reward which this period of suffering and uncertainty can offer to the social voyeur: the appearance of new social forms and tendencies. These forms and tendencies are not, however, simply responses to an immediate crisis: they express historical social patterns. These tendencies are first, the extension of commodity relations to every sector of social relations as a principle of social life that is elevated to the status of an academic and popular theory. At the same time, quite different social forms from the past return. The result is that extension of commodity relations and market-logic coexists with assertions about the importance of incalculable connections of family, and absolute tender of religious belief as primary constituents of society and nation.

This seemingly antagonistic combination of social forms – whether labelled capitalist and feudal, individual and collective, gesellschaft and gemeinschaft – is the central social tendency. It is not created by the current cyclical crisis of capitalism, but it is accelerated by it. This contradictory dynamic may, at least in the short-run, be moving toward a resolution in corporatism. In education, movement toward corporatist social forms is part of an identifiable institutional reorganization. In the institutional sector of education, reorganization of local school districts indicates more than fiscal crisis, with its attendant cutbacks of staff and resources. The social shape of US education has begun to shift. As a social institution, it is coming loose from its foundations of more than half a century. What is the meaning of this educational change and how is it related to wider social changes?

To ask now about the relation between education and the social crisis is to step already outside the prevailing discourse of American radical intellectuals. The division of discursive labor blocks analysis of education in the crisis; political economists and new sociologists of education are largely each in their own compartments. There is a tradition of radical political economic analysis in America. Currently, a central interest of this tradition is to go beyond a purely economic analysis toward a more general social one that particularly considers the role of the state. Many of the political economy radicals have moved from an abstract logic of capital view (for an early critique, see Aronowitz, 1978), toward an historical conjunctural analysis of the American economy that emphasizes placing capitalist dynamics in the context of this particular social formation. Yet, in their analyses of the social crisis, education is a rarely mentioned afterthought. More surprisingly, American educational radicals, the so-called new sociologists of education, slight analyses of the meaning of the crisis for education. Academic territorial division halts emergence of a substantial educational crisis literature. Division operates within new sociology itself (Wexler, 1982). Educational analysts look toward very general social theory, on the one hand, and detailed case studies, on the other. General theory discusses 'class' and 'state,' but as abstract categories. The 'specific' is consigned to ethnography, where it languishes within the school institution, outside of social history. Historically specific social relations of education are neither described nor explained. The ethnographic work complements an historical general theory with a structurally abstracted empiricism. Both idealist macrostructuralist and ethnographic microstudy, by denying history, become part of a larger silence within radical educational analyses – omission of politically interested social analyses of the infrastructure of education and of its social institutional dynamics.

That work has been left for the conventional political science or fiscal administration analysts of schooling. (See for example, Wirt and Kirst, 1982). Questions of finance, political regulation, governance, organizational dynamics, and specific historical, inter-institutional relations have remained underdeveloped within new sociology. The evident force of the general social crisis, and the place of education within it, finally calls these questions to our attention. The crisis undermines prevailing radical educational discourses both of cultural and structural reproduction.

Institutional crisis

Weisskopf's (1981:9–53) analysis rejects a structuralist, general logic of capital argument for an historical, conjunctural view of capital and crisis. He applies Gordon's (1980) long-cycle theory of capital accumulation to a periodization of US history. According to Weisskopf, the present crisis is the third major economic crisis in the past one hundred and thirty years, following Great Depressions of the 1870s to 1890s, and the 1930s. Each crisis of accumulation is a result of the heightening of contradictions in the modes of resolution of the previous crisis; contradictions are embedded in the 'institutional structure.' While there are important 'economic elements' in the present crisis – slowdown of growth, increased inflation, unemployment, decline in pay and profit – its source is the contradictory social institutional structure. The current crisis, for example, is a result of the breakup of 'Pax Americana' which continued the war's solution to the Great Depression well into the 1950s and 1960s and a domestic institutional structure of 'security capitalism' made possible by a combined capitalist-labor accord; economic stabilization through state management of demand; accomplishment and legitimation of economic redistribution through the social wage (unemployment compensation, transfer payments – e.g., social security) and increased social services. Each of these institutional solutions is now a source of current crisis. Pax Americana led to its own erosion through the advances it promoted among the other capitalist nations, particularly Japan, and through the cost of defending the empire. The domestic institutional structure which developed in response to earlier crises of accumulation disabled the American economy from adapting to a changed external, international situation. The capital-labor accord, state demand-management and protective role of the state diminished the range of action and confidence of the capitalist class to engage in their usual tasks of investments (due to declining profit rates – see Table 1) and economic streamlining.

At the same time that investment slowed, public demands on the state continued, despite declining output value, contributing to continued rising inflation. Labor victories in a stabilizing, redistributive, legislatively mediated restructuring of the capital-labor accord increased the range of labor's expectations for workplace control and self-determination. This meant still more demands placed on the state for increased regulation of the workplace, environmental protection and reduction of existing racial and sexual hiring practices. The economic cost of the political pressure to limit the bottom on recessions meant taking 'the lid off price and (money) wage restraint.' Thus the classical capitalist medicine of periodic economic downturn became increasingly ineffective as a restraint on inflationary pressures and as a stimulant to economic efficiency' (Weisskopf, 1981:24). The use of military spending as a stimulant was high-cost, inefficient spending, while the social wage raised expectations even further, increasing the economic costs of legitimation.

Weisskopf summarizes (1981:34):

> The liberal 'warfare-welfare-state' agenda, which was part of the *solution* to the economic crisis of the 1930s because it helped to stimulate profits via increased aggregate demand, is now part of the *problem* because it competes with capitalists for investible resources and limits the scope of their decision-making discretion.

Table 1 Profitability and investment in the post-war US economy

Variables*	1950s	1960s	1970s
Share of profits before taxes (as a % of national income)	22.5	21.9	18.3
Share of profits after taxes (as a %of national income)	14.3	15.1	12.2
Rate of profits before taxes (as a % of fixed capital stock)	12.1	12.1	9.2
Rate of profits after taxes (as a % of net national product)	7.7	8.3	6.2

Sources of underlying data: US Department of Commerce, Bureau of Economic Analysis, National Income and Product Accounts and Estimate of Capital Stock in the United States (published periodically in the *Survey of Current Business*); US Department of the Treasury, Internal Revenue Service, *Statistics of Income*.

* Profits are defined to include all forms of property income, net of capital consumption allowance; taxes include estimates of personal income taxes paid on property income as well as corporate profit taxes; fixed capital stock is measured by the replacement cost of net residential and non-residential capital.

Calculated as an unweighted average of annual percentages over the decade as a whole.

Adapted from Weisskopf, 1981:27.

He underlines the view of economic crisis as occurring within a series of historically transitory contradictory institutional reorganizations (Weisskopf, 1981:32): 'The long-wave historical framework developed earlier suggests that a resolution of the current crisis will have to be based on a new institutional structure.'

Bowles and Gintis (1982) have extended this view of institutional sources of economic crisis. They expand the institutional perspective through a more detailed analysis of the historically and contextually specific operation of the state as the central institutional mediation in class conflict. For them, the state is not, as in the functionalist-Marxist view, simply an agency of social control, working to gloss or resolve crises in capitalism. Instead, the state is seen as 'a site that is integral to the *production* of a crisis as well as its resolution' (Bowles and Gintis, 1982:60).

They reject both a functional view, which sees the state as an instrument of social-class stabilization, and also a structuralist view, that ignores the specific social practices that constitute a structure. They argue that as a result of working-class victories expressed in the labor-capital accord, there was a further rearticulation of social sites, a 'transportation of practices,' formerly considered specific to the separate sites of economy and polity. The traditional discursive boundary between polity as person rights and economy as property rights is dissipated by this social reorganization won in class struggle, and institutionalized through the legislation of the 'accord.' The discourse of person rights is applied to economic practices located in the state (Bowles and Gintis, 1982:70).

> The major distributional gains made by workers were not
> achieved in their direct confrontation with capital over the
> bargaining table, but in the State. The working class has
> increasingly relied upon the citizen wage as the concrete form of
> its distributional victories.

Because of past working-class victories in this rearticulation of the state and the accumulation process, the capitalist class has experienced distributional losses and a diminished capacity to discipline labor. Said simply (Bowles and Gintis, 1982:75): 'The accord promoted distributional conflict as the predominant axis of the class struggle, and the capitalist class lost.' Beyond the distributional victory, both the discourse and the site of class struggle have become political. Loss in surplus value and labor-disciplining power, under these conditions, leads Bowles and Gintis to believe that the capitalist class will seek a 'structural reconstitution of the accumulation process,' which means 'a new logic of class struggles.' Weisskopf's dialectic of historical institutional restructuring and reorganization thus becomes also a dialectic of historical class struggles. What this will now mean in the liberal-capitalist state is an effort of the capitalist class to '. . . curtail the transportation of practices from the liberal democratic State to capitalist production and to promote a transportation of practices from capitalist production to the liberal

Table 2 Sources of workers' consumption: the wage and the citizen wage, 1948–1977, in constant (1967) dollars

Year	Gross average weekly earnings[a] (1)	Estimated weekly direct taxes on earnings[b] (2)	Spendable average weekly earnings[c] (3)	Estimated weekly social welfare expenditures[d] (4)
1948	68	1	67	14
1950	74	2	72	16
1955	84	5	79	19
1959	96	9	82	25
1965	101	10	91	32
1972	109	12	97	61
1977	104	10	94	71
Average annual rate of growth, 1948–1977	1.5%	7.9%	1.2%	5.6%
Increase, 1948–1977	36	9	27	57

a   Gross average weekly earnings of production and non-supervisory workers, in 1967 dollars.

b   Estimated weekly direct taxation (including employee contributions to social insurance) for production or non-supervisory workers, in 1967 dollars.

c   Spendable average weekly earnings of production or non-supervisory workers, in 1967 dollars, for a worker with three dependants.

d   Estimated weekly social welfare expenditures under public programs per family of four, in 1967 dollars.

Adapted from Bowles and Gintis, 1982:73.

democratic State' (Bowles and Gintis, 1982:92).

Piven and Cloward (1982) emphasize the same historic transformation in the discourse and site of class struggle. Although they do not write about the transportation of practices, they do emphasize the 'renaissance of the idea of economic rights as political rights' (Piven and Cloward, 1982:100). 'How was it possible,' they ask (1982:70), 'for capital to triumph, and to triumph so fully, in the context of the most fully developed democratic laws in the world?' Their answer is through the ideology and institutions of laissez-faire, the mystified separation between political and economic democracy which has been the ruling-class American ideology. Yet, because of the insurgent movements of the 1930s and the 1960s, the 'walls have crumbled;' '. . . the state has finally become the main arena of class conflicts' (Piven and Cloward, 1982:125).

These political economists' awareness of historically changing sites and practices of class conflict belongs to the same historical conjuncture as the social crisis itself. The current transparency of past state structuring of class conflict is not now produced by the victories of the working class or the political accomplishments of insurgency movements. On the contrary, the allocative role of the state, the economic meaning of politics, is being brought home by segments of the ruling capitalist class, as it counter-mobilizes in an effort to reclaim its share of profit.

Although Reaganomics has not been the beginning of the counter-mobilization, the politics of capital have now been more directly expressed than at any time in almost half a century. Hammond and Martin (1982) call this counter-mobilization 'the corporate offensive,' and suggest that the strategy of this offensive is a 'reproletarianization of the U.S. working-class;' an attack on the state institutionalized social wage and on conditions regulating the sale of labor power. A new war on labor means reduction of the social or citizen wage by reducing and eliminating a wide range of government welfare programs; regressive taxation measures; and disciplining labor.

The working-class and insurgent movements once institutionalized their victories in the liberal state. Now, a counter-mobilization also works the state apparatus. The Reagan Program makes possible more direct exploitation, as a way to greater profit. Fendrich and Imersheim (1982:1) note:

> The Administration through its fiscal, monetary budget and
> taxing policies is attempting to dismantle the liberal democratic
> state by reconstituting the accumulation process and the state.

They conclude that (Fendrich and Imersheim, 1982:15): '. . . we find it extremely difficult to predict an optimistic political scenario to Reaganomics. The political economy is undergoing a major qualitative transformation away from the liberal democratic state.' In contrast to the radical political economists, mass news media have bombarded their audience with aggregate statistics of national *economic* crisis. They have consistently ignored social analyses of the data which they represent. Ruling-class intellectuals, however, acknowledge both an economic and a social crisis. Felix Rohatyn, a Wall Street banker, wrote of the need for a social-economic 'reconstruction' (1981, 4:6; 1982, 17:3). In this social crisis, one prominent line of reconstruction or reorganization has begun to emerge: corporatism.

From crisis to corporatism

Even if the United States is part, if not the leading edge, of a world-capitalist crisis, still it has its own historical and cultural specificity. It may be, as Weisskopf (1981) argues, that the current crisis is part of a long-cycle wave of 'institutional restructurings.' It is likely true that the crisis generates, as Hammond and Martin (1982) assert, a counter-mobilization, a 'corporate offensive' of the ruling class. These actions, however, may not be as alien to the American past as they now seem. While the economic and political moments of the crisis now seem paramount, they are, I suggest, embedded in historical cultural movements, particularly restorationist movements.

There are now two languages which are being spoken, two lines of action being favored, within the current rightward sociocultural movement. One is the language of the market; the other of morality. But, the two tendencies are dynamic parts of an internally contradictory structure that is in the process of resolution. The first is the language of laissez-faire, of the free market, the messianic American version of 'possessive individualism' (MacPherson, 1962), proclaimed as constituting Liberty and Freedom. This is the flag under which the attack on 'big government' has been mounted, particularly in the diminution of regulatory agencies. As Phillips argues (1982), this 'anti-government' revival is not Reagan's. It began in Wallace's campaign of 1968, proceeded through Nixon's pro-business policies, and was consolidated by Carter's defeat of the liberal wing of the Democratic party. The call for a free market has a long cultural history in the United States, where it has been associated with Social Darwinism (Hofstadter, 1955; Sutton et al., 1956).

The apparently opposing language is one that emphasizes social integration more than individual freedom. It values faith and loyalty more than the business virtue of rationally precise calculation. It speaks of primordial fixed ties rather than flexible choice, of stasis more than movement, order and continuity, not progress. Its most strident expression is the campaign of the 'moral majority.' Against all forms of cultural modernity, it asserts revealed truth of the Bible as a guide to contemporary conduct. It campaigns against abortion, homosexuality, and evolution. In the name of morality and decency, it claims the ties of family and religion as the basis of social relations. As Phillips (1982:27; emphasis added) observed, '. . . its fundamental loyalties are to antiestablishment cultural and social values, *not to the free market.*'

While these two languages cannot be neatly attached to different class factions and interests, they do indicate a central social contradiction. On the one side, there is a press toward total rationalization, toward the extension of the market to all social relations; a thorough triumph of the commodity form. In the other language, there is defense of the patriarchal family, fundamentalist religion, faith, and incalculability. Without denying that one side may represent the interests and commitments of a particular historical class faction, it is important to observe that this internal contradiction within the current rightist social movement is a central dynamic of the American institutional social structure. The development of market-commodity relations has taken place only with support of the surrounding social cushion of the maintenance and reproduction of the pre-market social relations of earlier social forms of sociation and solidarity. What the political economists generalize as production and state are internal, reciprocally related aspects of the historic pattern of social relations in America. This historical internal contradiction – market commodity exchange and family religion-integration – is surfaced and reorganized in the current crisis.

The social reorganization is corporatist. Corporatism surpasses the internal contradiction of conservatism by providing solidarity and integration through the organization of groups of market-commodity actors. It wipes the slate clean of pre-capitalist feudal forms by realizing their integrative possibilities within the logic of commodity production. The radical economists (Weisskopf, 1981; Hammond and Martin, 1982; Bowles and Gintis, 1982) project corporatism as one of several possible future social scenarios. Corporatism is an advanced form of capitalism. Panitch (1977:66) (emphasis added) defined the corporatist model as

> a political structure within advanced capitalism which *integrates* organized socioeconomic producer groups through a system of representation and cooperative mutual interaction at the leadership level and of mobilization and social control at the mass level.

Among corporatism's distinguishing features (Panitch, citing Bowen, 1977:62) are that it operates through '. . . collective agreements concluded among solidly organized "communities of interest" ' and that it is (1977:63) '. . . centered on the integration of central trade union and business organizations in national economic planning and incomes policy programmes and bodies.' The important thing about corporatism is that it is not state imposed, but only state coordinated. It is a product of 'voluntarist arrangements.' Corporatism does not mean the end of class society. On the contrary (quoting Jones) Panitch (1977:71; emphasis added) emphasized the fallacious pretence of egalitarianism in the corporate organization of society:

> *Authority remains with the employer*, it is he who still controls. But those who are controlled are taken into his confidence; their views are solicited; and so the control, by becoming less of an imposition, is made to operate more effectively.

Corporatism is a form of social reorganization which solves the capital and labor problems of the current crisis; and also resolves the antinomy between the marketizing, atomistic tendency of commodity exchange and the organicist solidarity patterns of pre-market anti-rationalist forms of social integration. Corporatism provides for social integration according to functional relation to the commodity. The social forms that grease the way for commodity, market, ruling-class consolidation, provide also for social integration. Conflicting demands of exchange and integration, of calculation and loyalty, of distantiation and communicative connection, are brought to the fore. Corporatism surpasses these contradictions with a less democratic form of capitalism. Yet, it is a form within the horizon of historical American experience (Hawley, 1978). The corporatist response to social crisis is now becoming especially evident in the reorganizing of a particular institutional sector: education.

Institutional reorganization of education

The American school is now not a social means to the creation of a messianic republican culture, as it was in the nineteenth century (Tyack and Hansot, 1982). Nor is it a vehicle for the gospel of scientific efficiency and progressive expertise that it was earlier in this century (Callahan, 1962). Education is no longer hailed as the method to attain social equalization, as it was for the past two decades. Education is now the site of another social movement. The present crusade is a fight against the public school as a central means of national integration and social development. This campaign aims toward the reorganization of US public schooling away from the model of a public institution serving a consensually defined national interest, which characterized the common school, Progressive and equal opportunity movements in American history. Both elements of the aspiring right hegemony – the cultural restoration of 'traditional' values and social relations identified with the New Right, and the fiscally and organizationally influential interests of the market-capital, commodity tendency – are now expressed in the educational activities of social movements. Their dismantling efforts preface a more extensive institutional reorganization of education. Schools are openly, repeatedly, and officially said to be in crisis.

Educational crisis

Signs of school crisis are withdrawal of institutional commitment and pervasive attention to inadequate performance – crises of legitimation and production. National opinion surveys (Kirst, 1981:45–68) show a decline of public expressions of confidence in the institution of education. The public consistently rates overall school performance as mediocre. Lack of discipline, according to the school surveys, is the number one educational problem. Attenuation of the legendary American faith in education (Perkinson, 1968; Welter, 1962) is shared by those who practice education: teachers. A National Education Association survey on the status of public school teachers reported that in reply to questions about willingness to choose teaching as a career again, fewer than half as many American teachers said that they certainly would enter teaching.

Table 3 Willingness-to-teach-again responses for all teachers, 1961–1981

Response category	1961	1966	1971	1976	1982
1	2	3	4	5	6
Certainly would	49.9	52.6	44.9	37.5	21.8
Probably would	26.9	25.4	29.5	26.1	24.6
Chances are about					
even	12.5	12.9	13.0	17.5	17.6
Probably would not . . .	7.9	7.1	8.9	13.4	24.0
Certainly would not . . .	2.8	2.0	3.7	5.6	12.0

Adapted from National Education Association, *Status of the American Public School Teacher, 1980–81*, p. 74; Table 51.

Behavioral indicators confirm withdrawal of commitment. Fewer college graduates choose teaching jobs. Scholastic aptitude test scores of future teachers are lower than those of other college students. Those who do choose teaching because of a stated interest in social justice are also the most likely to leave the teaching profession. 'Enduring' teachers are the ones who highly value job-security, and prefer not to state strong social and political opinions (Schlechty and Vance, 1982).

The public view of educational crisis is represented by an obsessive anxiety about standardized achievement test scores. Despite a slight recent upturn, there is a long downward slope of verbal and mathematics scores (*Education Week*, vol.II, no.4, September 29, 1982). 'But, the dominant message from the

Table 4   Percentage of selected subgroups of teachers who
certainly would become teachers again, 1961–1981

Subgroup	1961	1966	1971	1976	1981
1	2	3	4	5	6
Males	35.2	38.0	33.0	27.3	16.0
Females	56.6	59.2	51.1	42.5	24.8
Elementary	57.3	59.6	50.1	43.5	26.4
Secondary	40.0	44.9	39.1	31.7	18.1
Under age 30	[a]	49.2	41.4	35.6	28.5
Age 30–39	[a]	50.9	40.1	34.5	16.2
Age 40-49	[a]	48.9	47.1	41.6	21.3
Age 50 and over	[a]	60.2	53.0	41.3	27.3
Large systems	[a]	50.2	45.2	33.6	19.1
Medium systems	[a]	53.1	44.0	39.7	20.7
Small systems	[a]	53.6	45.9	36.9	26.1

[a]Data not available

Source as for Table 3, Table 52.

S.A.T.'s is that, even with the latest gains in scores, today's
students are performing nowhere near the level of their counterparts of the 1960's and 1970's' (Greenberg, 1982).

The 'discovery' of illiteracy further underlines failures of school
performance. According to one report (*Education Week*, Nov. 1,
1982:5)

> Some 23 million adult Americans, one of every five, are
> considered 'functional illiterates' – people who can barely cope
> with everyday reading and writing tasks. . . .And the number
> of functional illiterates doesn't appear to be dwindling. . . .it
> actually may be increasing. .
>
> Not only is functional illiteracy at a high level; the rate
> actually seems to be on the increase.
>
> 'Academic certification has nothing whatsoever to do with
> literacy,' says Sue White, research associate for a literacy study
> done at the University of Texas at Austin. A high school

student can take four years of English and still not be able to fill out a job application, she says.

'Crisis' is signalled not only by the loss of legitimacy and the perception of inadequate performance-production, but by images of indiscipline, disorder, chaos. In a description of a Boston high school, school appears unmanageable as well as unproductive (Roberts, 1982).

At English High School here, a security team patrols the graffiti-covered halls in an attempt to deter class-cutting, theft, trespassing and other disorders. Escalators no longer run in the 10-story building, making tardiness between classes an increasing problem. One biology class already has gone through three teachers this year, and the principal complains that students have only half the textbooks they need.

'English,' says Robyne Harris, a senior, 'has gone wild. It's a distracting environment.' Such distractions pervade the Boston school system where concern focuses as much on violence and expenses as on the quality of education.

Educational movement

The current perception of crisis is an early phase in a larger process of the institutional reorganization of education. As a preface to reorganization, it works to destroy the common national republican culture which the schools helped to create during the nineteenth century. There occurs a dismantling of the institutional infrastructure that standardized and solidified national culture through the social relations of twentieth-century education. Both tendencies within the rightward movement, social-integration and market, cultural restoration and reassertion of capital, are represented in the actions of these movements. There appears almost to be a division of labor: attack common culture on the one hand; undercut and dismantle organizational finances and forms on the other. Specifically, this means an attack on school curricula and budgets.

The aim of New Right groups like the Moral Majority is to change the content of schooling. They attack current curricula in public schooling as immoral, asserting that public schools teach a religion that they call 'secular humanism.' The attack on a 'secular humanism' is expressed in numerous efforts to censor schoolbooks. While censorship is fought against in the courts on constitutional grounds of the rights of free speech, book banning by local school boards occurs in every section of the country. Text censorship takes place at each stage in the process; from selection to removal of books from school libraries that are deemed 'dangerous' (Gabler and Gabler, 1982).

While American sociologists of education have turned little attention to this educational movement, educational reporters have (Brodinsky, 1982:88):

> The New Right produces more than 100 nationally circulated magazines, tabloids, and newsletters on a weekly, monthly, or quarterly basis. The New Right creates a new organization about every 30 days on national, state, or local levels. A recent count by the National Education Association (NEA) showed 67 major national organizations promoting ultra-right causes and working against the public schools. 'When it comes to getting rid of dirty schoolbooks, every board of education is a potential ally,' said one spokeswoman from the New Right.

Along with the attack on common civic curriculum, the fiscal infrastructure of public education is being reshaped, and struggle for national educational equality reversed.

The market commodity tendency in the educational movement is apparent in efforts to abolish the national department of education, and to end federal support for categorical educational programs for the education of minorities, women, and the handicapped. The capital offensive, through anti-government ideology and policy, works in education to redistribute educational financing back to the states, so ending national equalizing fiscal strategies. The key term in the fiscal reorganization is rescissions, cuts. The market reorganization involves reducing, decentralizing and disequalizing the financing of education. (For details of the fiscal reorganization, see Wexler and Grabiner, 1985.)

Educational reorganization

The reorganization of education is more than a turn against the national republican culture of the common-school movement or scientific Progressivism. During the same period that new sociology was articulating a critique of liberal public schooling as social class reproduction, an institutional disassembly of education had begun. Attack on the curriculum through censorship, and the so-called reprogramming of school finance were prefaces to this marketizing, commodifying alteration of the form of schooling itself. There is a move toward the marketization of educational activities (Wexler, Whitson and Moskowitz, 1981). There is a kind of de-schooling occurring – a de-schooling from the right.

While a commodifying de-schooling of American education may be taking place, this reorganization of education is hidden by the ideological binary, public/private. Only the private is now thought virtuous. Within the cultural restoration, the imaginary 'individual' has been resuscitated. In such a cultural moment, public schooling becomes identified with the indiscipline of the mass: social and dangerous. Meanwhile, familist and fundamentalist religious ideologies protect the reified market individual against charges of pecuniary heartlessness, and of organizing social relations on a purely exchange basis. Nevertheless, the core of the cultural restoration is market ideology. It is applied to a greater range of daily life activity, although enveloped in the mystifying mist of non-market affiliation and irrational hope. The ideologically restored, more privatized, free-market individual ironically serves the redistributive interests of an evermore social, internationalized capital.

While the current institutional reorganization of education includes processes that operate simultaneously and on several dimensions, and though the evidence is that these are still incipient tendencies, it is, I think, nevertheless possible to suggest a sequential description of this process of educational change. The first, most evident phase is the anti-humanist attack and effort to destroy and dismantle common culture and organizational homogeneity. That is the cultural work in the current educational movement; to be the conscious wreckers of 'secular-humanism' and 'big government.'

Commodification

The second 'phase' is the rationalizing commodification of education. Although its advocates are also within the current socioeducation movements, they speak a less apocalyptic and more educationally scientific language. Supporters are drawn from professional school workers, rather than entirely from the parent groups and political action committees. It is a segment of the movement directed more toward the transformation of knowledge. Already it has succeeded in redefining broad areas of curriculum content, and in de-skilling both the teaching-learning interaction as well as the process of evaluating learning. Its language is educational accountability, competency and 'back to basics' (Wexler, Whitson and Moskowitz, 1981).

The commodification of education is occurring within the framework of organizational and professional rationalization. Rationalization occurs at each point in the educational process. Thirty-eight of the fifty states now have minimum-competency tests for students. The tests represent and reinforce a *redefinition of the content of education* as specific skill learning, where skills are defined narrowly. 'Competency,' 'effectiveness,' and 'performance' are the cultural categories which begin to displace earlier educational terms like 'knowledge,' 'understanding,' and 'development.' Fragmenting rationalization of the school relations of education occurs through the redefinition of the learning process itself. Unlike earlier emphases on the classroom as a micro-community, where social and civic learning takes place, what is now most important about 'effective' classroom education is the amount of 'time on task' (Euchner, 1982:8). The meaning of teaching is also being redefined. Current practices of evaluating teachers, for example, are being de-skilled and rationalized through the establishment of competency testing for teachers (Boardman and Butler, 1981).

Taken together, these various processes of student and teacher de-skilling and expansion of methods of measurable organization and administrative surveillance constitute the commodifying aspect of a larger historic process of educational reorganization. They empty the content of curriculum and teaching of any cultural history that is not reducible to narrowly defined technical skill. The technical skill, by virtue of its method of acquisition and evaluation, is not the kind of generative capacity which engages the imagination. The routinizing emptying is legitimated by appeals to the specific job requirements of high technology, as well as by a more general appeal to an era of educational quality and intensified competition and sorting (Euchner, 1982).

Rationalization in the name of 'quality' is central in the commodifying phase of the reorganization of US education. The performance-testers are alienating the social relations of knowledge production in the mass public education system. The de-skilling of students and teachers in the service of technology and *quality* ('excellence') is an effective reorganization at the micro-level of the social relations of education. What is happening is that the educational process is being decomposed into smaller, more measurable, standardized units. In this way, educational activities are unintentionally being prepared for a macro-process of market-ization. The movement for 'quality in education' hides the reconstitution of education as an object of commodity exchange.

Marketization

For commodity exchange to be realized, there must be established a set of markets capable of accommodating the commodity which has been made in an appropriately alienated fashion. The establishment of a more macro-social, wider institutional net of educational markets is a third point in the process of educational reorganization. Once the definition of education as a necessarily marketable outcome-commodity is established, it becomes feas-ible to work towards appropriate distributive structures. The most obvious, of course, is to transform a public service sector, historically financed largely through community-local property taxes, into a set of private businesses. Privatization of education is an early and central component of the process of establishing an educational market.

The private schools are important; but not for their actual numbers (private schools still account for only a small percentage of enrollments in the US, about 10 percent). They are important as a version of what liberals once called 'demonstration projects.' The private school is now consciously seen as an exemplar for the future of US education. Even census reports on enrollment figures are reported with an eye toward relevance for the administration-supported idea of tuition-tax credits. Academic research adds legitimacy to beliefs in the virtues of what is now deferentially referred to, in the area of social and public services, as 'the private sector.' Coleman, whose national school study in the 1960s was a centerpiece in policy debates about how to achieve equality of opportunity, now reports another major research effort: a comparison of public and private schools (Coleman, Hoffer and Kilgore, 1982). In a review of the factors contributing to areas of relative advantage among private schools, Coleman argues that what is crucial are those factors under the heading of a 'more orderly school and more academic demands.' Acknowledging the interest in private schools as exemplars, he writes (Coleman, Hoffer and Kilgore, 1982:64):

> It would be sad to have to conclude that the constraints placed on public education are so harmful to academic achievement that a movement to the private sector is necessary for such achievement to flourish. Some parents have arrived at such a conclusion in their own local situation; it remains to be seen whether changes will come about in the public sector.

Coleman's findings follow rather than lead current folk knowledge. The move toward 'basic skills' is accompanied by an increasing emphasis on discipline in education. Among teachers, for example, an educational entrepreneur who promises effective discipline has become the leader of a popular professional movement (Canter, 1979:33). Parents are also being sold 'discipline' as an element of the educational product. The rationalization of parenting currently emphasizes 'toughlove.' But this interest in toughening-up, which the private school model promises, is not feasible for most parents – at least not in private schools. Money is a major issue in educational decision-making. Parents who send their children to private schools earn about a third more than do parents who send their children to public schools (Heard, 1982:16). A major perceived educational problem is lack of financial support (Mirga and White, 1982:1). 'Worry about financing education is especially acute with regard to higher education' (Ranbom, 1982:11). In one school attitude survey, almost half the parents said they would switch to private schools if they didn't have to pay the tuition (Mirga and White, 1982). When asked why, they said that they thought private schools had 'higher standards of education' (28 percent), 'better discipline' (27 percent), and 'more individual attention' (21 percent).

The ideology of educational privatization is only a beginning toward establishing so-called 'educational choice,' and transforming mass public schooling into a set of competing educational businesses. In addition to the tax-credit incentive for private schooling, producing an educational market is the stated aim of 'voucher' plans. 'Education vouchers,' Salganik (1981:263) writes: 'are tuition certificates that are issued by the government and are redeemable at the school of the student's choice.' Voucher plans are an extension of precisely the model of educational reorganization that I have described: destruction of civic culture and public social relations; commodification of the education relation; ideology of privatization; and then the conscious creation of educational markets. Vouchers mark the attempt to restructure the public social service sector of the liberal capitalist state into another arena of exchange relations – a market:

> . . . vouchers do not eliminate government control of education; they *redefine* it. Whereas its current function is to supply schools, the government's task under vouchers is *to establish and finance a market* . . . Their aim is to make the education system operate as much like a free market as possible. (Salganik, 1981: 278; 275; 263, emphasis added.)

While the ideal may be to bring education into a free-market economy, the changing form of education, its marketization, is no more of an individual, free-market choice than any other aspect of oligopolistically regulated commodity-markets. What now occurs is that as federal budget cuts are felt, educational administrators face increasing difficulty in financing their school programs (Hoover et al., 1982:124). State-level, educational financing is unable to take up the educational deficit produced by diminished Federal support. The percentage of state contributions to school revenues has decreased (*Education Week*, 1982, 11/3:13). Educators are told to emphasize training for high-technology jobs, particularly information processing (Foster, 1982:6). Yet, scientists are forced to organize to combat the fiscal crisis in science education (Federation of Behavioral, Psychological, and Cognitive Science, 1982).

The marketization of education proceeds through provision of private capital to fund schools. Schools are now being built by ways other than traditional methods of community balloting on school bonds. Rather, private investors are, in a spirit of helpfulness during the time of financial crisis, beginning to own the schools (Heard, 1982:6). Foundation plans move from pure fiscal marketization, private capital ownership, to the imposition of market practices in the running of schools. Bowles and Gintis (1982) might call this a 'transportation of practices,' across institutional domains. It points toward perhaps still another phase in the institutional reorganization of education: corporatization.

Corporatization

The first level of corporatization is intensification of business-involvement in public schooling. The history of such involvement has been ably documented (Spring, 1972; Lazerson, 1971). But (Toch, 1982): 'This new type of corporate involvement extends far beyond the traditional contribution to vocational programs, into such areas as curriculum development and financial management.' The Conference Board and the Committee for Economic Development, which are consortia of major corporations, are now supporting studies and plans for 'ways that business can play a direct role in improving elementary and secondary education' (Toch, 1982). Business-education 'partnerships' and various types of open agreements for joint planning and 'cooperation,' are being formed. These 'partnerships' may be through foundations, but increasingly they are direct business-school 'alliances.' New institutional arrangements include: 'adopt-a-school' – lending management executives from corporations to school districts; business-planned and supported curricula taught in the school; the possibility of 'career high schools,' directly financed and feeding into major corporations. School managers, foundation managers and corporate managers put aside conflicts to cooperate to solve educational and labor force employability needs.

This model of 'new partnership,' which includes teachers union leaves (Walton, 1982:1), follows the corporatist ideal. It is based on 'collective agreements concluded among solidly organized communities of interest' (Bowen, quoted in Panitch, 1977:62). It is 'a product more of general socioeconomic developments and voluntarist arrangements than of state imposition' (Panitch, 1977:65). There is a change in the organization of education that moves it closer to Panitch's definition of corporatism:

> a political structure within advanced capitalism which integrates organized socioeconomic producer groups through a system of representation and cooperative mutual interaction at the leadership level and of mobilization and social control at the mass level. (Panitch, 1977:66)

There is evidence for the occurrence of each point in the sequence: destruction, commodification, marketization, corporatization, for public primary and secondary schools. At the same time, there is also a reorganization of education at the pre-primary and post-secondary levels. Extension of schooling to younger ages, through day care, is one of the least-analyzed changes in educational everyday life. Corporate day-care complements the reorganization of public schools (LaVorgna, 1982:128, 129).

At the other end of the educational spectrum, historic business involvements in higher education are also reorganized. According to Noble, there are (1982:143–8) 'innovative arrangements for collaboration between universities and business . . .' He points to a number of such cooperating arrangements, describing the MIT case in detail. There is not only an intensification of corporate involvement, or even, as Noble observes (1982:143), 'that the multinationals are moving in, seeking to acquire privileged access to control over the form and flow of scientific research.' Rather, 'the new university-business affiliations,' like incipient changes in public education, are taking new social forms. In higher education, this goes beyond reductions in student loans and vast university institutional cutbacks. It means the spread of bridging institutions, between universities and corporations, the think-tank, the institute, the center. In a description of one such institution, Noble (1982:145) wrote: 'The debate at M.I.T. was conducted without regard for the public interest, with no public participation and with little public scrutiny. The press was barred . . ' Just as financing elementary school buildings through securities companies obviates a public election, or union-business partnership reduces participation to 'functional representatives,' establishment of new corporatist social forms for the production and sale of commodified higher scientific knowledge silences the public voice.

William   1-27-93

4
Movement

The ideology of new sociology

The new sociology of education did not escape this rightward social movement. Like other critical young American academics, new sociologists suffered from the still-undocumented university purges of the late 1970s (Parenti, 1980). The discourse of new sociology of education, particularly among educationists rather than sociologists, meanwhile continued in the process of paradigmatic rationalization, elaboration, qualification and diffusion (Wallace, 1978). Despite the political ideals of its carriers, their social contradictions between unemployment and incorporation, and their cultural contradiction between idealizing a distant working class and imitating high-status modernist academic languages, left them historically immobilized. The discourse of new sociology of education had become ideological. Mannheim (1936) wrote of ideology, that it 'conceals the present by attempting to comprehend it in terms of the past' (1936:97) and that it has unintended historically conservative consequences (1936:40):

> There is implicit in the word 'ideology' the insight that in certain situations the collective unconscious of certain groups obscures the real conditions of society both to itself and to others and thereby stabilizes it.

The ideology of the new sociology of education was that in trying to systematically understand the role of education in social domination, it had adopted some of the ahistorical theories and terms more appropriate to the classes and social order that it aimed to oppose. As new sociologists, both among educationists and sociologists, turned to empirical research, they unwittingly replicated the methods and epistemology of the cultural system that they wanted to demystify. When they spoke of educational practice, it was in a language that ignored the historical practices of the social movement that they were intellectually recouping and revising. The concept of 'hegemony' that was intended to describe the process through which social reproduction is achieved (Wexler and Whitson, 1982), now ironically captured the historical difficulty of an academic discourse, albeit a radical or critical one, in transcending the cultural limits of the conditions under which it is produced. This is the problem of opposition that Raymond Williams underlined when he wrote (1977:114):

> That all or nearly all initiatives or contributions, even when they take on manifestly alternative or oppositional forms, are in practice tied to the hegemonic: that the dominant culture, so to say, at once produces and limits its own forms of counter-culture.

What was true of American counter-culture was true also of a more rationalized academic counter-culture: continuing indirect expression of assumptions of the dominant culture, even in the terms of opposition to it. This hegemonic tendency was underlined and exacerbated by the cultural restoration and reassertion of capital which, together, comprised the overall social rightward movement of the 1980s. Its effect on new sociology of education was to weaken the theoretical bases and practical culture of an historical collective movement point of view among the very academic intellectuals whose professional identities were based on such a movement. As the memory of that movement dimmed, and rightist movements prevailed in society and education, the claims of new sociology took on an ideological character, in theory, in research, and in practice. At the same time, however, new forms of collective action and incipient social movements emerged that implied social and educational forms beyond both rightist reorganizations and paradigmatic residues of the academic New Left.

Theory

The view that education operates as a means of social reproduction, despite contestation and resistance, is central to new sociology of education. The ideological aspect of reproductionism is the extent to which it ignores specific historical changes and reorganizations in education. Its theory is ideological to the degree that it remains caught within an historical, organicist social view that it unintentionally shares with the cultural restoration. This ideology dehistoricizes, naturalizes, individualizes and reifies the historically specific collective actions and movements through which organized social life is continually produced and changed. By an overarching imagery of systemic reproduction, a substitution of individual cultural resistance for collective interaction, and inattention to social class as an historical process of conflictual formation, theory in new sociology occupies, as I have suggested, the place of negation. It fills the oppositional space by remaining within the theoretical terms of the hegemonic class.

Internal critiques of reproduction, especially among educationist new sociologists (Apple, 1981; Giroux, 1981), modify, but preserve the basic logic of analysis. Adding terms like 'contested reproduction' or 'structural autonomy' does not displace an organicist view of society as a natural integrated social order. Because it reifies historical action in favor of systems operations, the image of society as social reproduction supports the cultural view of the hegemonic social class, which is that what they do constitutes the natural order of things. Reproduction images thus slight an alternative view of social life as a collective, conflictual, historical accomplishment. Reproductionism makes it appear as if social action takes place only within some pre-existing order. Apple (1981: 36), for example, describes contestation and resistance which 'occur on the terrain established by capital.'

Reification of an historic social accomplishment – the collective production of social relations – is one of the ways that reproduction theory supports the naturalistic, ahistorical and organicist logic that is revived during the cultural restoration. Functionalist organicism merely translated earlier sacred justifications for feudalism into the newer secularized language of society. Reproduction theory is not fully 'functionalist' because reproduction occurs, in part, through contestation and because the society which is reproduced contains hierarchy. What is neglected is how much functionalism is a way of thinking that accepts the ruling groups' social victories and pronouncements of its hegemony as social order. It accomplishes that by reifying and naturalizing collective history as systems operations. The way that this reification works theoretically appears in analyses of social change.

The possibilities of social change are thought of as occurring against a given social order. Social change is not understood as a path of development, as a goal-oriented, collective process in which the appearance of order is only the result of class conflict on the field of historical action. The theoretical effect of the reduction of historic class conflict to contestation on the grounds of an evolutionary pre-existing social order is underlined further by the way that the ensuing conflict is then understood. Class conflict is not theorized and studied as a struggle over the forces of societal self-production, of all the social apparatus on the battlefield of recognizably shared cultural orientations. Conflict, in the logic of reproductionism, is reduced to 'resistances.'

The reduction of class conflict to resistances has several effects. Conflict is limited to opposition as defined by the superordinate group, rather than as an expression of an ascendant group's struggle to realize its own goals and identities. Opposing collective actions are reified, as if resistances were things that could be easily identified, picked out of the conflict of historical groups. But, as E.P. Thompson (1978) has argued, so-called resistances need to be decoded, which means that they must be placed within an historically specific context of symbolic struggle.

The emblematic theoretical practice of organicism, however, is not historical, but classificatory. Instead of decoding opposition by contextualizing it as an aspect of collective conflictual action, new sociologists and educationists have done exactly the opposite. They substituted a fragmenting de-contextualized labelling for historic cultural analysis. They asked which resistances are 'reproductive' and which ones are 'transformative' (Anyon, 1981b). Yet, without symbolic contextualization in collective struggles, resistance comes to be defined from the point of view of dominant groups; if it is not interpreted from the point of view of the formation and struggle of subordinate groups for ascendance, resistance becomes a naturalized and reified label that comple-ments social organicism.

The class analyses of new sociology show the effects of a growing distance from practical movement of its origin. It is a type of class analysis that first reduces the meaning of class from that of a collective, historical actor to a location or place in an order, and then to that of a salient, static attribute describing group differences. Anyon's class analysis (1981b) is a good example. In relating class distinctions to school knowledge, she first reduces class to a location, and then to a multidimensional set of attributes. Class becomes an attribute that can be correlated with other attributes in a thoroughly cross-sectional way and in separation from other aspects of social relations. This is the customary practice by which conventional sociology removes political meaning from the term 'class.' It eliminates from usage the meaning of class as an *historical process of group formation in social antagonism*. E.P. Thompson wrote of this reductive practice (1978: 147):

> From this (false) reasoning there arises the alternative knowledge of class as a *static*, either sociological or heuristic, category. The two are different, but both employ categories of stasis. In one very popular (usually positivistic) sociological tradition, class can then be reduced to literal quantitative measurement: so many people in this or that relation to the means of production. . . .

Like reproductionism, the discourse of static class analysis relegates collective action to an artifactual product of society, denying that it is its dynamic constituent and formative process. It speaks of distinctions and resistances, but not of historical collective social action and movement.

Criticism of reproduction did not lead to a reassessment of the new sociologists' own social situation or of what the rightist educational reorganization could mean for their path of collective class action. Instead, the view of education as an instrument of social reproduction was criticized because it pays insufficient attention to individual human agents, to consciousness, critical and dialectical thinking and liberation. (See, for example, Giroux, 1981.) Against a static reproductionism is posed the activity of subjective human consciousness. Like naturalistic organicism's historic internal binary complement, spiritualism, opposition to new sociology's reproductionist emphasis remained abstract, ahistorical and individualistic. Talk of agentic subjective human consciousness extracted from concrete historical class specificity was reminiscent of the abstract humanism Marx had so roundly ridiculed among the Young Hegelians (in Feuer, 1959: 246–62). The criticism of reproductionism also ignored an historical, collective understanding of society as the material cultural accomplishment of conflicting groups of collective actors.

Research

When research in the new sociology of education, like other forms of social knowledge, is understood as an historical, contexted cultural practice, then it too appears to belong to the current broad rightist movement in social life. Research in the new sociology plays a socially conservative role as an ideology, in its operation as a social technology, in its confirmation of historically suppressive social relations, and as a locally defined instance of a new imperialism. This research, which for the most part references itself as Marxist or critical 'ethnography,' is not only subject to the kind of criticism that anthropologists like Ogbu have offered that these field researches are not ethnographies at all. The irony of current so-called Marxist ethnographies and qualitative researches is that they abandon the traditional methodological organicism of anthropological interpretive organicism (Geertz, 1973) for an imitative display of unquantified positivist variable analysis. While the language of the analysis is vaguely anthropological, its logic is that of the ordinary quantitative correlational study of conventional sociology. This logic is simply the selection of an independent variable, of school knowledge, which is then plotted against a series of social attribute differences.

This way of doing research is based on a pre-modern, pre-Kuhnian philosophy of knowledge and science that antedates the important discussions about meaning, language, history and science that have been going on for several decades (see, for example, Bernstein, 1983). This research exemplified the cultural practices of objectivism; doing research as if there were no subject-object relation, as if the subject were simply absent, as if the research reported were a reflection of the externally objective facts of the case.

Inter-relation of events within the setting, description of the *interpretive work* of the researcher in making sense of the structure and her/his own relation to it, and to the categories of the members, becomes totally unproblematic in this type of abstracted correlational approach to fieldwork. For radicals, this kind of positivist objectivism is an objectivist practice that is antithetical to collective theoretical and practical struggles against reification and commodification. Naturalization performed by combining structural abstraction and interpretive agnosticism negates the potential value of ethnography as a de-reifying interpretive practice. A field study that does not examine for a moment the external and internal conditions of its own production, and the methods by which it actually accomplishes the production of an account, diminishes the capacity of interpretation that is the subjective aspect of the work of de-commodification. By reaffirming a naturalized, commodified social view as radical science, research in the new sociology of education ideologically supports the particular, current historic form of educational reorganization: commodification. This research objectivism confirms also the more general cultural ideology that knowledge is an unmediated, unproduced representative reflection of 'the real.' As an ideology, realism denies the symbolic labor of the process of knowing and the socially organized processes through which representations are produced.

As with the theory of reproduction, there is an internal, but complementary and continued opposition to research objectivism. Against naturalizing description, research critiques emphasize the 'experience' of research, the importance of subjective self-awareness, consciousness of the observers' own life, how it impinges on the research act, and how the self is liberated through research (see, for example, Ruby, 1982). While interpretive awareness prides itself on reflexivity in research, reflexivity is not seen as an historical practice and the researcher's autobiographical account of the research experience is not seen as an historical class practice. Collective history and the collective production of meaning fade in the face of cultural performances of personal individual remembrance in accounts of reflexivity.

Against both tendencies – the research objectivism which is a local rhetoric of a more general ideology of the illusion of realism, and, on the other side, interpretivism that easily slides into idealist subjectivism – there is, as I have suggested, a 'new contextualism,' in which knowing is understood as an historical cultural practice. In this view, methods of research, as well as concepts and theories, are *tools* for producing knowledge. These tools are themselves socially and historically produced, and their *use* has social consequences. Walter Benjamin (1969:222) eloquently foreshadowed this view of the social character of research as knowledge when he wrote that

. . . the mode of human sense perception changes with humanity's entire mode of existence. The manner in which human sense perception is organized, the medium in which it is accomplished, is determined not only by nature but by historical circumstances as well.

The current prevailing medium in which sense perception is organized is television. Television watching (Livant, 1982; Feuer, 1983) is the quintessential activity of a broader regime of social knowledge, in which, I suggest, the so-called radical educational ethnographic researches are local, specialized cultural expressions. Radical research in education shares a variety of perceptual social practices with the procedures of television. The structure of the narrative is segmented and its serial dispersion is like the research reportage use of isolated vignette field quotes. The aesthetic procedures of stripped-down images, use of close-ups to type character presentations, and talking-heads of television, are similar to the kind of abstractedness, and bare-bones classificatory logic of new sociology of education ethnographies (Hargreaves, 1982). The naturalized positioning of the viewer, television's comfortable voyeuristic spectator relation that places 'us' safely viewing 'them,' reappears also in decontextualized field research.

The hegemonic effect of the specific cultural practice of research in the new sociology is to support the general regime of social knowledge, the prevailing social organization of sense perception. Indirectly, but certainly contrary to its oppositional intent, if radical research amalgamates with television-watching, then it too may play social roles: in the formation of a disciplinary society; in the establishment of a new imperialism; in the reinforcement of the perceptual realism that blocks awareness of historical change and cultural movement. That reform efforts may have unintended effects, and may be less emancipatory than their advocates realize, was argued persuasively by Foucault (1979) in his history of penal reform and practice. Foucault's late eighteenth-century 'reforming jurists' (1979:130) played their discursive role in forming the discourse and practice, the technology of everyday power, that trained the 'obedient subject' of the early disciplinary society. One element of this technology of controlling obedience and surveillance is 'the great tradition of the eminence of detail' (1979:140).

What roles does field research of young people in schools play? What is the effect of enlightened 'qualitative evaluation,' in the further development of new political anatomies of detail, and then their use in surveillance, discipline and punishment? Similarly, to what extent do cultural practices in the social relation of naive spectatorship, whether in research or television-watching, create the epistemological insularity that is a condition of imperialism? As Ellis writes (1982:166): '. . . TV confirms the domestic isolation of the viewer, and invites the viewer to regard the world from that position.' The new imperialism's psychology is not simply racism, but familism. It is the distanced perception of the 'other,' looked at by us and television (or the researcher and 'the working class'). It is the unification with the apparatus, which is confirmed by our identification with the anchorpersons of news (Stam, 1983:26). We are the 'protected witnesses' (Stam, 1983:39) who are learning to be confirmed and secure in television's 'fictive we' ('the radicals,' 'the new sociologists'). Perceptual practices of the 'update,' the interpersonal psychology and the repetition of 'the news' stabilize the world of the spectator against changing outside forces. The electronic contradiction is that ethnocentrism is produced by the expanding horizon of world-wide news. How is the ethnocentrism of the sociologists' ethnography of the working class, women and minority students different from that of the process of television news?

The ideology that radical field research in education shares with television watching is the regime of realism. Representational illusions of the real prevent understanding that social 'facts' and cultural meanings are not naturally given, but historically produced in the course of conflicts and struggles or collective life. Realism stabilizes and naturalizes the objects and apparatuses of perception and knowledge. Views of social life as historical collective social action and of culture as an interdeterminate field of symbolic movement are antithetical to objectivism and realism. In theory and in research, the new sociologists aimed to free themselves from the stabilizing practices of dominant social groups; but they remained caught inside the complementary internal oppositions of dominant cultural ideals and practices.

Practice

Radical professional identity placed a contradictory demand on the new sociologists. They had at once to articulate and rationalize a radical or critical paradigm within the academy – in conditions of depleted and dwindling resources – and also, especially as radical educators, to act on the social world by developing a radical practice. The experience of contradictory pulls from professional institutional demands and from traditional radical political ideals was further complicated by continuing professional and political uncertainties in a climate of defeat. The solution that developed in the new sociology, again, particularly among the educationist new sociologists, was equally contradictory and complex: an abstract academic theory of practice.

On one side, the radical tradition requires a commitment to 'praxis.' On the other side, historically, new sociology had belatedly displaced, in theory, a social movement, only to then find itself routinizing and legitimating that accomplishment within a reorganized rightist social hegemony that it was unable to appropriate, even theoretically. The contradictory solution was, therefore, to espouse 'practice,' but outside of any historical specificity, and above all, with no reference to any real, concrete, social movement.

There are many statements of historically emptied general practices of radical pedagogies. They had in common that they made no mention of anything historically and socially specific. The effect was to create a transformative pedagogy in general. I offered an ahistorical plan for 'a pedagogy of mobilization,' in which education would be modeled on the general stages of revitalization movements (Wexler, 1981). Anyon (1981b:131) and Giroux (1981:81) wrote about 'transformative pedagogy,' 'radical pedagogy' and a 'pedagogy of critical thinking,' *in general*, without regard to the specific historical conjuncture, the level of collective development, or the specific needs of a particular group. If they had any wider cultural effect, it was that these theories of educational practice helped to consolidate and defend the reactionary reorganization of society and education from historical collective movement practices. They removed education from processes of class formation by making historical educational practice within social movements into a universal radical pedagogy. Historical movement was again displaced into radical academic theory, even in the arena of practice (Wexler, P. et al., 1988).

This radical academic theory of practice in the new sociology is now called critical pedagogy. Critical pedagogy occupies the space of practical educational movements with exhortation and formula for the creation of critical consciousness and dialectical thinking. In his definition of critical pedagogy, Simon (in Husen and Postlethwaite, 1985) writes of a

. . . procedure that consists of three inter-related moments. First, transformative critique views knowledge as socially produced, legitimated, and distributed . . . Second, knowledge is apprehended as expressing . . . particular interests and values . . . Third, seeking to negate the 'objective' nature of knowledge and forcing the educator to confront the relation between knowledge, power and control, critique additionally requires the articulation and consideration of transformative action.

Similarly, Giroux (1983:151 – emphasis added) writes that the importance of 'radical' or 'critical' pedagogy

. . . is the goal of developing an understanding of the immanent possibilities for a radical critique and a mode of social action based on *the creation of a culture of critical discourse*. The aim of such a discourse is to create the ideological and material conditions for a radical public sphere.

The effect of critical pedagogy is to further distance new sociologists from past, contemporary and emergent social movements; to replace with generality, the specific requirements of an educational politics; and, finally, to diminish social understanding that prohibits flight from history and from politics – even in times when movements for social change are blocked both by defeat and subsequent exile, and by institutional incorporation and success.

Movement

Theory

An alternative to the ideology of a theory of reproduction, objectivist research, and decontextual practice, is to reconnect theory, research and practice in the new sociology of education to historical movements in society and education.

Against the view of social life as systemic reproduction and individual resistance that unintentionally reinforces a static naturalistic perception of society, the historic alternative understanding is to recognize the production rather than the givenness of society. The practical alternative is to identify and articulate what Marx called (in Bottomore and Rubel, 1956:66) 'the historical movement,' and further, particular historical movements. It was an identification – albeit a delayed displaced recoupment – with an historical movement that is at the origin of the new sociology of education. Beyond the limitation of academic paradigmatic routinization and the current social blockage of the rightist hegemony, it is within identified expression of both Historical Movement and historical movements that a non-ideological sociology of education is possible.

Such a sociology would first reject the view of society as a natural, hierarchical and evolutionary order. Instead, society is seen as the *product* of historical collective action, a view that has been notably developed in the work of Alain Touraine. For Touraine, society is produced through social action. He writes (1981: 50, 25):

> . . . nothing can be further removed from this self-production of society than the image of *reproduction* . . . A society has neither nature nor foundations; it is neither a machine nor an organization; it is action and social relations. This idea sets a sociology of action against all the variants of functionalism and structuralism.

Social movements are quintessential representations of social actions. Understanding social life depends less on mapping structural locations, and more on grasping social dynamics of the historic movements which produce the relational patterns that ideology stabilizes for us as 'order.' Touraine writes (1981: 29):

> Social movements are not a marginal rejection of order, they are central forces fighting one against the other to control the production of society by itself and the action of classes for the shaping of historicity.

In developing the point that social movements are central, Alberto Melucci (1980:199) contrasts the social action approach with traditional Marxism and functionalist sociology. Melucci writes (1980:199):

> Centering its investigations on the logic of the system, it has underestimated the processes by which collective action emerges, as well as the internal articulation of social movements (mobilization, organization, leadership, ideology) and the forms through which revolt passes in becoming a class movement.

Like Touraine, Melucci highlights the importance of analysing the path from one to another type of collective action (Melucci, 1980: 200):

> In order to extricate itself from this theoretical impasse, the Marxist tradition must, therefore, move from a structural analysis of class relations and the logic of the capitalist system towards a definition, first, of class action, and then, of political action. Reflection on social movements is a crucial theoretical issue that cannot be avoided.

From the vantage point of social action and social movements, class analysis is also seen differently. Adam Przeworski (1977: 343) defines such a class analysis as: '. . . a form of analysis that links social development to struggles among concrete historical actors.' Przeworski states the dynamic class movement position quite plainly (1977: 363, 377) (emphasis added):

Classes are not given uniquely by any objective positions because they constitute *effects* of struggles and these struggles are *not* determined uniquely by the relations of production.

Social relations are objective with regard to processes of class formation only in the sense that they structure the struggles that have the formation of classes as their potential effect.

Edward Thompson also argues against an organicist view of class analysis. For Thompson, classes are constituted in the processes of movements of collective action, conflict and struggle, and not as positions in a grid, markers in the logic of natural evolution (1978: 149, emphasis added):

. . . to put it bluntly: classes do not exist as separate entities, look around, find an enemy class and then start to struggle. On the contrary, people find themselves in a society structured in determined ways . . . they experience exploitation . . . they identify points of antagonistic interest, they commence to struggle around these issues and in the process of struggling they discover themselves as classes, they come to know this discovery as class-consciousness. *Class and class-consciousness are always the last, not the first, stage in the real historic process.*

The point that class is an historically formed product of collective action, and not a location in a grid of places, represents a disagreement about the character of social life and about the course of practical action. To take just one example, I see the analysis of social action in school as 'resistance' that parallels a contested labor process as an 'economism' of educational action. It represents an economist argument for class formation from the shopfloor of the school. If it is then argued in reply that qualified reproductionism does not display a new economism of the school because it relates education not only to the labor process, but also to the state, it becomes even more evident how much reproductionism misses the point: *class formation is an historical process of collective movement in which education plays a role.* Social structure is not assembled from bits and pieces of structuralist discourse about labor process and state. It is the real movement, constituent and resultant, of concrete historical collective action.

The collective social movement cannot be made economic by talking about the labor process or made political by talking about the state, and then made social by glueing these pieces together. On the contrary, in the earliest phases of the movement, class action, as Melucci writes (1980: 203): 'goes beyond the institutional limits of the system and challenges its fundamental relationships.'

Movements and education

It is now difficult to see the relation between education and the collective action of social movements. In part, it is because we are now accustomed to think of education as a process that reproduces social domination. In part, it is because early phases in historical movements may not be evidently political.

Collective action is historically formed outside of liberal discourse, in the language of custom and religion. The American Restoration is recent evidence of the power of religious rhetoric, and also of the instrumental importance of education in social movements. The role that education has played in social movement rather than social reproduction (see, for example, Welter, 1962; Silver, 1965) appears to have been forgotten, with a few exceptions, by new sociologists of education. One such exception is Julia Wrigley's (1980: 1982) study in the social history of American education.

Wrigley revises the revisionist description of American educational history, which has provided an empirical justification of reproduction and its continuing documentation. In her history of public education in Chicago, she shows how educational policy, even in that highly organized bureaucratic context, was the result of a series of concrete historical struggles between labor and business groups; not, as revisionists have argued, an 'imposition of reform' from above. The unions, for example, while they may have lost the major educational battle of Chicago, fought for public schooling, held an educational ideology quite different from the business view of education, and one articulated to a wider process of class struggle. Wrigley summarizes (1980: 167):

> The image of a disordered mass of people on the bottom rungs
> of the society who were basically confused and

uncomprehending and lacked any sense of collective consciousness or clarity about their political strategies, is not borne out by the record of educational controversies in Chicago.

The role of the popular societies in the French Revolution, the Corresponding Society in the making of the English working class, the labor victories against the platoon school in Chicago, provide no formula for the relation between education and class formation; they are historical examples of education not as a moment in social reproduction, but in social movements and historical change.

There are historically new social movements that are different from, oppose, and can surpass the rightist movements of the current social regime. The new social movements are movements of identity and not simply traditional economic or political movements. The 'new movements,' as Melucci (1980) calls them, are not fighting directly against the state. Rather, they are attempting to reappropriate identity from an encroaching apparatus. They are the movements of the body, of personal freedom in daily life, integralist movements which aim to provide meaningful bases for personal identity that may be expressed in religious languages and even academic movements. As Melucci notes, these movements contain the possibility of degeneracy to immediacy and terrorism. But they also provide a basis for developing a more articulated sense of *how* and *why* it is worth struggling on the social field for the sakes of control of the resources of societal and self-production. The path from that initial identity politics to the 'struggle over society's stakes,' in Touraine's terms, is precisely the path of class formation.

In the United States, even during the restorationist moment of the crisis, there were signs of a common path of development from among the still-fragmented Black, Women's, Gay, Ecology, and Anti-Nuclear movements. For example, from segments of the Black and Women's movements there were explicit assertions of the possibilities of a common social movement. Manning Marable (1980) traced the recent path of the Black movement from a liberal integrationist course of demands for equal participation, through the appearance of various expressions of the identity politics of Black nationalism, to the current period of political reaction and the ascendance of the 'pro-capitalist' politics of the Black elite (1980: 98). Particularly significant about Marable's analysis was the extent to which the failures of the movement were not simply attributed to 'hegemony,' the 'inner logic of capital' or the 'reproduction of racial distinction.' This imagery and language is totally absent from Marable's view. Instead, the analysis depends on the actions of the movement (1981: 176; 178):

Each little formation was so concerned and involved with meeting the reformist needs of its primary constituency that most neglected to raise issues that transcended the narrow boundaries of ethnicity, sexual preference, neighborhood control, etc. Thus, the politics of particularism and self interest in the 1970s inevitably became the politics of chaos in the 1980s. . . .

What we must do in the 1980s is struggle together, along parallel lines of development, finding those points within our own agendas that promote common work . . .

While Marable spoke of a 'Common Program,' Betty Friedan wrote of a 'second stage' (1981). Friedan described an historically parallel development from the politics of equal participation, through the politics of identity and separatism through the present reaction, to a 'second stage.' This stage may involve men and will '. . . transcend the battle for equal power in institutions and transform the nature of power.' Insisting on women's fight in both the family, broadly defined, and workplace, Friedan argued for the convergence of gender needs, and urged a consequent struggle against a common enemy. While neither Marable nor Friedan speak for a unified movement, they did speak from a history of identity politics, for a common program toward a movement of the whole.

The new movements are movements through identity and knowledge. Because of the distance between social interest and social knowledge that is the result of effective ideologizing of the population, the political process of movement necessarily works in the media of redeeming knowledge and identity. In these conditions, collective action importantly includes things other than coordinated instrumental activity. Social movements require historically specific processes of the re-formation of a group's members' knowledge of the world and definition of themselves. The first stage in such contemporary movements is the formation of a collective subject. The place where this formative work occurs does not have to be on the shop floor of either the factory or the school; and it does not immediately require a recognizably political or economic language. The activity of forming collective historical subjects is political education; fight for the generation and control of self-defining and socially orienting knowledge. The discourse of new sociology increasingly represents expression of these movements. But it is an unintended hegemonic expression, because it blocks the re-formation of the language of knowledge and identity in the course of trying to include the voices of oppressed groups within its paradigmatic formulation. Because it occupies the space of negation within a binary ('old' and 'new' sociology of education, for example) that is encompassed by overarching prevailing cultural assumptions, the discourse of new sociology represents a discursive action of incorporation in relation to the new movements that it seeks to champion.

New sociology, particularly through its practical sub-discourse of 'critical pedagogy,' operated the prevailing, rather than the political, educational function: distortion and silencing of oppositional speech and the sociocultural conditions that make it possible (Wexler et al., 1988). This discourse included 'gender,' but in a male language. It included 'the working class,' but in the language of critical theory that suppressed the articulated speech of working people. The category of gender was placed into a reproductionist view of education, alongside the category of class, in order to study '. . . the way in which schooling produces *both* class and sexed subjects' (MacDonald, 1980:13; see also Clarricoates, 1981; Anyon, 1983). The new sociology view of the working class as a primary source of resistance to reproduction disabled the nurturance of working-class collective self-constitution by suppressing even 'pock-marked' (Trotsky, 1975) working-class speech with the language of radical academic theories for emancipation of the working class. Yet, outside the established, though insecure, critical discourse of new sociology of education, practical theories of education were being developed, even within the academy, that were not directly appropriative of social movements. Instead, these inchoate educational theories emerged as historically integral to the course of the new movements, accepting their self-defined prioritization of knowledge and identity as the vanguard elements in contemporary educational politics.

Within the academy, a new social history – that might offer the same historically appropriate meaningfulness to a symbolic social analysis of education that revisionism provided the new sociology of education – began to democratize historical writing (Stearns, 1980:212):

> The clearest general definition of social history in the United States focuses on its concern with the general membership of a society, and not just individuals among the elite. Second, not only the mass of people but also the framework of their daily lives – their families, artefacts, community life, their births and deaths – was to be studied to fill out the historical characterization of a period.

Academic and popular studies of life history through methods of oral history have developed to the point of a life-history movement that promises to: '. . . provide[s] a means for a radical transformation of the social meaning of history' (Thompson, 1978: 18; 65–90; 138–69). The practice of oral history counters the elite assumption of the unreflected silence of ordinary people and makes their self-representing expressions authoritative. Where traditional history plays a role in social legitimation, the life-history movement works to disperse authority. Among sociologists, the political dimensions of modern existence gathered together in the life-narrative begin to be recognized as the proper focus for social investigation. Daniel Bertaux argues 'The only knowledge we may hope to reach is of a *historical* character: our present *is* history' (1981:35). Life history research offers as a model of social relations in education not system reproduction and resistance, but hermeneutic conversation. As research, it refuses to separate research and practice. It aims to amplify the capacity for intentional and historical memory. Life history as a practice is an act of constitution, of first description of the human subject in context. The practice of oral history underlines the narrativity of individual lives and asserts the mutuality of social relations through the telling of stories (Thompson, 1978:18):

> It makes for contact – and thence understanding – between
> social classes, and between generations. And to individual
> historians and others, with shared meanings, it can give a sense
> of belonging to a place or in a time. In short, it makes for fuller
> human beings. Equally, oral history offers a challenge to the
> accepted myths of history, to the authoritarian judgement
> inherent in its tradition.

The hermeneutic process of oral history research interrupts the
commodified culture that dissolves the capacity for interactional
speech in favor of unilateral, monopoly communication (Horkheimer and Adorno, 1972:120–67).

On the same borderline between an academic and a wider
cultural movement, a new politics of knowledge and identity is
asserted by French feminism. Within French feminism, the
movement 'politique et psychanalyse' rejects the inclusionary aim
that new sociology attributes to the oppressed (Gauthier, 1981:200):

> . . . How imposing the phallocratic system must be for women
> to have doubted themselves to the point of asking for equality
> (?!) with men! How great our alienation must have been to let
> us think for one instant that we should be like men, to let us be
> tempted for one instant to take our (?) place inside that
> hierarchical jungle . . . Now that women are entering history, it
> would be heartrending if they were in a hurry to become men.

Like the life history movement, it is a struggle against clouds of
silence or misrepresentation. It is a struggle to write the moving
and multiple feminine subject against the stereotyped 'woman.'
But this feminism is not a hermeneutic interruption of commodified language. It is a disruption of the male symbolic order that
refuses to accept a complementary, negative position in a binary
('men' and 'women'). Rather, it opposes binary dualism as the
epistemological foundation of a phallocentric society. First,
through a self-knowledge that refuses to replicate binaries in
sexual pleasure (Irigaray, 1981:101): 'She is neither one nor two.
She cannot, strictly speaking, be determined as one person or two.
She renders any definition inadequate.' Then, through subjective
re-presentation by a creative symbolic re-formation, a new

collective subject produces itself by a practice of writing (Cixous, 1981:250, 253, emphasis added):

> *Write yourself*, your body must be heard. Only then will the immense resources of the unconscious spring forth.
>
> It is impossible to define a feminine practice of writing and this is an impossibility that will remain, for this practice can never be theorized, endorsed, coded – which doesn't mean it doesn't exist. But it will always surpass the discourse that regulates the phallocentric system.

The authoritative, commodified phallocentric knowledge that suppresses collective self-formation is the social knowledge that is the substance of cultural reproduction in education. The symbolic social analysis that begins after the new sociology of education begins with this social knowledge. As in larger historical movement and the particular social movements from which it develops, this symbolic analysis places the cultural content of education in relation to social structure and collective subject, in a process of historical movement.

5
Knowledge

School knowledge in new sociology

While it recognized their importance, new sociology encoded in the hegemonic way that Williams described, demands and cultures of historical movements into its own professionally ahistorical, and incorporated discourse. Likewise, it recognized the centrality of knowledge, yet without grasping the specific historical reasons for the importance of a sociology of educational knowledge. As a result of this partial understanding, the question of knowledge was placed on the new sociology agenda; indeed it was declared the successor to the individual mobility concerns of the old sociology (Young, 1971; Brown, 1973). But, the relation of knowledge to historical movements was disconnected from what became a paradigmatic rather than socially formative interest of new sociology in a sociology of school knowledge. It was as if new sociologists had anticipated that the social analysis of knowledge might be salient to historical movements, but could only operate such an analysis with the analytic tools developed and used in unconscious reminiscent replication of earlier movements. The new sociology hinted at a link-up with new discursive and social movements by its interest in the knowledge question. But even as it moved toward new methodological approaches that surpassed ideology-critiques, it remained historically encapsulated.

Throughout the 1970s in England, sociology of school knowledge remained as a centerpiece of the new sociology of education (Young and Whitty, 1977). The ambiguous situation of this new sociology subdiscourse – sociology of school knowledge or curriculum – was that, by the late 1970s, American new sociologists began to come into contact with the attractive high cultural discourses of structuralism and literary theory that were engaged in mapping and understanding of knowledge. However, even when they borrowed terms from these academic movements, new sociologists did not see them as part of a deep 'refiguration' (Geertz, 1980) in the social sciences, or a broad new epistemological movement (Bernstein, 1983). Certainly, they did not view them as heralds of broader mass movements in which discourse, language, meaning and knowledge would become central topics for historically newer mobilizations.

What I want to show in this chapter is first this ambiguous position of the study of knowledge in new sociology. School knowledge was studied, but largely inside the categories of the reproductionist phase. Second, I want to begin to show possible applications to a sociology of school knowledge of perspectives and methods from the broadly 'interpretive' academic movement that uncomfortably joined literary criticism, semiotic structuralism and post-structuralist philosophy as 'textualism.' In this discursive movement, it became possible to understand knowledge not as a frozen object, or reified essence, but as a process of symbolic activity or signifying labor. Third, I want to indicate how the study of knowledge becomes a bridge not only toward interpretive and textualist academic discourses, but also to processes of class and subject formation in implicit symbolic movements for knowledge and identity – movements through which a new educational politics emerges, and, along with it, a more historically social analysis of education.

The analytic categories of new sociology show how an intellectual shift can be indicated, yet contained and retracted into familiar prevailing codes. Take, for example three categories that have been especially influential in new sociology of education. In opposition to the socially abstracted study of the communication of facts and values – curriculum – new sociologists of education discovered the existence of social relations in the classroom-hidden curriculum. Rather than see schools as stable repositories of accumulated truth, they were increasingly studied as social sites where partial knowledge – ideology – is taught. The older individual voluntarism of learning was displaced by emphasizing the imposed character of knowledge – socialization. Such concepts replaced the earlier idealist, objectivist and privatist analyses of the old sociology. But they continued to represent the concerns of the hegemonic social class. Hidden curriculum asserts the primacy of social relations over knowledge and technology in the same way that human relations replace technicism as a managerial strategy (Edwards, 1979). The concept of ideology relativizes knowledge in an historical, social context where cultural relativism and cognitive pluralism have the effect of confirming apathy and serving as sustaining rationales for sociopolitical inaction. The category of socialization affirms the powerlessness of the individual against a reified collectivity, a system, which purportedly reproduces itself.

The new sociologists did not, of course, advocate managerialism, social apathy and individual powerlessness. In hidden curriculum they found social control; in ideology the display of economic and political inequalitites; and in socialization, training for social class reproduction. Though 'critical,' these categories of hidden curriculum, ideology and socialization remained outside emergent textualist movements within academic culture, embedded instead in prevailing cultural assumptions. The combined use of the concepts hidden curriculum and system reproduction is an unintended reinforcement of reification (Lukács, 1971). Conscious rational human activity is dissolved between poles of manipulative human relations and iron-like systems laws. Popularity of the hidden curriculum concept has the effect of replacing knowledge with interpersonalism. The system reproduction perspective leads to forgetting that social structures are the result of collective actions, not its origin. The analysis of ideology, that was the first critical moment of new sociology, was traditionally a critical, unmasking activity (Mannheim, 1936). When, however, social domination works through the symbolic and the analyst portrays the symbolic as secondary by translating it away into something else, like a privileged, anterior material base, then critique operates as affirmation. The concept of socialization surrenders in advance the capacity for collective appropriation and transformation, to a system view, in which individuals are merely structural supports.

Rather than relegate questions of social knowledge and information to the realm of interpersonalism, under the tantalizing rubric of hidden curriculum, I begin a social analysis of educational knowledge. Rather than allow this analysis to be exhausted by hypotheses about system needs and subsumed in the magical metaphor of cultural reproduction, I describe structured processes of knowledge production. Rather than reduce ideology to antecedent material causes, I acknowledge the power of symbols. School knowledge is analyzed as a meaningful text rather than accepted as the alienated social psychology of role socialization, I see as the student, a subject, making and being made, within the history of discourse and production.

Representation and transformation

The sociology of knowledge is still the basis for new sociological analysis of school knowledge or curriculum. This sociology is built on a theory of representation or naming. One thing stands for another, usually an idea for a social position. Naming, or representation, is already an audacious act against the autonomy of the object. It is a claim of ownership, in which one set of words, objects or relations is subsumed and repossessed by another. Representation destroys the integrity and aura of the object, which is why the most sacred objects of knowledge are so resistant to naming (Benjamin, 1969). In the sociology of knowledge, representation means the translation of knowledge into a social matrix, ordinarily that of classes, system requisites, social statuses, and patterns of social organization. Since types of knowledge are stratified, social translations are selectively applied, depending upon the power of the knowledge bearers and the closeness of knowledge to the core of the sacred.

In this culture, scientific knowledge resists social representation. The sociology of science, particularly in the United States, avoids social translations of scientific knowledge. Sociologists of science analyze instead the social relations of science, using the models of normative consensus, competition and social mobility which are characteristic of American sociology generally (Ben-David, 1978). There is a minority interest among British (Whitley, 1977) and American (Brown, 1979) sociologists of science in a social analysis of the content of scientific knowledge. But even Marxists respect the 'purity of science,' and usually exempt scientific concepts from sociological representation (Young, 1973). The less prestigious knowledge domain of literature is more likely to be translated as a representation of the social. Plekhanov, Caudwell, Fox, and Goldmann depict literature as a reflection of a more fundamental social reality (for a summary see Eagleton, 1976b; also Fox, 1945; Goldmann, 1976).

The familiar base-structure model may be modified so that form rather than content mirrors social reality; the representation of the social in knowledge is not seen as direct, but mediated; culture may represent social contradiction in addition to social unity (Goldmann, 1976; Young, 1973). But, as Eagleton (1976a:65) observes: 'One does not escape from reflectionist models by imagining a somewhat more complicated mirror.'

Sociologists of school knowledge use this qualified representational sociology of knowledge. School knowledge reflects class interest (Anyon, 1979:379):

A whole range of curriculum selections favors the interests of the wealthy and powerful. Although presented as unbiased, the historical interpretations provide ideological justification for the activities and prerogatives of these groups and do not legitimate points of view and priorities of groups that compete with these established interests for social acceptance and support.

School knowledge is the unequal representation of the experience and culture of social classes (Bourdieu, 1973:84):

By making social hierarchies and the reproduction of these hierarchies appear to be based upon the hierarchy of 'gifts', merits, of skills established and ratified by its sanctions, or, in a word, by converting social hierarchies into academic hierarchies, the educational system fulfills a function of legitimation which is more and more necessary to the perpetuation of the 'social order' as the evolution of the power relationship between classes tends more completely to exclude the imposition of a hierarchy based upon the crude ruthless affirmation of the power relationship.

School knowledge is an organizational representation of different class languages (Bernstein, 1975:11, 22):

Thus from this point of view, power and control are made substantive in the classification and framing which then generate distinctive forms of social relationships and thus communication, and through the latter initially, but not necessarily finally, shape mental structures.

The class assumptions of elaborated codes are to be found in the classification and framing of educational knowledge, and in the ideology which they express.

School knowledge develops as cultural representation in response to the system needs of capitalism (Apple, 1979b:118):

We shall need to look at schools as aspects of the productive apparatus of a society in two ways: first, as institutions that help produce agents for positions outside of the school in the economic sector of society; and second, as institutions that produce the cultural forms directly and indirectly needed by this same economic sector.

This work replaced the earlier portrayal of knowledge in schools as the socially transcendent, taken-for-granted occasion for invidious individual differentiation. New sociology of school knowledge and curriculum showed how social power is culturally represented, and that knowledge and culture are essential moments in the process of social domination and capital accumulation. In this view, the selective transmission of class culture as common culture silences the cultures of the oppressed, and legitimates the present social order as natural and eternal.

Like their counterparts in the sociologies of science and literature, new sociologists of school knowledge are also aware of limitations in the reflectionist perspective. Apple writes about the pitfalls of reflection and correspondence models, notes the importance of contradiction and resistance in the school and in the work place, and urges the use of '. . . metaphors describing other modes of determination such as mediation and transformation,' to 'complement' the metaphor of reproduction (Apple, 1981:18–19). Yet, qualified representational analysis is still representation. It moves away from the object or the knowledge toward its context. It tells a story of how one thing fits in with another, how, for example, school knowledge contributes to social legitimation. The problem is that representation and reflection are themselves modes of thought that now operate as ideologies. While they challenge the autonomy of the object, they quickly reposition it within social structure. They are ways of thinking which put things in their place, and permit the flow of present thoughts and social relations. The *representational mode of thought* is naturalizing; it prevents awareness of tenuousness, disjunction, interruption, and possibility. 'History,' as Aronowitz (1979:110) declares, 'is not and can never become a seamless narrative.' A critical analysis which hides uncertainty and disjunction in a coherent story is also ideological.

Where the view of knowledge is that it represents reality, the critique of ideology requires a mode of analysis which makes the tenuousness of the object apparent, not by contextualizing it, but by deconstructing it. To deconstruct the object, whether it is school knowledge, film or social organization, means to show how it is itself an outcome of its own composition, a result of its own internal series of transformative processes, its own production, and not an entity among other self-generating entities. Objects, knowledge, and relations are not simply representations of something else, but stabilized moments of the internal process of transformation out of which they are made, and which it is the task of ideology to naturalize by freezing the present into an objective, realistic, natural representationally convenient snapshot.

The language of class interest, class reflection and cultural reproduction emphasizes the role of school knowledge in a broader social context; but it neglects the collective activity, the production, which makes knowledge possible. This language relates knowledge to social structure while ignoring the internal construction which gives knowledge its appearance as natural fact. It encourages a strategy of social change that demands systemic change, while overlooking strategies for changing the course of everyday perception and action.

An alternative to the representational and systemic view of school knowledge is to see knowledge as a process of transformation; made by a series of transformative activities which end at the point where knowledge is a recognizable commodity. The end point, the labelling of activity as knowledge, and the process of transformation which leads to that, is socially patterned. The source of knowledge, collective human labor, the transforming activities which constitute it, and the definition and distribution of the product are socially variable. Artisanal knowledge is different from bureaucratically made knowledge. Schoolbooks written by a single author present a different meaning from schoolbooks produced through editorial collage and organizationally prescribed formulae, even when they are about the same event (Fitzgerald, 1979).

The apparatus which makes the reality that we experience is more complex than a mirror. Describing the operation of that apparatus as a mediation between anterior reality and final product places the process of knowledge production into the background. But, to paraphrase McLuhan, the mediation may be the message. The socially organized process by which knowledge is produced makes its own reality. The more that we live in the world of constructed knowledge, the more does the translation of knowledge into something other than its own production lead us away from understanding what shapes our lives. The informationally overloaded subject is propelled toward a secure external code. Representational translation offers a handle on the present, but only at the hidden cost of affirming it.

The early Russian film-makers, who insisted that conscious assemblage, editing and montage make a new reality (Henderson, 1976) offer us an alternative to the device of the mirror and the concept of cultural reproduction. If we ask about the process of assembling knowledge, instead of horizontally mapping its relation to exterior domains, we can begin to think about knowledge production as a series of editings and recodings. During this process, raw materials are continuously transformed until they reach the social definition of a product. Although this is a humanly directed series of activities, in contrast to individual auteur theories, in this view the directed activity which makes each knowledge frame and its subsequent assemblage and transformation is social rather than private. Social montage, and not representation, reflection or reproduction may be the more appropriate metaphor with which to pursue a social analysis of school knowledge.

The montage metaphor would lead beyond system mapping of qualified reflectionism to an archeology of knowledge. This would not be, as it is for Foucault (1970), a history of discourse, but rather an effort to reconstruct the series of socially organized labors through which knowledge is made. This labor includes representation, as part of knowledge-making, but it emphasizes transformative translation – how knowledge is constantly reworked and made anew. This is not a simple process of selection, but a process of transformative selection, of recoding as knowledge is pushed through the apparatus – the social organization of meaning production.

Empirically, this requires working backward from a description of the internal structure of the finished product, to the history of its coding and recoding. One research strategy is to assume an hierarchical process, in which official, socially hegemonic knowledge is a recoding of popular knowledge. The production of knowledge can be seen as a systematic practice of cultural exploitation. The social relations of knowledge production not only make official knowledge, but remove from its earliest producers any claims or awareness of ownership. In a cycle of fetishized production-consumption, recoded knowledge is then sold back to the producers, now acting as consumers (see Ewen and Ewen, 1982). They are taught that what they are buying is an opaque object, and not one which has a history of production, a history to which they are themselves attached by their own labor. From this assumption, a history of science, for example, could be written as a series of socially organized transformations of popular cultural beliefs and practices, which as Shapin (1980) points out, have contextual social uses. A second research strategy emphasizes the organizational determination of the transformative collective labor through which knowledge is produced. Epstein underlines his thesis that the apparatus alone makes knowledge by entitling his book *News From Nowhere* (1973). The content and form of the official knowledge that we recognize as television news is not made, according to Epstein, through a biased representation or reflection. Rather, the news is made according to organizational criteria based on internal organizational social routines, technologies and formulized definitions of what constitutes a saleable product or commodity. Epstein quotes a network executive (1973:4):

Every news story should, without any sacrifice of probity or responsibility, display the attributes of fiction, or drama. It should have structure and conflict, problem and dénouement, rising action and falling action, a beginning, a middle, and an end. These are not essentials of drama; they are the essentials of narrative.

The transformation processes through which school knowledge is produced have hardly begun to be described. There are some chatty descriptions of the school textbook industry. Black (1967), for example, provides anecdotes about corporate consolidation and conglomeration in the textbook industry, and the interlocking network of corporate, educational and government elites who initiate curricula reforms. Boyd's discussion of professional and local curriculum politics provides another link in the series of transformative practices that result in official knowledge. The production of school knowledge involves, as Boyd (1978) began to explicate, a politics of knowledge distribution. Fitzgerald (1979) working outside the academy, has written an insightful account of the changing content and style of American history books, suggesting how the rationalization of the textbook industry has affected the texts. Apple (1984) has begun a political sociology of educational publishing. Anyon (1979) has examined history textbooks, showing how economic change, labor unions and social problems are presented within conservative ideologies. There are additional instances of critical analyses of school curricula (Apple and Weis, 1983). But there still remains absent a coherent description of the politics of distribution, the organization of the knowledge-producing industry, the internal structure and content of school knowledge and texts, and their relation to the broader cultural formation through which school knowledge is produced. Even critical analyses of curricula are safely embedded within the representational cultural theory of new sociology of education.

If old sociology of education reduced social knowledge to the objective and the private, new sociology, despite its outlines of a critical study of school knowledge, risks translating cultural processes of knowledge into correlates of the interpersonal and the social structural, reassimilating the critique to the hegemonic aspects of concepts of hidden curriculum and cultural reproduction. An alternative path is to follow the opening that the study of school knowledge offers toward the language of symbolic movement.

Textualism: preview

Assertions of the importance of non-reductive analyses of knowledge are typical of the new criticism in literature, and of broader intellectual trends of formalism, structuralism, and semiotics. New criticism insisted on analysis of the literary work itself, the 'words on the page,' without any antecedent or exterior points of reference. It is an analysis of literary techniques which, according to Hawkes (1977: 152) 'never goes "beyond" the work to validate its arguments.' Russian formalists share with the new criticism what Jameson (1972: 43) characterizes as a 'stubborn refusal to be diverted from the "literary fact" to some other form of theorization.' They are different because they are less concerned with exemplifying tradition, balance and 'intelligence,' and aim instead toward the critical goal of textual work through 'ostranenie' – making strange or defamiliarizing perception.

Structuralism is a broad intellectual movement that spans linguistics, literary analysis and anthropology, and that may be briefly described as a synchronic (rather than historical) study of the internal relational rules of difference which constitute language, literature, and (for Lévi-Strauss) mind and society. Semiotics builds on Peirce's pragmatic philosophy and on Saussure's analysis of language, which posits a system of signs made possible by a set of rules, a langue. Semiotics is an attempt to create a general science of signs, of all meaning or message systems. Each of these traditions suggests methods for analyzing school knowledge. According to Jameson (1972: 101): 'We may therefore understand the Structuralist enterprise as a study of superstructures, or in a more limited way, of ideology.'

It is, however, a study of ideology – not as a collection of entities, ideas, but as itself a production, a set of practices, structures, or methods which make meaning. The value of structuralism and semiotics for a study of school knowledge is that by viewing the curriculum as a set of rules or symbolic practices, it avoids reducing knowledge to a static representation of social process – a representation that subverts its critical intent by reifying symbolic activities. Instead, ideas are understood as the result of the symbolic practices which make them, just as cultural reproduction is the contingent outcome of collective social practices or activities. Deconstructing concepts and facts of curriculum into the patterned methods out of which they are made, attacks the opaqueness of knowledge as object. This covering over of process, the naturalizing of dynamic, internal relational production as solid appearance, is what now constitute the ideological effect. To take an example from formalism, in Propp's analysis of fairy tales there are a limited number of functions. Hawkes (1977: 68) defines textual function as 'an act of a character defined from the point of view of its significance for the course of action.' Wright (1977), who borrows from Lévi-Strauss, and more directly from Propp, has analyzed Hollywood Western film as a set of sixteen functions that define a classic Western plot (e.g. the hero is unknown to society; the hero is revealed to have an exceptional ability). The functions are expressed through a narrative which includes the use of elemental binary opositions (good/bad, inside society/outside society, strong/weak, civilization /wilderness). The semiotician, Umberto Eco, analyzes the 'Myth of Superman' (1979), which he sees as organizing time so as to destroy the concept of historical time, creating an 'immobile present' (1979: 116–17):

> In growing accustomed to the idea of events happening in an ever-continuing present, the reader loses track of the fact that they should develop according to the dictates of time. Losing consciousness of it, he forgets the problems which are at its base, that is, the existence of freedom, the possibility of planning, the necessity of carrying plans out, the sorrow that such planning entails, the responsibility that it implies, and finally, the existence of an entire human community whose progressivism is based on making plans.

Jameson, in his critical interpretation of formalism and structuralism, describes the formalist literary techniques which defamiliarize (1972: 60–1). He emphasizes their method of 'laying bare the device' by choosing a text which '. . . takes itself for its own subject matter, and presents its own techniques as its own content' (1972: 76). Eco (1979:120–1), in his analysis of popular culture, describes the structural practice of redundance, which reassures the consumer-reader, and itself becomes an expectation. The pleasure of repetition blocks the possibility of using a text as an occasion for imagining possibilities for change.

Within the new sociology of education, there have been only scattered examples that can be related to this broadly structuralist, semiotic interest to textualism. In his analysis of children's Revolutionary War fiction, Taxel (1980), for example, used Wright's model to analyze historically changing textual structures. Apple (1981) stressed that it is the form of curriculum modules used in science education which acts as a mode of technical control. His description of how pre-packed school materials eliminate the need for conscious planning parallels Eco's (1979) semiotics of the redundance and timelessness of a popular culture which eliminates the imagination of planning. Pinar's (1979) work made its own production a topic and attempted to bare the experience behind the text. By doing that, he violated the seemingly natural form of the academic narrative. All of this work, in different ways, moves from base-superstructure representationalism toward meaning production, and toward an analysis of the activities and practices which constitute the school text.

Semiotics of school text, descriptions of the operation of structure to produce textual effect, counter the reification of knowledge as a solid, though socially reflexive, object. In this sense, it supports opposition against the pervasive commodifying processes (Lukács, 1971: 81) that incorporate even such critical analyses as those of cultural reproduction. It makes it possible to understand knowledge production as a chain or series of transformative activities which range from the social organization of text industries, to the activities of text producers, through the symbolic transformations of the text itself, and to the transformative interaction between text and reader, or school knowledge and student. Various kinds of remakings can be traced across the boundaries that ordinarily label the social, the cultural, and the personal. The problem of textual analysis is that it may become reified, abstracted and frozen as scholasticism. Formalism may lead us, in Nietzsche's phrase, to forget why we ever began. The 'text' replaces the system as the cardinal denial of the collective production of historical social life. If cultural reproduction theory can become a new objectivism, formalism and semiotics can surely become a new idealism.

School knowledge and class consciousness

The sociology of school knowledge can be redirected away from the ideological paradigmatic routinization of new sociology and the ahistorical, formalist tendency that inheres in textualism. The sociology of knowledge returns to processes of historical movement not only through engagement with interpretive and textualist movements. The de-reification of knowledge that is promised by the symbolic, textualist transformative view which supplants representational and reproductionist system logics returns to historical movement when the production of knowledge is seen in relation to processes of class formation. School knowledge plays a role in these processes in the production of class consciousness; the study of school knowledge is an analysis of class consciousness and class formation.

This occurs at several levels. The first level is the study of representational bias, class-specific narratives, which are naturalized as History, Science, Literature and Truth. Anyon's (1979) analysis of American history texts is a good example. A second level describes the concepts which order and stand behind specific representations. These concepts constitute a social theory of class consciousness and can be seen as the textual functions of history, totality, exploitation, class and contradiction which comprise the structure of school knowledge. History, totality, and exploitation are not only static concepts which are largely absent in ordinary school knowledge. They are modes of relation, practices of making sense which stand behind and structure specific representations. They are at once descriptions of social relations and rules of information processing. A critical social analysis of school knowledge as class consciousness takes these constituents of class consciousness as the organizing practices, whether present or significantly absent, with which to deconstruct the text. The most important of these operations, the human social making of relations and products, is perhaps the most general of these rules. It is the assumption required for confident action, and it is the relational rule, the organizing principle, without which knowledge is reified.

A critical social analysis based on class consciousness must show how the text symbolically shuts out awareness of collective human labor as the continuing source of what we are and what we have. The construction of causality, like the text's production of a seemingness of time, stands behind particular textual discussions of whether entrepreneurs or labor unions are more potent historical determinants. Such differences of representation offer the student significantly different narrative accounts. The symbolic practices which together produce as effect the constituent categories of class consciousness are considered. Conceptual elements such as history, totality, exploitation and human production, class and contradictions which make specific representations likely are themselves results of more microscopic textual practices. To describe these transformations within the text, what stands behind, or more precisely operates to produce these concepts (or to omit them) within the school text, is to show the process of textual production of class consciousness in school knowledge.

The third level of analysis, beyond class consciousness as the recognition of biased historical representation, and beyond class consciousness as a deeper conceptual structure which stands between representation and the methods of the text, is the class consciousness which is still another degree removed from reification – class consciousness as more actively and materially realized, class consciousness as a participatory remaking of the text. False consciousness, in this model, is more than class misidentification or historical onesidedness. False consciousness is, increasingly, pseudo-participation. Bernstein's analysis of codes of curriculum structure (1975: 79–84) suggests that the structure of the curriculum makes possible different types of social actions. In another textual domain, Eco (1979: 47–66) differentiates between open and closed works in music and in literature. Describing the classical composition (1979: 48–9):

He converted his idea into conventional symbols which more or less oblige the eventual performer to reproduce the format devised by the composer itself. Whereas the new musical works referred to above reject the definitive, concluded message and multiply the formal possibilities of the distribution of their elements. They appeal to the initiative of the individual performer, and hence they offer themselves, not as finite works which prescribe specific repetition along given structural coordinates, but as 'open' works, which are brought to their conclusion by the performer at the same time as he experiences them on an aesthetic plane.

The open text invites participation. It refuses the assumption of a reproduction of fixed forms as the basis of expression and communication. The open text is class consciousness because its incompleteness underlines that the work is a process of activity rather than a dead object. Eco calls it 'a work in movement.' It is class consciousness not only because its form serves as a reminder that the work has been made, but also because it calls for further making, for the interpretive and constructive activity which characterizes transformation, as opposed to reproduction. Texts can be open to the continuing work of transformation, which is a form that teaches activity rather than passive consumption as its message. Even highly structured musical compositions can demand nonproduction by the performer through the use of extensive pauses, just as works of literature may have what Iser (1978: 169) calls the 'blanks,' the less narratively enclosed spaces, which stimulate the participation of the reader. The text, which contains its own internally stated negation, communicates contradiction, and makes it more likely that the reader or 'addressee' can stand 'in relation' (Iser, 1978: 169) to the text, instead of being captured and included in it. The presentation of ambiguity, of a text which remains unexhausted even after systematic interpretive grids are placed over it, 'structurally prefigures' a world of indeterminacy, of possibility, and itself makes possible interpretive activity. A Brechtian play refuses to close contradiction with an advance resolution: 'A solution is seen as desirable and is actually anticipated, but it must come from the collective enterprise of the audience. In this case the "openness" is converted into an instrument of revolutionary pedagogies' (Eco, 1979: 55). Barthes (1974) applies the open work to the whole text. The 'readerly text' is the closed, classic text, literature, but the 'writerly text' is the openness to transformative activity generalized (1974: 5):

> the writerly text is not a thing, we would have a hard time
> finding it in a bookstore. Further, its model being a productive
> (and no longer a representative) one, it demolishes any
> criticism which, once produced, would mix with it . . . The
> writerly text is perpetual present, upon which no consequent
> language (which would inevitably make it past) can be
> superimposed, the writerly text is ourselves writing.

If class consciousness is fundamentally the opposite of reification, then the texts which reveal and produce further transformation, rather than those which absorb and hide production, affirm class consciousness as an activity, and not just as a set of conceptual entities. Ironically, an ahistorical semiotics leads toward class consciousness through an emphasis on the internal practices of textual production, while a representational commitment to class consciousness leads us toward its denial in reification.

Text and subject

The reproduction metaphor slights the process of social production. Representationalism misses the internal productive practices of the text. The concept of socialization expresses a particular way of relating the sociocultural formation of the individual, identity, to collective life. This concept works to eliminate the imagination of an historically produced but active, transformative individual subject by dehistoricizing and naturalizing historical processes of the collective production of identity. In the model of socialization, whether as transmission of social value and roles, or as textual positioning, the subject becomes an inevitable object of a social or cultural system. The question is not whether the social apparatus *can* make, objectify or fully position the subject. Goffman (1962) and Lifton (1961) described how a person can be destroyed and remade according to the routines and ideals of social organization. Literary structuralists have argued that the narrative text can constitute the subject (Coward and Ellis, 1977: 50):

> Narration rather sets the subject in place as the point of intelligibility of its activity: the subject is then in a position of observation, understanding, synthesizing. The subject of narration is a homogeneous subject, fixed in a relation of watching. It is precisely this relationship of specularity that becomes clear in the analysis of film.

The inmate and the spectator may be the social types of our times. Advertising becomes the paradigm of a culture in which transformative labor is reduced to the acquiescent roles of employee and consumer. The human commodity belongs in the social gallery of inmate and spectator (Horkheimer and Adorno, 1972: 167):

The most intimate reactions of human beings have been so thoroughly reified that the idea of anything specific to themselves now persists only as an utterly abstract notion: personality scarcely signifies anything more than shining white teeth and freedom from body odor and emotions.

The point of the socialization model is that it affirms as natural fact rather than as an historical accomplishment, these processes by which an active, transforming subject is eliminated. Both old and new sociology of education advance the socialization model: old sociology of education, by naturalizing historical alienation as role socialization; new sociology, by accepting – with an only qualifying addendum of 'resistance' – that the economic apparatus defines the subject of identity as its objectivized medium of reproduction.

There are, however, other historical subjects, who rupture the apparent naturalness of the systematic objectifying pacification of self-conscious subjective identity and intentional action that is assumed by the term 'socialization.' The subject who makes the rupture brings to awareness the signifying practices of the text and the structures of social relations as traces of human activity. This is not the socially roled subject of conventional sociology, not even the sometimes resistant-though-structuralized subject of the new sociology. No, as an individual identity, she/he is not the market actor who assimilates profit to conscience. She/he is a self-parody, an ephemeral self in movement, a multidimensional, decentered and decentering subject. The social apparatus creates not only the inmate, who is the paradigmatic object-subject of socialization theory, but also the spectator and the human commodity. And, in its contradictoriness, the apparatus also produces the contradictory, decentered divided subject. To this subject the false sanity of the inmate, tolerance of the spectator, and rationality of the human commodity are the result of narratives of repression (Cooper, 1971; Deleuze and Guattari, 1979). This historically decentered subject perceives socially rationalized repression and recognizes that behind the text stands individual transformative human action. In the brief moment when the divided subject appears, the solid positioned subject of socialization models is revealed as the subjective aspect of the ideology of reification. The dialectic of fragmentation diffuses and weakens the integrated subject, while making possible the unexpected and disjointed activity of the decentered subject.

Each type of subject, the inmate, the spectator, the human commodity and the divided subject, has a different relation to knowledge. Each is adapted to a different text. To the veteran inmate, knowledge can only be read as a command. The habit of acquiescence to instruction generalizes to all information, and the inmate's social context, the asylum (whether mental hospital, school or society), is organized in ways that accommodate and reinforce this need. The bureaucratic announcement/memo is the form of the closed text to which the inmate is accustomed. The spectator awaits excitement. Conditioned to the narrative of suspense, the time between the tantalizing opening and the overcoded reassuring closing passes without notice. It is the limbo in which the extra dream-work of surplus repression operates. The spectator rises to every icon of beginning, and breathes easier with every demarcation of sequence. Intertextuality, connotation, bringing the familiar to each event, affords protection from new experience and feeds addiction to pleasing redundance. The spectator loves to cry, 'foul! density! incomprehensibility!' at every violation of the encratic code (Barthes, 1975: 40):

> Now, encratic language (the language produced and spread under the protection of power) is statutorily a language of repetition: all official institutions of language are repeating machines: school, sport, advertising, popular songs, news, all continually repeat the same structure, the same meaning, often the same words: the stereo-type is a political fact, the major figure of ideology.

The human commodity wants knowledge that will buy and sell easily, even offering itself for the same price. Efficiency is its watchword, and condensation and commonality are its practices. The best knowledge is emptied of content, since commensurability is what the commodity market requires (Horkheimer and Adorno, 1972: 7):

> Bourgeois society is ruled by equivalence. It makes the dissimilar comparable by reducing it to abstract qualities. To the Enlightenment, that which does not reduce to numbers, and

ultimately to the one, becomes illusion; modern positivism writes it off as literature.

The divided subject seeks over-interpretation and under-interpretation. Knowledge which is elusive, associational, and complexly connotative enables the fragmented decentered subject to push forward, interiorly, toward realizing a residual desire for integration. Knowledge which requires no interpretation, the pop-art of the everyday, that blares itself out from every node of the communication network, permits a disconnected wandering. In its midst, the decentered subject asserts itself through short spurts of deafening and stylized activity.

In this view of the individual-collective relation, the socio-cultural text is understood. The text is viewed as an interactive invitation to interpretive activity, rather than as the socializing imposition of behavioral rules. Nevertheless, not all texts leave open the same space in which the transformative action of subjects can occur; the subject is not always able to appropriate the presented text. The relation between text and subject, socio-cultural formation and individual identity, is a moving, historical relation. Now, the text and the subject, I suggest, are moving in opposite directions: the text to closure; the subject to opening.

The press toward capital accumulation and rationalization of economic production is a broad social tendency that affects processes of knowledge production. Knowledge produced in every domain (while each has its own rules and practices) is unified by an overriding social logic of the commodity (Lukács 1971: 83). Its attributes are standardization and calculation. Its requirements of saleability imply an intensification of exploitation to increase profit. It includes making the social relations of production invisible, through agglomeration, dispersion and opaque govern-ance by bureaucratic rule. Commodity-logic is extended to language, meaning and perception by the generalization of a specific organization of human labor, and not as a magical response to the needs of capital (Marcuse, 1968).

Culture is made continuous and homologous with the social organization of production by being forced into a commodity form. The means of production, including the most powerful means of the mass production of signification, are privately owned and controlled (Golding and Murdock, 1979). Signification, like every other commodity, is made for sale. It is made through commodified social relations. The knowledge of culture which is produced through such relations, whether television, film, or school and academic knowledge, is an extension of the commodifying practices that characterize labor in other spheres of production. The labor of signification is also commodified. That is why knowledge and culture appear as the textual practices which occlude the transformative activity of the subject – redundance, reduction, simplification, and self-advertisement. The text, then, is not an object, but a set of commodifying signifying practices. It invites the participation of the subject, but as a human commodity. Such participation carries over the commodity experience of other areas of social life (Aronowitz, 1973) to symbolic work, and an appearance of objectivity and closure.

Commodity production has a different effect on the subject. Faced simultaneously with powerlessness in production, decay of earlier bases of identity in family and community, and a continuing ethos of individualism, the integrated ideal subject of early capitalism becomes the new decentered subject (Turner, 1976; Wexler, 1983). Potentially collectivizing tendencies within production, which include centralization and the use of human relations techniques to regulate the social relations of production, press toward a new sociality. The social character of the subject changes from the earlier interiority of conscience to an anchoring of meaning in others. But this outwardness is not solidified by collective social power. Instead, the field-dependence, which results from the habit of communication without power, combines with the ethos of individualism to make the subject hungry for symbolic affirmation of selfhood (Dannefer, 1980; Wexler, 1983). The norm of self-realization is underlined without the economic and social resources necessary for its accomplishment.

In these circumstances, the subject is pushed toward the arena of consumption as the site for self-affirmation. Simultaneously, self-realization through the control of productive labor recedes from the horizon of imagined possibility. Denuded of the centering bourgeois virtues, needful of social validation, yet without social power, the subject becomes open to vicarious sociality. The subject attains a sense of social participation through the imagined activity that mass culture provides (Brenkman, 1979). The outcome is that as commodity-production encapsulates knowledge within commodifying practices, and closes the text to the open work of transformative activity, the subject stands open, awaiting the newest symbolic product to provide confirmation of his/her existence. If the text, even the closed commodifying text, is an invitation to transformative activity rather than an imposed socialization, it is an invitation with few takers. Yet it is passivity of the subject, assumed by the socialization model, that is not a natural but an historically social condition.

Although ascendant knowledge texts may be closed, history is not. The mass production of cultural commodities, of which school knowledge is an instance, bases its claim for consumption on individualism. Even while consumption is practiced as imitation, the advertised commodity promises that individual differentiation can be accomplished through ownership. Individualism remains also a buttressing incentive in the world of work. Within the homogenizing bureaucratic organization, career advancement stands in for the earlier rule of morality. Compliance is offered because estimations of self-worth are attached to organizational conformity. Achievement complements consumption. Both require some appeal to the self-referential and self-directive power of the individual. Industrial systems management requires the ideal of self-direction in the middle, as well as in the higher places. It generates a self-regulating subject as a device within a cybernetic system.

The individualism which serves commodity production is a basis for opposition to it. Production-required autonomy and the ethos of freedom pass beyond expected bounds of organizational containment. The subject learns to want more space. When she/he is included in planning, even if it is in the pseudo-participation of human relations management, she/he may recognize that his/her autonomy is defined by a larger and more constraining apparatus. Acceptance of limited self-direction in production is challenged also by the unbounded egoism which commodity consumption urges upon the subject. A combined taste of power and hunger for meaning can induce the subject to ask who controls the production of meaning.

Once the text-subject relation is historicized, it becomes possible to think of the collective production of meaning and identity, despite the naturalizing grip of a commodified society. It is not only the culture of individualism that has contradictory and socially disruptive implications. Deepening and extending the social commodification of text and subject requires further rationalizing and denaturalizing of signification and identity, increasing a market-prompted need for understanding processes by which they are produced. In this rationalization, not only social structure and system, but also culture and person, are necessarily revealed as results of production by collective historical action. Even during the historic defeat of the rightist Restoration, a larger historical movement – commodifying all aspects of social relations – brings to awareness the dynamic constituents of social life, creating conditions for the discourses and social movements through which its course is altered. The capacity to articulate historical awareness of this possibility is an unanticipated effect of new sociology's continuing struggle for legitimation and status, which leads it toward textualism.

PART THREE
Social analysis of education

6
Theory

New sociology and critical theory

The meaning of critical theory is changing. Critical social theory, in Marxism and, to a lesser extent, in Frankfurt school philosophy and sociology, has been the main source of analysis and legitimation in new sociology of education. Early on, the field emphasized a sociology of school knowledge and culture that drew from Mannheimian, Durkheimian and interactionist traditions. Later, theory and research were affected by conventional functionalist and empiricist logics of sociology. But theoretical development in the new sociology of education was, most of all, linked as virtually a vassal discourse, to the historical path of critical social theory.

During the societal restoration, general critical theory began to fall into academic disrepute; and to lose even the small foothold of legitimacy it had attained in sociology (van den Berg, 1980). This decline was part of a sociocultural movement that included a profound retreat of the culture of liberalism, and cuts in academic employment, especially among socially critical intellectuals. New sociologists of education, who still lagged behind general social theory within the procession of academic discourses, continued to claim status on the basis of their use of the language of critical theory (see, for example, Giroux, 1981; 1983). They too were soon assailed as educationally, socially, and politically irrelevant and 'rhetorical' (McNeil, 1981). At the same time, the distance of new sociology from wider social movements increased, underlining the academic paradigmatic uses of the discourse, rather than any more general socially formative role. Left professional middle-class institutional intellectuals became a socially residual remnant, rather than the institutional vanguard of an ascendant social class segment.

In such circumstances, and with a history of discursive appropriation, new sociology might have been expected to turn – in its own terms – toward newer forms of academic 'cultural capital.' For, while critical social theory was receding before the reassertion of conventional positivist sociology that accompanied the social restoration, a broad intellectual new wave was rising toward academe: *textualism*. Textualism included post-structuralism as well as structuralism and semiotics. It brought a new store of literary theory and philosophy to the familiar academic task of simultaneous use as a currency of critique and legitimation.

The symbolic virtuosity claimed as a unique strength of the professional or 'new middle class' (Gouldner, 1979) might have been the basis of textualist and other varieties of symbolic anti-positivist intellectual movements (Bernstein, 1983). Post-structuralism might be understood, as Handelman (1982:163–223) wrote, as a form of 'exiled speech.' Its ethos of decomposition could be coded as a symbolic adaptation to political defeat and institutional historical exclusion. Recession in the critical social theory which had intellectually distinguished the New Left academic professional middle class from both the old political left and positivist sociology, and simultaneous inflation of varieties of symbolic theory as *the* general academic currency, could have been grasped as part of a larger historical movement. But instead, new sociology borrowed only a few fashionable surface terms from the new discourses. It did explore their traditions and methods of understanding. It did not attempt to locate the discursive shift within a sociocultural transformation. Nor did it look ahead to the prospects for education and its social analysis to a time beyond both new sociology and the societal restoration. For their part, advocates of the symbolic discourses, the new literati, like socially ascendant strata everywhere, did not inquire into the historical conditions of their own success. Nor did they scarcely imagine, or wish to imagine, that their cultural victories could have educational implications. (For an example, see Yale French Studies, 1982.) New sociology, like old critical theory, could dismiss symbolic theories as idealism, denying the academic and social changes they might signal. Discursive division and denial again contains and blocks development of a critical social analysis of education. I want to avoid that blockage, and instead to entertain a vision of the historic importance of symbolic theory for a critical social analysis of education. To surpass the discursive blockage of the new sociology requires an acceptance that the meaning of critical theory is changing.

From social theory to literary theory

There are now *two* accessible traditions of critical theory that can be directed toward social analyses of education. The first tradition, Marxism and the dissident, Frankfurt school variant, has until recently entirely defined what it means to do new sociology of education. As we have seen, critiques of ideology, class analysis of schooling, macro-structural political economy, reproduction and resistance and radical cultural theory, have all been modes of critical work in the new sociology of education.

I want to bring the second, less evidently social, tradition of critical theory to bear on a social analysis of education. This bringing to bear is not a private mental gymnastic. The aim is to articulate what is occurring as part of a wider social and cultural transformation, that includes a change in the meaning of critical theory. Recall only Marx's observation (in Bottomore and Rubel, 1956:66) that there are times when 'theorists . . . have no further need to look for a science in their own minds; they have only to observe what is happening before their eyes, and to make themselves its vehicle of expression.' While it may be the appropriate vehicle of expression of an historic movement, this second tradition of critical theory still does not see itself as part of a sociocultural movement or historical transformation. In its self-definition, it is not a social analysis. Rather, it has historically belonged to literature and philosophy, and not to political economy. Its theoretical root is not Hegelian historicism, but linguistic structuralism. Its object is not a political economic critique of industrialism, but the analysis and critique of language and discourse. It directs its attention to the symbolic order of the signifier, more than to that of the so-called 'objective' referent. These are good reasons to accept the self-definition, and to believe that symbolic theories are not social theories. Yet, I suggest that it is not only a social theory, but also a critical and historical social theory. The symbolic and literary tradition provides a social theory because it analyzes the central social practice of signification; the process through which meaning is produced. The contemporary importance of this theoretical interest is that we are at an historical moment when significatory or knowledge processes are of crucial and growing social importance. If, for example, as Bell (1979) argues, we are in a post-industrial society distinguished by (1979:22): '. . . fact that, for the first time, innovation and change derive from the codification of theoretical knowledge,' then understanding the process of that knowledge itself is an analysis of society's determinative locus of energy. From quite a different perspective, Finlay-Pelinski (1982) argues for a social-historical justification of interest in the symbolic theories of what I have called the 'second' critical tradition. The study of discourse is a fundamentally *social* study in particular historical conditions (1982:257, emphasis added):

> If at one time, in a certain episteme, the dominant conditions of production were economic, it is possible that in this present context *the dominant conditions of production have indeed become discursive or communicational.*

The importance of symbolic theory for social analysis of education is that it addresses processes and effects of social changes that exceed even incipient social-institutional reorganizations of a potential corporatism. Beyond institutional reorganization, are possibilities of a change in the basic forms of social energy, that Bell calls 'transforming resources.' Realization that knowledge is a transformative energy, and that it is itself a process – a symbolic movement or labor of internal signification – leads to a combination of the projections of post-industrialism and informationalism with the insights of philosophical and literary post-structuralism. By its general prioritizing of analysis of social forces of production, such a view is traditionally Marxist. By operating specific analyses in new languages and discourses appropriate to an historically new force of production, this view helps recast symbolic and literary theories as a new type of critical social theory. This new social theory is critical now simply because it de-reifies processes of signification or meaning-production in knowledge and culture, although in a commodity society, de-reification is a cardinal form of social criticism. It is socially critical not only because it describes the transition to a new type of post-industrial/post-structuralist, semiotic or, as Baudrillard (1981) disparagingly calls it 'semiurgical society.' It is critical also because it represents an ambivalent attitude toward that new society. Symbolic theory is a socially critical and historically specific theory in still another way. The current historical conjuncture includes processes of cultural restoration, critiques of liberalism, reassertions of capital, academic underemployment, and dissipation of the New Left's socially based enthusiasm and momentum of critical social theory. In this conjuncture the 'second,' symbolic tradition offers an *historically relevant theory of social practice.*

The relation of the new sociology of education to social practice has been twofold and contradictory. On the other hand, interest in transformative practice is constantly asserted (Wexler, 1981; Giroux, 1983; Apple and Weis, 1983). But, as we have seen, the new sociology begins at a point of decline in practical left social movements, and later asserts educational practice generally and ahistorically. Its own practical historical relation to a theory of practice is belated and reminiscent. Memory of the 1960s movements fuels images of practice that in the 1970s are then recycled in the rediscovery of academic traditions of Marxist and critical theory. In this sense, the new sociology of education is historically backward-looking and ideologically reactionary, although its ideals combine the values of the New Left and traditional socialism. As the egalitarian and cultural revolutionary movements of the 1960s and early 1970s faded deeper into memory and gave way to popular New Right movements during the restoration, the critical theory foundation of new sociology was both academically routinized and assaulted from the academic right (van den Berg, 1982). The interest of critical theory in the practical and socially transformative aims of theory began to sound like ritualized memory. It was detached from the unarticulated practical needs of a changed situation and still unformed mass movement of the new historical period.

The second, reluctant tradition that I claim for critical theory is not reminiscent. It is anticipatory. My claim is: *theories which operate in the realm of symbolic processes and discourse, that might broadly be called 'literary' or symbolic theories, are representations of historically new forms of critical social practice.* With regard to a theory-for-practice, new sociology, while occupying the space of negation and opposition, continues to rationalize historical memory as practice, in the unconscious service of academic legitimation.

Sparse and beginning interests of new sociologists in literary theory, semiotics, hermeneutics and post-structuralism are in the discourse-gathering mode of academic production that occludes critical understanding of the practical meaning and social uses of the newer discourses. Ironically, literary theory is sought after for its academic theoretical currency; I think its real importance is that it contains the outlines of a contemporary critical practice. But the practice has to be redeemed by reading through textualism and replacing it, against its will, into an historical social context.

Textualism

This view of the social historical basis and the critically practical value of symbolic theories is not the ordinary view, even among those who advocate the importance of literary theory for social science. American academic intellectuals like Richard Rorty (1982) and Clifford Geertz (1980) do, however, acknowledge a change in the character of academic social theory, though it is not immediately seen as a practical change or as part of an historical transformation. The philosopher Rorty (1982:155) asserts the extension of the contemporary influence of literary theory even beyond social science in his view that there is 'the plausible claim that literature has now displaced religion, science, and philosophy as the presiding discipline of our culture . . .' Rather than literary theory, Rorty uses the term 'textualism' to refer to an intellectual movement of historians, social scientists, and philosophers, as well as literary theorists, all of whom (Rorty, 1982:137) 'write as if there were nothing but texts.' He describes (1982:140) the textualists as the 'spiritual descendants of the idealists.' But, unlike nineteenth-century idealists, they aim (1982:141) 'to treat both science and philosophy as, at best, literary genres.' In its abandonment of philosophical foundationalism (Rorty, 1979), textualism shares also nineteenth-century Romanticism's distance from science and commitment instead to a relativity, in which, as Rorty writes (1982:149) 'everything can be changed by talking in new terms.'

Textualism, however, is a twentieth-century cultural form, which, though it inherits idealism's distrust of science and Romanticism's literariness, is itself a 'post-philosophical form.' It takes final shape passing through pragmatism, which does not claim to represent the discovered truth of reality, but only a more useful way of talking. Textualism, as the historical effect of idealism, romanticism and pragmatism, has its counterpart in literary modernism (1982:153) 'which prides itself on its autonomy and novelty rather than truthfulness to experience or its discovery of pre-existing significance.' True to his own form, to his 'philosophy without mirrors' (Rorty, 1979), Rorty does not offer some correspondence external to the textualist discourse, beyond intellectual history, in order to reflexively 'explain' its historical emergence. He steps outside of textualism's historical text only to admit that it presents another 'new form of intellectual life.' Rorty would like to go beyond the text to argue his own moral preference for humanism. In the end, however, he forgoes the moral argument. Textualism is an intellectual movement that is left outside social history.

In quite a different vocabulary, Geertz also asserts the replacement of traditional social theory by literary theory. His way of saying it is that there is (1980:168) a 'revised style of discourse in social studies.' The revision is that the analogies which are the bases of understanding 'are coming more and more from the contrivance of cultural performance than from those of physical manipulation.' The imagery of the humanities now supplants the physical and mechanical metaphors as the mode of understanding in the social sciences. These images of cultural performance are those of games, drama, and (1980:175): 'the text analogy . . . in some ways, the broadest of the recent refigurations of social theory, the most venturesome, and the least well-developed.'

The view of social life as a text underlines the so-called 'interpretive turn' (Rabinow and Sullivan, 1979) in modern social science generally, and a contextualist approach to symbolic action. It takes Geertz close also to Rorty's anti-foundationalism, and pragmatism's non-correspondence approach to 'reality.' Although not quite a 'textualist' himself, and unwilling to surrender the traditional science approach to 'causes' and 'effects,' Geertz does grant that (1980:178) 'explanation comes to be regarded as a matter of connecting action to its sense rather than behavior to its determinant.' Unlike Rorty, he doesn't want to abandon the 'mirror of nature.' But he does want to understand social life differently; not as an object to be reduced by imposing metaphors, but as symbolic action to be interpreted by reading.

The interpretive turn carries analogies of the humanities, particularly literature, to the heart of social science understanding. The source of this change is unclear to Geertz. In his terms, it is a 'genre mixing,' a 'cultural shift' that is itself a new interpretive convention, part of a 'democratic temper' and an accommodation to a (1980:166): 'situation at once fluid, plural, uncentered, and ineradicably untidy.' There seems to be no more suitable explanation of the source of this change than there is of its effects. According to Geertz, the relation between (1980:179) 'thought and action in social life,' like the reasons for the 'refiguration of social thought' itself, remains 'very far from clear' (1980:179).

Social context of textualism: preview

There may be a general discursive shift occurring among academic social theorists. It may become more generally accepted to see textualism, rather than say psychology or sociology as 'the presiding discipline of our culture.' But where is the implication for a social analysis of education or, as I have claimed, for a social theory of practice? Drawing that implication requires a social contextual reading of textualism itself; to read the textualist movement in terms of social use, inside social history.

Marxism would read signs of a shift in social science, from social to literary theory from within social, economic, and political history. There is, in fact, a valuable Marxist review of the varieties of literary theory (Eagleton, 1983). But it does not intend to explain the claim that there is currently a totalizing replacement of critical social theory by the traditions of literary theory. Marxism could, however, offer an explanation that is alternative to Rorty's intellectual history or Geertz's cultural shifts in an effort to grasp this change – a change that I have suggested is importantly a change not only in academic social science, but also for a contemporary theory of practice. Although he is not writing about modern literary theory, Perry Anderson's (1976) view of the history of 'Western Marxism' can be extended as an historical explanation of the current importance of what I am calling symbolic, or literary, theory.

Anderson's view is that since the political defeats of the post First World War period, Western Marxism has been characterized by a (1976:29): 'structural divorce of this Marxism from political practice.' What he calls Marxism's 'unending detour' away from the masses and from political practice was the result of a series of political defeats that have so deeply affected the Marxist tradition that it is possible to say that (1976:42): 'The hidden hallmark of Western Marxism as a whole is thus that it is a product of defeat.'

The 'formation in defeat' has meant neglect of concrete materialist analyses of strategies of class struggle and of studies of modes of production and 'political machinery.' Instead, Marxism became a theory of academic philosophers, who brought it into the ambit of (1976:55) 'contemporary bourgeois culture.' The theoretical representation of this cultural embourgoisement was that the central topic of study in Western Marxism became 'superstructures.' 'Theoreticism,' the separation of theory from practice, that has characterized this Marxism, is ahistorical, except that it follows the historical path of bourgeois academic culture. 'The most striking single trait of Western Marxism as a common tradition,' writes Anderson (1976:56), 'is thus perhaps the constant presence and influnce on it of successive types of European idealism.'

If we extend Anderson's argument to symbolic and literary theory, textualism, as the successor to idealist and romantic philosophy, is simply the most recent instance of Western Marxism's detour into bourgeois culture and the study of superstructures. Continuing to underline both the depth and the legitimated acceptance of the defeat of revolutionary practice, this latest idealism does not merely concentrate on superstructure. It declares that the theory of superstructure is all that there is to social theory. To say, as Derrida does, that there 'is nothing outside of the text,' appears to remove from consideration not only political practice but also its basis in social history. Textualism can then be understood as a fitting culmination to Western Marxism's historic pattern of defeat and denial of political practice.

Literary theory as practice

I agree with Anderson that the study of superstructures has operated as a displacement of socially transformative political practice. But, unlike Anderson, I want to suggest that these

131

superstructural 'displacements' do not simply represent a denial and avoidance of political social practice. Rather than effective denial of practice, I see the superstructural displacement as a *redeemable* sublimation of historically specific forms of social practice into general ahistorical social, cultural and philosophical theories. It may be, as Anderson claims (1976:32) that Western Marxism does 'speak its own enciphered language.' But is not part of the work of a theory-for-practice, within any ideological formation, the politically interested *re-ciphering* of that language which has been academically sublimated as 'theory'? Literary theory, by its totalizing replacement not only of political practice, but of social theory generally, has gone beyond the historically antecedent, milder, partial displacements of superstructural Western Marxism. It has exaggerated the sublimation to the point of parody; and as is the function of such a distortion, draws attention to itself and invites inquiries about its real intentions and substance. Textualism is unmasking itself as a theory of practice.

Textualism's critical practice is symbolic. It describes how the operation of relations among signs produces the effect of meaning. It encourages symbolic actions which take apart the thing-like essences that stand over and block the transparent fluidity of processes of symbolic movement. Textualism is an anti-reifying practice. What is involved in deconstructive readings, discontinuous histories and semiological sociologies, is a *continuous de-reification of the sign and the concepts that occlude and deny significatory activity.*

In this sense, the analysis of symbolic movement parallels the analysis of the commodity fetishism that obscures movement and energy in the internal relations of labor power. The relation between a symbolic practice which seems to move only within the meaning-webs of the text, and the social processes of commodification and reification that are exposed by the study of the labor process, is not just analogical. Study of symbolic processes is a requisite of the critique of the historical commodification of language and discourse. Where social production is importantly accomplished by discursive, communicational or informational means, study of signification *is* a de-reification of production.

Foucault reveals this de-reifying practical interest when he writes (1972:47) 'What, in short, we wish to do is to dispense with "things" . . . To substitute for the enigmatic treasure of "things" anterior to discourse, the regular formation of objects that emerge only in discourse.' Similarly, Derrida (1970:257), in his discussion of Lévi-Strauss, refers to the 'work of decomposition.' In a more direct critique of the reification of symbolic processes, Derrida writes (1982:10) 'The elements of signification function due not to the compact force of their nuclei but rather to the network of oppositions that distinguishes them, and then relates them one to another.'

Such terms as 'origins' or 'social basis' are anathema to the textualist discourse that works to free itself from presignificatory determinants. Literary theory, like the new sociology of education, does not self-reflexively seek the reasons for its coming into being outside of the history of language and discourse itself, outside its own 'text.' When, for example, Foucault writes about (1972:204) 'the crisis in which we have been involved for so long,' he is referring to the history of European philosophy, to humanist discourse, and not to the socioeconomic crisis of capitalism. When Derrida (1970:249–50) pauses for a question of origins, of sources of the critical significatory practice of the decomposition of reified or essentialized language, he asks:

> Where and how does this decentering, this notion of the structurality of structure, occur? It would be somewhat naive to refer to an event, a doctrine, or an author to designate this occurrence. It is no doubt part of the totality of an era, our own, but it has already begun to proclaim itself and begun to *work*.

If discourse is a dominant condition of production, then its de-reification becomes *the* historically appropriate critical practice. Rather than dismiss literary theory as another 'bourgeois idealism,' as a quintessential superstructural displacement of political practice, the work of theory-for-practice is to perform a socially de-sublimating reading of literary and symbolic theory. Here I take an example that obviously does not include all of what might be considered literary theory; textualist hermeneutics (Palmer, 1969; Howard, 1982; Gadamer, 1984; Bernstein, 1983) and general semiotics (MacCannell and MacCannell, 1982; Scholes, 1982; Hawkes, 1977; Whitson, 1985) are omitted for now. I look toward post-structuralism as the iconographic speech of a postmodern symbolic 'era.' Read socially, the historic importance of post-structuralism emerges.

Post-structuralism: a practical social reading

The object of criticism for post-structuralism, in philosophy, literature, history and sociology is humanism. Whether against a 'metaphysics of presence' or 'man,' or any centered, essentialized, transcendental signifier, the aim is always to differentiate from the language and thought of European humanism. Rather, the desire of post-structuralism is to assert instead terms for describing the decomposition of those historic fixed centers; to oppose to them, as Foucault writes (1972:203): 'movement, spontaneity, and internal dynamism.'

The discourse against humanism is, at a more profound philosophical level, and despite itself, also a critique of the historical cultural bases of the social practices of liberalism. The 'second' critical tradition, like the first, sees the crisis of liberal society. It sees it, however, displaced as Anderson would argue, and ironic to its own anti-philosophical project in what appears to the social analyst as the transcendental terms of philosophy. Despite its own anti-foundational self-definition, it offers a foundation for 'another form of life,' against liberalism.

The post-structuralist movement shares with new sociology, though at a deeper (or more sublimated) level, this critique of liberalism. Its critique of liberalism is, however, not of the ideology of individualism, but rather of its discourse: *of the means of producing its meaning*. In choosing the discursive means of production, rather than the reified products which have been taken for 'things' or 'ideas', this more distantiated form of critique *anticipates* a new politics in a society in which: *the struggle over the means of producing discourse, over language and the practices of forming discourse, becomes the major locus of social life*. In its sublimated critique of liberalism, through its critique of philosophy, post-structuralist literary theory anticipates the more general terms of social criticism in a symbolic or semiotic society. Its practice of textual 'decomposition' points it toward the future of the commodity. The course of the commodity, I shall suggest, is one in which it alternatively reifies and makes itself transparent, according to the profit-driven demands of production.

Will the post-structural academic movement, like the new sociology of education, remain caught in liberalism's negation? Or will its practice go beyond criticism of society toward its transformation? The capacity to grasp this possibility depends in part on a willingness to socially desublimate this theory into its social practice; on a practically oriented, de-sublimating social reading of the academic theory.

Post-structuralism begins, textually and appropriately, by differentiating itself from structuralism. Derrida (1970:1982) sets his own terms by differentiating from Lévi-Strauss, and more importantly from Saussure (1982:10):

> Now Saussure first of all is the thinker who put the arbitrary character of the sign and the differential character of the sign at the very foundation of general semiology, particularly linguistics.

The sign, the signifier and the signified, attains its meaning not by a natural relation to a referred object, but in its relatively arbitrary difference from other signs within a system. Language, as discourse, does not emanate from the individual authorial mind or imagination. Particular expressions, 'parole,' are products of the operations of relational differences within the structure, 'langue,' of the linguistic system. Structuralism is consciously anti-historicist, and more importantly, anti-substantialist. In Saussure's statement (quoted in Lentricchia, 1980: 123):

> Everything that has been said up to this point boils down to this: in language there are only differences. Even more important: a difference is set up; but in language there are only differences *without positive terms*. Whether we take the signified or the signifier, language has neither ideas nor sounds that existed before the linguistic system, but only conceptual and phonic differences that have issued from the system. The idea of phonic substance that a sign contains is of less importance than the other signs that surround it.

So begins the assault against the view of language as the expression of a primary, central being, of the view that there is a pre-linguistic transcendental present signified. Derrida, Foucault, Barthes, Kristeva and Baudrillard begin their various theories of a network-like dispersion of signification and of discursive practices generally, on the ground cleared by the de-essentializing linguistic model of Saussurian structuralism. The de-naturalizing effect of the structuralist world-view prefaces later attention to signifying practices, not only in language, but in the sign systems of cinema and television (Nichols, 1981; Ellis, 1982; Kaplan, 1983).

Realism is the aesthetic parallel to foundationalism in philosophy and physicalism in the human sciences. Its assumption of natural mirroring reifies the symbolic practices through which meaning is the produced effect, rather than of which it is the natural representation. The appearance of natural representation is seen as illusionism, the mis-representation of the image as solid and coherent, the ideology of the 'imaginary' as opposed to the significatory labor of the 'symbolic' order (Nichols, 1981:246). Realism is no longer then an abstract epistemology, but the everyday ideology of reified symbolic relations.

The decomposition of realism into its constituent signifying practices, the 'aesthetic procedures' or 'organization of meanings' (Ellis, 1982) is the critical practice read out from symbolic theory and directed against the current commodification of the symbol and the image in mass culture. Analyzing the process of symbolically producing the object, either by institutionally organized discursive practices, for Foucault, or by the signifying aesthetics described by film theory, is an antidote to the prevailing structural ideology: symbolic reification.

Post-structuralism carries this work forward from structuralism: in Derrida's extension of the possibilities of the arbitrary and differential character of the sign; and, back behind it, toward Baudrillard's semiurgical society. Across these disparate symbolic domains and analyses, emerges not only the common structuralist tradition, but a new language, thought and practice that both describes and tries to live through what Derrida has called 'our era.'

From structuralism to post-structuralism: Derrida

Structuralism may have interposed language to disrupt the ideology of the natural tie between nature's substance and the 'glassy essence' of the individual subject's representing consciousness. But, structuralism remained within the orbit of the 'metaphysics of presence,' of dependency on something being outside and anchoring the symbolic relations of the text. Above all, it is attachment to some center in the relational system of signs that ties and limits processes of symbolic movement, of *textuality*. The centering of the sign, despite the non-representational appearance of structuralism, returns language to being rather than signifying. Centering stabilizes the structure, allowing its predictive generalizability. But, the price is the presence of some foundational essence which operates to make discourse secondary.

Derrida aims to take structuralism further by refusing to moor the operation of relational symbols to the *presence* of a 'transcendental signifier,' something outside of the text. The centering of structure not only regresses toward essentialism, toward the view of symbols as 'expressing' some prior unitary being or thing, but it stops the *movement* that inheres in language. Structuralism limits itself. Derrida writes (1970:247–8):

> . . . the structurality of structure – although it has always been involved, has always been neutralized or reduced, and this by a process of giving it a center or referring it to a point of presence, a fixed origin. The function of this center was . . . above all to . . . limit the *free-play* of the structure.

Lentricchia (1980:168) explicates Derrida's concept of free-play:

> So by his refusal to accept uncritically the traditional Western metaphysics of the sign, which speaks of sign as 'sign of', and which requires a signifier rigorously distinguishable from a signified, Derrida collapses all signifieds within signifiers; his version of play . . . wants to do without ontological anchors.

The sign according to Derrida (1982:9) 'is deferred presence.' It is a '*differance*' in the sense that as in structuralism, it is relationally defined in a system of signs, but it is a 'difference' also in a second sense, as a deferral, because it (Derrida, 1982:9) 'defers the moment in which we can encounter the thing itself.' This 'differance,' writes Derrida, is (1982:12) 'the movement according to which language, or any code, any system of referral in general, is constituted "historically" as a weave of differences.' Differance attacks both the deductive fixity of the structuralist model and humanism's foundational philosophy of an essentialist metaphysics of being (Derrida, 1982:21): 'it is the determination of Being as presence or as beingness that is interrogated by the thought of differance.'

Refusal of the priority of presence through the sign's operation as deferral, is, at a still deeper level, a rejection of a view of individual 'consciousness.' The persistence of the philosophy of being, 'ousia,' even in structuralism, is manifested in the privileging of speech over writing. The privileging of speech, as the expression closer to self-consciousness, is part of the logocentric, metaphysical tradition. Writing, '*ecriture*,' on the other hand, enables the operation of the free-play of signification. Without the transcendent centering philosophies of consciousness, writing can display the 'infinite substitutions' of the '*movement of signification*.'

Textuality: Barthes

Mobilization of the structure, and dispersion of centering presences asserted in the medium of, but against philosophy, by Derrida, also appears in the critiques of foundational humanism in literary criticism and in history. In literary criticism, the former structuralist Barthes (in Young, 1981:44) proclaims, 'it is the whole of criticism . . . which is outdated.' Criticism now becomes writing, because the structuralist activity of classification is to be replaced by 'the mobile play of signifiers' (1981:37): a shift as Young succinctly observes (1981:31): 'from the analysis of structures to the analysis of signification.' Derrida's 'bottomless chessboard' of significatory play is, for Barthes, its 'signifiance' in which 'the text becomes erotic' (1981:38). As 'ecriture' replaces speech's phonocentric display of logocentrism, so does writing replace reading and criticism for Barthes (1981:42): 'Full reading, on the contrary, is the kind in which the reader is nothing less than the one who desires to write, to give himself up to an erotic practice of language.'

Derrida's dispersion of significatory play, cut free of referential responsibility is shared by Barthes's reformulation of the theory of the text, to a mobile, decentered, and decentering operation of processes of signification. 'Signifying practices,' he writes, 'even if it be provisionally permitted to isolate one of them, always belong to a dialectic, not to a classification.' This 'dialectic' is polysemic, playful, erotic, mobile and dispersed. The dispersion without fixed signified or abstract ideal, forms the common image of post-structuralism's difference from both humanism and structuralism. Barthes (1981:39):

> The current theory of the text turns away from the text as veil and tries to perceive the fabric in its texture, in the interlacing of codes, formulae and signifiers, in the midst of which the subject places himself and is undone, like a spider that dissolves itself into its own web.

Lentricchia's (1980:198, emphasis added) definition of 'textuality' captures this post-structuralist moment in philosophy and literature:

> a potentially infinite and indefinite, all-inclusive series of networks of interrelation whose connections and boundaries are not securable because they are ruled by never-ending movements of linguistic energy that recognize neither the rights of private ownership nor the authority of structuralism's centralized government of interpretive norms.

The movement of post-structuralism attacks the knowledge of humanism-liberalism. The aim of decentering is to release the reified energy of textuality, and to offer an enlightenment not of reason, but of movement. The movement is not simply self-referential linguistic eroticism, the playful 'coming' of a textasy (Young, 1981:32). It is, in philosophy and in literature also, more than an over-coming of the other side of emanations from the fixed center; the passive absorption of 'reading' which is to be reversed by knowledge as active writing. Socially and practically, the transcendent signifier and the self-consciousness entailed in metaphysical philosophy, classificatory literary structuralism, and indexed by that whole constellation, 'humanism,' are also themselves signs of the totalitarian society and false individualism that are being opposed.

Discourse and subject: Foucault

Foucault (whom we should honor enough to say that it is not the name of the author (Rabinow, 1984:101–20), but of the discourse) not only practices the counter-transcendence and de-humanization in his 'effective, genealogical history' (1984:76–100;1972), but acknowledges its social, historical, practical meaning. Reflecting on his own work in the contemporary period, he observes (1982:213):

> Never, I think, in the history of human societies – even in the old Chinese society – has there been such a tricky combination in the same political structures of individualization techniques and of totalization procedures.

Even more openly committed, he indicated that (1982:216) the 'problem of our days [is] to liberate us both from the state and from the type of individualization which is linked to the state. We have to promote new forms of subjectivity . . .'

The topic of Foucault's works is not an 'application' of post-structuralism to history, or, as it may seem, the institutional history of power. 'Thus,' (1982:209) 'it is not power, but the subject, which is the general theme of my research.' But it is not the 'idea of the founding subject,' the central, essential being from whom expression emanates. Rather, Foucault aims to show the historical specificity of this founding subject of history, the 'man' that is the product of the operation of the dispersed practices of discourse but who has been mistaken for a center and an origin (1970:xxiii):

> It is comforting, however, and a source of profound relief to think that man is only a recent invention, a figure not yet two centuries old, a new wrinkle in our knowledge, and that he will disappear again as soon as that knowledge has discovered a new form.

What Foucault accomplishes is to show that significatory processes are more than playful: they are formative of the subject, unto the very body. It is through discourse, 'the power to be seized,' that the central object of the prevailing humanism, man, is formed, stratified and regulated. The bio-power of the practices of social, discursive regulation are described as (1979:140–1):

> the supervision of the smallest fragment of life and the body

. . . the meticulous observation of detail . . . a whole set of
techniques, a whole corpus of methods and knowledge,
descriptions, plans and data. And from such trifles, no doubt,
the man of modern humanism was born.

The power of discourse, which, unlike the centered metaphysics
of both humanism and structuralism, is not an expression or
representation of anterior objects. It is discourse, the socially
regulated and constraining practices of that dispersed plane of
active knowledge, the episteme, that forms the object, referent,
and being of last appeal, the subject, 'man.' The dispersion of the
sign is here not an inclination, a textualist disposition, but for
Foucault the actual practical historical grid, 'effective history,' in
which events occur (1981:68): 'The fundamental notions which we
now require are no longer those of consciousness and continuity
. . . nor any longer those of sign and structure. They are those of
the event and the series . . .'

With Foucault, post-structuralism moves more openly toward its
social commitments, and to an historical analysis of 'our era.' This
history, however, is not a history of continuity, of development, of
accumulation from points of origin. The aim is to (1972:203) 'free
the history of thought from its subjection to transcendence . . . to
cleanse it of all transcendental narcissism; it had to be freed from
that circle of the lost origin . . .' Like the anti-foundationalism of
Rorty, and like Derrida's bottomless chessboard, it studies not
how discourse (1972:47–8)

> define[s] these objects without reference to the *ground, the
> foundation of things*, but by relating them to the body of rules
> that enable them to form as objects of a discourse and thus
> constitute the conditions of their historical appearance.

The aim, Foucault continues, is: 'To write a history of discursive
objects that does not plunge them into the common depth of a
primal soil, but deploys the nexus of regularities that govern their
dispersion.'

No origin, no 'constituent consciousness,' no symbolic reification, we would say: neither above communicative social practices,
in historical transcendence through a unitary, telic, continuous
view of history; nor below, through centered individuals, authors,

unified subjects. Instead (1972:47) 'to dispense with "things". To depresentify them.' Rather, an 'effective history' that (Rabinow, 1984:88) 'uproot[s] its traditional foundations and relentlessly disrupts its pretended continuity.' A general history is opposed to a total history (1972:10): 'A total description draws all phenomena around a single centre – a principle, a meaning, a spirit, a worldview, an overall-shape: a general history, on the contrary, would deploy the space of a dispersion.'

In those spaces, Foucault describes in detail how the interlacing codes of discourse are now connected, now dispersed, to constitute their human objects, subjects. To show the institutional sites where through discursive practices the subject is formed and regulated: not as a unitary product, but as a discontinuous one, the effect of discontinuous practices, full not of continuity and loyalty to origins, but marked instead by 'thresholds, ruptures, and transformations.'

The discourses operated, we would say, as stratifying methods, 'procedures of exclusion,' through which the meliorist claims of liberalism betray themselves. The betrayal occurs not only as the denial of discontinuity and dispersion, in liberal-humanism's mode of writing history, but also in its unintended effects as a succession of technologies of control, surveillance, and fractionating self-pulverization. Liberalism is a practical, 'wirkliche' (effective) denial of any transcendental illusion of a unified subject. For liberalism as effective discourse, in psychiatry, criminology, medicine, religion, and the social sciences, is activated in the network of discursive formations to play its unintended and unacknowledged role in a series of strategies of domination.

Foucault is not the name of the author; and when it is, it plays the ideological role that 'Foucault' foresaw: it stops interrogation of the mode of existence of discourses and (Rabinow, 1984:117) 'the manner in which they are articulated according to social relationships . . .' The reappropriation of this discourse – the hegemonic function, we would say – to the name of the individual author shows how the interplay of discourse and institutional practice reintegrate dispersed elements within the social grid, reducing their difference (1981:66), 'annulled in its reality and put at the disposal of the signifier.' Here too, writing is the last hope of an anti-transcendental urge for social transcendence, for overcoming the reintegration of difference. 'Do not,' writes Foucault

(1972:17), 'ask who I am and do not ask me to remain the same: leave it to our bureaucrats and our police to see that our papers are in order. At least spare us their morality when we write.' That is the voice of a faint hope against Foucault's realistic knowledge that writing too belongs within a 'dispersion of matter,' inside social history.

Post-structuralism in society: Baudrillard

Foucault brings the post-structuralist philosophical and textualist critique of metaphysics to history; to the writing of an effective, genealogical history, and to the analysis of the practical discursive accomplishment of a 'tricky combination' of individualization and totalization that characterizes the 'disciplinary society.' Baudrillard does not bring post-structuralism to the study of society. Rather, we see in Baudrillard how structuralism and post-structuralism *belong to society*.

The very logic of difference through which structuralism and post-structuralism distance themselves from essentialist, substantialist, metaphysical humanism, is the logic which Baudrillard repositions inside of society. For him, the logic of difference is not a critical textual practice, neither free-play nor preface to the possibility of an historical dispersion. Rather, the appearance of the logic of difference is itself a sign of an historical change in society: the triumph of consumption. The object of consumption does not find its meaning in a symbolic relation to the subject or in an instrumental relation to the world. Instead, 'it finds meaning with other objects, in difference, according to a hierarchical code of significations.' 'The definition of an object of consumption,' writes Baudrillard, 'is entirely independent of objects themselves and *exclusively a function of the logic of significations*' (1981:65,67).

A society of a political economy of signs is one in which the sign plays the same role that the commodity once did in a production-centered society. It is abstract, reductive generalization of the 'labor of signification.' Now we see 'the same process that lends the commodity an appearance of autonomous value . . .' (1981:145). Like the commodity in the labor process, the sign is a reification of the symbolic process. It no longer functions within social relations, but only by reference to other signs, which define the structural

143

code. This code, as a structure of differences, is the new fetish. Now there is a 'passion for the code' (1981:92) which goes beyond attachments to objects, and moves toward symbolic reification. That is the ideological process in a society in which the natural environment has been totally 'semanticized' – 'total functionality, total semiurgy' (1981:183).

The sign that operates in a code of difference reduces the ambiguity of difference to a 'distinctive opposition,' and then to an ideology of positivity in communication emptied of any relational ambivalencies. In such a society, where ambivalent symbolic relations have been reduced to positive signs that function through their differential place in a structured code that absolutizes speech, post-structuralism is no longer a critical theory. We can say that which Baudrillard argues, but does not say: structuralism and post-structuralism are representations of the semiurgical society. What Baudrillard says of design (1981:147) can also characterize the relations of post-structuralist theory to the society of the political economy of the sign: it is 'an operational semiology.' Textualist post-structuralism presents itself as a critique of humanism. But the same logic reappears, in Baudrillard's account, as the historical form of social domination at a (1981:147) 'stage where the commodity is immediately produced as a sign, as sign value, and where signs (culture) are produced as commodities.' 'The sign,' (1981:206) 'is the apogee of the commodity.'

The production of meaning by the operation of difference, the assimilation of the signified to the signifier, and the general displacement of beings and things by signs, are not only the logic and practices of structuralism and post-structuralism. They are the social properties of a society in which the elevation of consumption activities reveals that the system of social communications has become symbolically reduced, ideologized to the point where the symbolic disappears, and the sign prevails as a reified and reifying commodity. Baudrillard's goal is not simply to name as homology the relation between post-structuralism and the operational societal semiology that I have drawn here. It is his aim, however, to develop a critique of this political economy of the sign in which the logic of difference operates and in which the prevailing social form is one where everything is both commodity and sign.

Of this society, Baudrillard writes (1981:163)

As the functional and terrorist organization of the control of meaning under the sign of the positivity of value, signification is in some ways kin to the notion of reification. It is the locus of an elemental objectification that reverberates through the amplified systems of signs up to the level of the social and political terrorism of the bracketing of meaning.

The fulfillment of the social form of the sign-commodity as the (non)-relational mode of consumption is in the institutional apparatus of the mass media. For what mass media practice does is what the sign does to the symbolic: it reduces the ambivalent mutuality of ambiguous communicative relations to abstract value. Sign value is 'irresponsible'; it has no need of response. It is mass media which finally monopolize and absolutize speech, and ultimately, discourage symbolic relations. After all, what need is there for conversation, when the maximization of value in consumption capitalism insists on the reification of significatory labor, and suppresses expansion of speech relations that goes beyond the bounds of the commodity sign form? The 'passion for the code' 'abolish(es) the cardinal reference to the individual,' while the abstract sign logic of difference 'engulfs the Referent as surely as it does the Signified' (1981:152) – not as anti-meta-physical textual decentering, but as an historical social process within capitalist society. Baudrillard's response? (1981:162): 'Only total revolution, theoretical and practical, can restore the symbolic in the demise of the sign and of value. Even signs must burn.' Short of total transformation, the practical critical response to the intransitivity of communicational media in a thoroughly semant-icized environment of a signified society is to strike against commodified value in the symbolic medium of communication (Baudrillard, 1981:150):

Only ambivalence (as a *rupture* of value, or another side or beyond of sign value, and as the *emergence of the symbolic*) sustains a challenge to the legibility, the false transparency of the sign; only ambivalence questions the evidence of the use value of the sign (rational decoding) and of its exchange value (the discourse of communication). *It brings the political economy of the sign to a standstill* . . .

Like Derrida's textual free-play and Foucault's discontinuous history that works through the transgression of limits (Lemert and Gillan, 1982:68), Baudrillard too, aims to counteract constraints on symbolic movement. The symbolic counter-practice that is for him an active critique in the political economy of the sign is exemplified by the language of the streets and the transgressive discourse of graffiti. Such discourse, by its very immediacy, 'breaches the fundamental role of non-response enunciated by all the media' (Baudrillard, 1981:183). The aim of the counter-practice: to restore the 'reciprocity of speech.' The significatory culmination of commodity logic, which in the communicational mode of the consumer society bears a remarkable resemblance to the logic of post-structuralism, is simply that (1981:172) 'people are no longer speaking to each other.'

Baudrillard dampens our expectations for post-structuralism as the critical theory and practice of a semiotic, post-industrial society where knowledge processes are the central social resource. He argues instead for awareness of how signification itself is socially re-integrated as mass consumption practice into the cycle of commodity production. The means of symbolic production are quickly commodified in the consumption apparatus of mass culture. Baudrillard's own critical practice remains, however, within the symbolic medium-discursive transgression in the service of a truly symbolic reciprocal and ambivalent *speech*; a communication that manages to transgress and rupture the historically most recent expression of the logic of commodification.

7
Society

From discourse to society

Return of the dialectic

Baudrillard's analysis of communication in consumer capitalism insists on the continuing power of the commodity form. Overturning the ideological regime of realism, decentering and dispersing the transcendental essentialism which masks the operation of symbolic processes, is no guarantee of an unreified social form of life.

Post-structuralism brings the labor of signification to the surface, out from the suppressive weight of humanism's essentialist and substantialist reifications. It asserts the formative, active role of symbolic processes. That is one sense in which post-structuralism is, even against some of its own claims, a discourse directed toward a critical social practice: bringing symbolic processes to awareness and then to the active and creative possession of intentional practice. Beyond that, in its enunciation of the ideal of freer movement of the signifier, of discontinuity rather than accumulative growth as characteristic of historical change, and, with Baudrillard, in the ideal of 'the symbolic,' post-structuralism offers a series of social practices: dispersion, decentering, deferral, rupture, and ambivalence in the mode of signification.

Both the foregrounding of significatory processes, of which 'reality,' 'being,' 'essence,' and 'things' are the effects, and the series of practices of disruption, the 'work of decomposition' as Derrida called it, are critical social practices, especially in historical circumstances where signification is of inescapable social import. But just for that reason, where symbolic communicational or discursive practices begin to be understood as socially important, they are not left to their own anti-metaphysical 'play.' The importance of the means of signification, although they may be made transparent as part of the intellectual work of criticizing the philosophical assumptions of the hegemonic social regime, also makes it more likely that they will be assimilated to the prevailing social form. That is Baudrillard's point. The 'sign' is extricated from the mutuality of symbolic social relations only to operate as a commodity.

The commodity fetishism of labor in production is complemented by the commodity fetishism of the sign in consumption. Reading or writing with and beyond Baudrillard, by placing post-structuralism into his political economy of the sign, I would say, following Deleuze and Guattari's (1979) dialectic of libidinal energy, that the symbolic energy which is released by decompositional practices of de-centering or dispersing the structure is re-integrated into the neo-symbolic, 'the sign.' *Commodifying the sign is the historical social practice that operates to limit the symbolic freedom heralded by post-structuralism.*

This too is a symbolic movement. Not the end of movement, the regression to metaphysical realism's suppression of the symbolic movements which produce its appearance of stolid, bourgeois facticity; rather, the simultaneous emergence of symbolic processes *and* their re-integration into the commodity form, as the commodification of culture. This simultaneous event defines a tension in the symbolic domain, a dialectical tension between the freer movement of signification on the one hand, and its capture to a predictable and familiar commodity exchange value form, on the other. Symbolic movement is then relational, *between* transgression and integration, disruptive differences and routinized positivity. Or, in Baudrillard's terms, the tension that produces symbolic movement is between the ambivalent social 'symbolic' and the intransitive commodity 'sign.'

This dialectical movement takes place in concrete social history. It operates in the medium of signification. Signification, for Baudrillard (1981) is where the 'object,' now really the code, of consumption is found. Yet it has a social pragmatics, a context of operation. It operates according to the dialectic of the commodity: fractionalization and transparency of the processual parts for purposes of sale, that alternates with a masking denial of processual composition, again for purposes of sale.

Transferring emphasis to the significatory level of social life heightens the inevitability of the transparency of this alteration. Both the compositional process and the solidified product are now more openly matters of signification. The first, the compositional process, appears as a new cultural form at the reflexive level. Here, literary theory displaces so-called social theory, critical or otherwise, and takes its place, according to Rorty (1982) as the 'presiding discipline of our culture.' The second, signification as product, assumes a pivotal position in the production of value by culturally regulating labor-power and consumption. 'Advertising' is the emblem of mass culture, of signification as the regulative product, which now extends to the entire cultural realm. Horkheimer and Adorno's aperçu (1972) that 'thought amalgamates with advertising' has become an accurate historical description of the repressive everyday workings of signification as sign.

Social pragmatics of discourse

Baudrillard's emphasis on the commodification of the sign in mass consumption is potentially misleading for a theory of practice. There are two sides, two directions of movement in the dialectic of commodification. To limit the accomplishment of change to practices of transgression and rupture accepts the timeless effectivity of commodified life and ignores the dialectical logic of transformation. There is, however, another side to any dialectic; it is one of historically dialectic movement, rather than socially dominative reproduction. In the dialectic of commodification, it is the de-reifying moment that is a condition for conscious social practice. The commodification of signification may be the cultural result of de-reification, which is but an ephemeral moment within commodity logic. But, it is not an inevitable result.

In the process of commodification new areas of social life are denaturalized and demystified while being readied for social use. Without intervening either disruptive or appropriate languages and practices, whatever is de-naturalized soon becomes a social resource to be commodified. What post-structuralism and discursive theories of the subject indicate, though in abstract, theoretical cultural form, is that the twin pillars of bourgeois ideology are themselves being more intensively and openly de-naturalized and readied for commodity use. Ideology itself – culture-as-individualism – is placed into the cycle of commodification. In order to become a socially useful resource, the natural has first to be de-reified, and to some extent decomposed, so that it is more rationally manipulable. Between this dynamic of de-reification and commodification, historically new discourses and practices are created, which have the power to illuminate and revision the social order, but also, as Marcuse (1964) and Baudrillard (1981) have seen, to confirm it and to block the imagination of change.

The most evident new discourse created in the moment of de-reification is subsumed by the terms 'literary theory,' or textualism. Here, culture is de-naturalized, and processes of symbolic labor, signification, are made transparent. The de-naturalization of individualism, in new forms, appears in the as-yet less familiar terms of a symbolic economy of identity. But, the same dynamic operates in the medium of identity. I think that textualism's insistent assertion that 'discourse forms the subject' overlooks the structure of social interaction through which discourse operates in society. So, in our current research (Wexler et al., 1988), we try to show how signs are used in an ordered social process in which individual identity is produced. I call this a 'symbolic economy of identity' because while the medium of relation is symbolic (with a heavily coded use of subculture and mass cultural signs), the process of relation among the signs is mediated through interactions that follow the form of capital-logic, particularly of exploitation and commodification. Individual identity, like 'things' and apparently natural 'culture,' is a reification of a symbolic economy. This economy combines labor and sign, as interactional resources like trust and status are produced and distributed symbolically.

Identity, however, is not ordinarily being de-reified in academic discourse. Rather, any historic unfreezing of selfhood that reached popular awareness during the cultural revolution of the 1960s, has been replaced into direct processes of self-commodification (Wexler, 1983: 120–6) and naturalizing individualist ideologies of survivalism (Lasch, 1984). The working-up of identity-elements for entry into a symbolic economy of identity remains a generally opaque process, and the rules of that economy are still ignored in favor of the iconized identity commodity of the individual self and the process of socialization.

The commodifying moment is now more apparent in the domain of meaning. The de-reifying discourse of de-reified culture in literary theory and textualism generally, and post-structuralism particularly, can be reintegrated into a semiotic class society. In Baudrillard's terms, it is the culturally commodified and commodifying 'positivity of the sign.' But the same process may await the unfreezing de-reification of identity. Social economics of individual identity, in which interactional resources are constantly mobilized to create loci of value, as individual identity, can be centralized, rationalized, and appropriated to leave only defensive, 'minimal selves' (Lasch, 1984).

Nevertheless, the outcome of this dynamic of de-reification and commodification is not an automatic, more complex version of the functionalist system logic of social reproduction. It depends on collective social practice. It is not simply that the discourse of literary theory and economy of identity supplant critical theory in a new historical moment. The point rather, is that the articulation of the new discourses within the de-reifying moment enables historically appropriate collective practices. The displacement of traditional critical social theory by literary theory and textualism contributes to theorizing the practice of collective criticism and collective cultural creation. Beginning to de-reify social psychology (Wexler, 1983) enables imagination of an economy of identity that makes the collective production and private appropriation of symbolic identity value transparent, and leads toward questions of the ownership of socially produced identity values. The practical dynamic is between an expanded territory of commodification that includes even pillars of the ideological apparatus, and the socialization of value, in the forms of identity and meaning.

How identity and meaning both operate within a dynamic of de-reification and commodification circumscribed by the value logic of capital may become evident only with the realization of those practices which, in fact, breach that logic. Transgressions of commodity logic that do not directly return from social historical possibility into post-structuralism's ahistorical individualist Romantic heritage, may point a way toward these practices: the socialization of identity and of meaning in the mobilization of collective action.

A second potentially misleading aspect of Baudrillard's commodified cultural emphasis and, perhaps of textualism generally, is that symbolic analysis is entirely a question of culture and consumption. An alternative view, to recall Anderson's thesis, is that textualist descriptions of symbolic processes are important because they are displacements. As I have argued, textualism is a theory for the practice of symbolic de-reification. But, it may indicate both the semiotic productivity of symbol as process, and a displacement: the historically new importance of symbol as the means of production. Textualism may be a double displacement: first and transparently, as a de-reifying practice of social significa-tion; and, second, as an abstract theoretical de-productionized, de-economized statement of a change in production. Textualism is both a practice and itself a sign of the emergence of a qualitatively new social formation or society. That formation entails changes in the character and organization of production, consumption, and the organization of persons. In this view, textualism is a rationalized, reflexive, and academically specialized aspect of the culture of this new formation – the semiotic society.

In an effort to avoid a purely formalist textualism, a merely semantic study of discourse that would leave post-structuralist and discursive movements outside of history, Finlay-Pelinski (1982: 229–366) takes a similar view; a bridge to social pragmatics that specifies the historical presence of textualism (1982:257): 'the dominant conditions of production have indeed become discursive or communicational. The "real" would be the discursive proced-ures of communicational interaction; it would be the pragmatic' (1982:257). With this leap, discourse is linked to history through pragmatics, through the conditions of discourse. A similar view of historical transformation that states the textualist movement's significance less directly, but converges on the point of an historical change in the means of production, comes from the other-social, historical, pragmatic-side of the relation between text and context. It comes in the form of an hypothesized informational society, where information and knowledge play the same central role that modern textualism attributes to signification.

Semiotic society

Informationalism

The rise of informationalism as a social form paralleling the rise of textualism as an intellectual movement is neither a direct nor full equivalent. They do both, however, indicate a common point and practice of transformation. The hypothesis in both cases is of extensive effects in intellectual and social formations. It is, I think, fairly clear that the new social formation from within which textualism speaks is less and less that of the corporate liberalism from within which new sociology of education reassessed the social meaning of education. Just as textualism is itself embedded in the intellectual pragmatic of academic metaphysics, and the social pragmatics of the dialectic of the commodity, so too any informationalist, socially revolutionary transformation is located within existing historical institutions.

The most salient of these historical institutional and cultural processes within which transformation in the means of production is occurring is the rightward reorganization that I have linked to both a cultural restoration and a social reorganization as corporatism. Marx's comments on the restoration of Louis Bonaparte captures the cultural mood of the current restoration (Feuer, 1959: 323–9):

> Society now seems to have fallen back behind its point of departure . . . They had given out the watchwords of the old society, 'property, family, religion, order' . . . Every demand of . . . the most ordinary liberalism, of the most formal republicanism, of the most shallow democracy is simultaneously castigated as an 'attempt on society' and stigmatized as 'socialism'.

While the current 'restoration' may have a similar appearance, it is the result of a peculiarly contradictory twentieth-century dynamic. On the one side, the language and pre-modern social practices of local attachments and integration to family, religion and nation become highly valued. At the same time, there is an intensified social rationalization, instrumental and technical regulation of everday social life, and marketization and privatization of social domains such as schooling that had formerly belonged to the public sphere. What appears on the surface as a cultural restoration turns out to be part of a much more profound reorganization of social life, a reorganization toward a form of society that, together with its critics, I have called 'corporatist.' As I indicated in discussion of tendencies toward an institutional reorganization of education, corporatism describes the most general new institutional form that is emerging in response to capitalist crises.

Yet, there are other long-run sociohistorical developments that are in part responses to these same crises. Beneath the cultural restoration, and apparently even more basic than the emergent tendency to organize social life along corporatist lines, there are occurring deep and large-scale social changes. Fundamental changes are taking place in social production, in the culture of consumption, and in the structure of persons which I think are part of a broad social transformation, toward a new type of society that I call here 'semiotic.'

The change is that signification has itself become a force of production to unprecedented degree. Textualism is a relatively autonomous, indirect, yet I think integral, aspect of this historically new form of social energy: the basic productive energy or force of production is becoming information. Information is becoming central in production, distribution, communication and services. The view of the centrality of information in society is advanced by critics and apologists of the current social order alike. A critic of American capitalism, writing in a critical social theory journal, reports on 'informationalism' (Luke, 1983: 61–4):

> American producers increasingly are engaged either directly in the production of *information* or indirectly in the informationalization of goods-production and services provision . . . industrial capitalism has been greatly augmented if not nearly displaced by American informational capitalism . . . informational capital has not eliminated industrial or agricultural capital. Rather, it has begun to informationalize industrial production . . . just as industrial capital industrialized agriculture.

In a succinct statement of the extent of the social effects of informationalization in America, Luke wrote (1983:62): 'An entirely new social formation tied to the production, interpretation and distribution of information has emerged from within American industrial capitalism since the mid-1950's.'

From a perspective that is less critical of American capitalism, writing in a leading business journal, Bell (1979: 20–42) indicated a similar fundamental shift in the basis of production and social organization. He describes what he refers to as a 'revolution' toward an 'information society.' Bell suggested this emergent society is 'postindustrial,' partly because there is a redistribution of the labor force from industrial to service sectors. More importantly, however, he used the term in order to underline a basic shift in society's 'transforming resource' from one of created energy, like electricity, to information. Bell wrote (1979:26):

> The crucial point about a postindustrial society is that knowledge and information became the strategic and transforming resources of the society, just as capital and labor have been the strategic and transforming resources of industrial society.

There is serious disagreement among social analysts about the reasons for the development of informationalism in production and about its social and political consequences. While Bell may see the information society as somehow ending the capital/labor distinction, Schiller (1981;1984) sees the development of informationalism as part of a general pattern of corporate concentration and as a strategy used by transnational capitalism in response to current capitalist socio-economic crises. There is much less disagreement about a change in the actual means of production than there is about its source and consequences in the social relations of production. A change in the means of production, Rada (1980:9) writes about information technology: 'At this stage machines are being substituted for human intelligence, much as they were substituted for human muscle power in an earlier epoch.' King, in his Report to the Club of Rome on microelectronics and society, reiterates the theme of a revolution in the forces of production (1983:13): 'We are inclined to accept that the impact of the integrated circuit *is* revolutionary. No other single invention or discovery since the steam engine has had a broad impact on all the sectors of the economy.' In the same report, Lenk (1983: 261–96) suggests how the technological innovations of micro-electronics can extend beyond the economic means of production in a narrow sense, to redefine the organization of social life (1983:262):

> The present explosion of information technology and of microelectronics is much more closely related to the functioning of society as a whole than was the Industrial Revolution. To a much greater extent than other technologies, microelectronics affects the very essence of social cohesion, i.e. communication.

Disagreement about the social implications of the technological change are not blunted by an apparent consensus about the force and extent of the change itself. Dizard (1982: xiii) presents the democratizing view of information technology, when he describes the 'coming information age' where there will be a 'universal electronic information network, capable of reaching everyone everywhere.' For Mosco, diffusion of micro-electronics and telematics leaves the defining characteristic of a socially undemocratic capitalist society unchanged (1982:135):

> The post-industrial information society does not tame power relations . . . in the shift from the mechanical to the electronic, from the conveyor belt to the computers, from typewriter to videotex, . . . shifts the site of conflict, the instrument of struggle . . .

While he criticizes the role of 'post-industrial' fantasies in maintaining the present social order, Mosco acknowledges the extent to which changes have already occurred toward an informational base of production (1982:121):

> The post-industrial paradigm has inspired extensive empirical work that specifies some of the details of the information society. Whereas in 1900 only 10% of the U.S. labor force was engaged in information occupations, information workers now comprise 45% and collect 63% of all compensation. Other research has pointed to the remarkable growth in the capacity of information technologies and the equally remarkable decline in their costs. All of this is enhanced by the convergence of

computer technology and telecommunications into national and transnational data-base networks.

Beyond effects on the distribution of employment, information technology does appear also to have rather direct organizational consequences. Heydebrand (1983) suggests that a precondition for the kind of fusion of professional and administrative social forms that Derber describes (a kind of technocratic-professional organizational control structure) is (1983:11) 'the enlargement and increasing sophistication of the intelligence function, rapid information and data processing and long-term planning.' Heydebrand describes an emergent social organizational form that de-bureaucratizes and de-hierarchizes to create a more informal, though not less centralized, system of organizational control. System control, as well as production and distribution, take not only an informational form, but resonate to the symbolic language and imagery of textualism. Networks, dispersion, de-centeredness and the determinative power of the signifier, are neither merely erotic textualist play nor portents of greater freedom for subjective self-definition. They are, at the same time, the organizing concepts of a post-modern *administrative control apparatus*, a social practice in a society that is semiotic at the cultural-consumption level, informational-production level, and at the communicative regulative or power level. The sign is also a cybernetic control device in a system. Note the symbolic, textualist turn of Heydebrand's description of the administrative apparatus in neo-corporatism (1983:21):

> Central to this technocratic form is a concept of systemic power
> or systems guidance conceived as a medium of communication
> and influence based on an underlying symbolic code which is
> diffused throughout the whole system. . . .Such symbolic codes
> function essentially like signals and directions in traffic control
> systems, i.e. they constitute a system of pre-arranged options
> which are built into the control structure. . . .Technocratic
> control structures are thus not embedded in monocratic
> positions, but in the systemic nodes of communication of the
> organizational system as a whole.

Augured changes in the social organization of production

subsequent to the diffusion and deepening of informational production are, like the dialectic of commodification, two-sided. On the one side: informationalism communicationally cements the global networks of transnational capital; de-skills labor; streamlines and centralizes administrative organization control and intensifies the exploitation of consumptive as well as productive labor by accelerating consumption – producing and packaging the audience power that is as necessary for consumption exploitation as labor power is for exploitation in traditional sectors of production. On the other side: the de-centering of symbolic production and network diffusion of telecommunications offers potentially democratizing access to understanding and controlling the means of production. Network social organization de-hierarchizes not necessarily to re-control informally, but enables a disaccumulation of symbolic stores that can be used in projects of individual and collective self-definition. Most of all, in the service of more efficient techno-coordination, commodity production is much more transparent, so that the socially dominative effects of commodity fetishism, of the reification of the process of production, are reduced and dissipated. Between the Taylorist degradation of more centralized labor in a systems-guided network that dominates less by reifying than by fractionating the capacity for *assembly*, and a transparent network of democratic, accessible symbolic power, is where the tension and dialectic of production operates. Degradation, meaninglessness, and authoritarianism are one set of intermediate resolutions to the emergent social changes. On the other hand, informationalism promises release from surplus labor and an electronic community that will re-define and revive democratic society.

Mass culture

There is a less evident, but no less important change occurring in the organization of culture. It is no longer a question of whether advertising is acknowledged as an important cultural form. It has historically succeeded in establishing its cultural preeminence. Ewen and Ewen (1982) describe how not only advertising (Ewen, 1976), but fashion, movies and the mass culture of the urban landscape now follow such an effective, collectively constitutive form that non-mass-produced alternative images and understandings, and, perhaps even the capacity for interpretation itself, are obliterated (1982:280): 'Images and words proliferate; all people have access, yet increasingly the interpretations are ready-made, alternatives are expelled – a kind of democratic despotism.' The pervasiveness of the effects of the symbolic environment – semanticization – the mass discursive definition of the subject, occurs quintessentially in television-watching, where its constitutive effects have been documented. In a survey of television effects studies, the 'symbolic world of television' becomes the 'real world' for television watchers (Roberts and Bachen, 1981:328): 'In all cases, the responses of heavy viewers revealed a conception of the world that differs from reality but that is characteristic of television's world.'

But that is television's role. The depth of the modern transformation of cultural organization – against which textualism represents a movement for a counter-hegemonic de-reifying symbolic practice – is that it communicates belief and absorption in *itself*, in the naturalness of its own apparatus as the mass ideology enabling the continuing commodification of culture. Post-structuralism's fight against essentialist realism is also a struggle against the illusion of mass cultures' 'reality,' that denies its own productive apparatus. Kaplan (1983:xv) writes of television's role that:

> Television, like films, has at once to satisfy the need for illusionism (i.e. that the television world will *look like* the external world) and the craving for the world of the Imaginary where the viewers can find identification with the Ego-Ideals of the pre-symbolic, pre-oedipal phase.

Stam (1983: 23–43), in a discussion of television news, explains this qualitative shift in cultural organization that television embodies. It is an identification with the apparatus of cultural production which, by offering a sense of immediacy, totality and power, really disempowers the critical distance and separateness that is an interactional or pragmatic condition for understanding cultural production. 'The primary identification,' Stam (1983:24,25) writes, 'then, is not with the events or characters depicted on the screen but rather with the act of perception . . . this illusory feeling of presentness, this constrained impression of total immediacy . . .'

What Stam is describing is the constitution, positioning or re-definition of the cultural consumer as a *spectator*; a social role that requires an extended moment of passive absorption in the apparatus of cultural production in order to gain active efficacy as a successful consumer. This psycho-cultural process, that is now integral to the operation of the socially necessary consumption cycle, works especially well in the domestic darkness of television's living room, and the sexual anonymity of the invisibly, and therefore, falsely public, movie-house. The cinematic effect is, as Ellis (1982:44) describes, 'a series of identifications on the part of the spectator,' of which the most important is 'identification with the cinematic apparatus itself.' While the context of television's illusionist realist text is the domestic imperialism of the family's non-conversation, cinema's context is the men's room of a social form of attention in which the voyeuristic gaze of male sexual curiosity organizes the meaning of movies' narratives (Ellis, 1982).

It is the narrative itself, which already represents a cultural change because of the pervasiveness of the self-indexing, self-aggrandizing, identification message of the cinematic and television apparatuses, that is now changing even more. The post-narrative anti-diegetical forms of modernism, like the language of textualism in relation to the changing forms of administratively controlling production, are practically emergent forms, beyond their currency in intellectual textualist movements such as post-structuralism.

There is a shift in cultural genres, from realist narrative representation to a dispersed, modernist, and non-representational use of cultural resources. Realism versus modernism is not simply a dispute among the literati; it is an historical conflict within the sales culture of an emergent new society, and a change in mass cultural forms.

The prevailing culture which is the sales culture, is increasingly de-narrativized, less realistic and more modernist. What is happening, in Baudrillard's (1981) language, is that the intransitive sign is replacing the ambivalent relational symbol. The preeminent cultural form, advertising, is itself changing. The 'sign,' which acts as an associatively effective signal, replaces more traditionally coherent narrative and relational symbols, as the cultural means of engagement in consumption.

The sign which literary theory de-naturalizes is reclaimed by the logic of commodity production. The same non-referential, bottomless chessboard of post-structuralist theory that de-reifies the sign also operates as a new logic of commodity consumption. This is what I think Baudrillard means when he writes of the 'object' of consumption that (1981: 65, 67):

> . . . it finds meaning with other objects, in difference, according to a hierarchical code of significations . . . The definition of an object of consumption is entirely independent of objects themselves and exclusively a function of the logic of significations.

As with the informationalization of production, de-narrativization inside the operation of the mass consumer culture has contradictory consequences. A culture of signs rather than stories, of cultural fragments rather than integrated and realistic narratives, means a further reduction in already assaulted communicative capacities. A society of the political economy of the sign is one in which the sign plays the same role that the commodity once did in industrial society. It is the abstract, reductive generalization of the 'labor of signification.' Like the commodity in the labor process, the sign is a reification of the symbolic process. Culture becomes 'semanticized,' and even more extensive cultural resources can be used in the interactionally destructive and exploitative production of cultural commodities. Any moment of de-reification in the de-narrativization of culture passes quickly into an expanded cycle of value production in the commodity form.

On the other side, the diffusion of cultural narratives can unchain the means of signification from traditional emplacements. Attacks on coherent representational realism free signs for less burdensome use in continously negotiated rather than fixed meanings. Less stable and less rigidly integrated forms of cultural organization provide the kind of flexibility that actualizes communicational technologies, enabling realization of the ideals of democratically negotiated communities.

Identity

Change in the structure of persons, or in the language of post-structuralism (Young, 1981) 'subjects,' occurs along with changes in production and consumption. The diffusion or so-called 'de-centering' of traditional narrative culture corresponds to an historically different sort of subjectivity. The structure of a new type of personal functioning is better characterized by poly-morphous fluidity rather than moral integration. There is already extensive debate about the existence and value of this historically 'new self' (Wexler, 1983: 117–40).

The view of traditional critical social theory (Frankfurt Institute, 1956) is that fluidity and de-centeredness are potential ego weaknesses that make new selves susceptible to the mass appeals of authoritarian unifiers. The person or 'subject' is being re-positioned and reorganized as part of the transformation in production and in the cultural organization of consumption. Marcuse's concept of 'repressive desublimation' (1955) was only a preface to what now becomes a reorganization in the *form* of subjectivity. There is a diffusion of the person, in the name of liberation, freedom, and pleasure. There is a release of repressed energy into decentralized, signifying nodes, that produces the de-centered subject of modern textualist discourse only momentarily freer, liberated from the weight of selfness, open to socially negotiated self-constitution; but also more readily accessible to activation by the eroticized signifiers of culturally patterned positive signs. The post-modern, de-centered subject is only one tendential aspect of de-narrativized positive sign culture. An integrated ideological subject is simultaneously being formed in a quite narrative, organized collective symbolic structure.

The mass cultural content through which integrated individual identities are still socially produced are not only television's family myths and Oedipal identifications, but also through newer myths of late capitalism. These myths are sexual and domestic myths. This does not mean that sexuality and domesticity are not activities, but points rather toward their current cultural ideo-logical role: *the subjective denial of production*. *Penthouse* and *Harlequin* romances are examples of mass-gendered sexual wishes. *Good Housekeeping* and *Better Homes and Gardens* represent the mass domestic fantasies. These modern mythologies are structured, in both the form of their presentation and reception, not like a bourgeois novel, but like television's serial maintenance of narratives – the soap opera. These illusionist everyday realisms replete with false concreteness, these pseudo-realistically structured scenes, are the ideology of the unconscious. They produce the drives and motives that are the subjective aspect of historically particular modes of production; the specific fears and hopes of particular kinds of labor-power. The ideological work in this text – subject relation is to encode or translate the drives of psychologies of labor power from the mass cultural, serialized scenes of sex and domesticity. The relation between text and subject is to de-productionize desire. The persistence of this unconsciously narrativized individual subject is immediately accomplished in the collective text/individual subject relation by the work of processes of identification. For identification to operate, a false, though believable, individual identity has to be continuously produced in the symbolic operations of identity economies.

Description of identity economies will necessarily be contextually specific. But, I want to begin to suggest – omitting for now the requisite pragmatics of social interaction – the kinds of text/subject, culture/person or collective/individual relations that appear as historical possibilities. I risk the tentative speculation on identity because I think that the contradictory tendencies within the emergent semiotic society – between degradation, symbolic incapacitation, and authoritarian integration of identity, and, on the other hand, electronically enabling democratic community, open cultural negotiation, and voluntary, rational self-constitution – will not be decided by the inevitable reproduction of system logics, but by the historical action of a collective subject.

Collective subject

Within the dialectic of commodities, there is both a de-naturalizing, de-reifying, dis-articulating moment, and another moment of reintegration, reorganization, and commodification. When these two moments are viewed across the domains of production, culture and identity, the competing tendencies for the future shape of the semiotic society come into view. There is clearly a possibility for the renewal and strengthening of capitalism. This is the highly integrated, interactional systems-guided intensification of the exploitation of labor and control of capital. An apparently backward-looking cultural restoration combines with a futurist semiotic corporatism to produce a post-modern capitalism. There are also possibilities within the present for a democratic, informational global community, in which post-modern culture has successfully shattered the essentialist myths and stabilizing processes of the metaphysics of industrialism, and where its parallel psychology of over-controlled personality is replaced by fluid, contextually negotiated identity. This is the hope of new democrats, like Luke, who looks toward the second possibility, in ecological terms (1983:73):

> The struggle centers on the different meanings being reassigned to acts and artifacts in industrial life by informational capitalism. One syntax of signification points towards an official informational pragmatics in labor and leisure that would revitalize the reification of labor in the production and consumption of information. On the other hand, a more subversive ecological pragmatics derived from localist vernaculars can empower producers and consumers with their own meanings for informationalizing development, which could turn labor and leisure into emancipatory works of ecologically sound living.

In order to avoid the forced integration of informational corporatism, as well as the irrational, uncontrolled and dangerous disorder that results in moments of decomposition and disarticulation in production, mass culture, and identity, the de-reifying practices of textualism as theoretical icon of the semiotic society require a path and a direction. The achievement of a democratic, ecologically sound, alternative from the present occurs through a series of practices that aim, I think, toward the socialization of production, meaning, and identity value. What are the practices, methods, or process through which a modern socialization of value becomes possible?

I want to outline a path that combines the very general textualist view that the subject is formed in discourse, with an acceptance that the modern subject has already de-centered, a signifier that is floating apragmatically, without freedom.

This path begins with Kristeva's (1980:124) assertion '. . . that every language theory is predicated upon a conception of the subject that it explicitly posits, implies, or tries to deny.' I turn this from an epistemological argument to an empirical observation that there are prevailing forms of discourse, each of which 'posits,' predicates and produces its appropriate subject. These discourse-subject matches, that I refer to as discursive logics, are each capable of transformation, textually and contextually. The relation among the logics is not of an immanent evolution, as in models of individual moral and social development. Rather, the process of movement from one discursive logic to another ('from one identity to another,' writes Kristeva) is one of change and re-formation in the course of social action.

The re-constitution of the subject of discourse takes place outside of Oedipal immediacy of even the institutional replications and reminders of familied, Oedipal relations. Rather, a wider collective historical experience, the movement of the collectivity, is the dynamic stage and crisis that become the substance of subject-formation. Developmental turning points in individual maturation models are replaced by the developmental crises of the collective that occur in the process of formation. This formation is the process of collective movement itself. *The 'long march through the institutions' is a symbolic movement of the socially pragmatic, discursive formation of historical, collective subjects.* Discursive logics are descriptions of language and desire, though their medium in language is described from my interested point of view: a path of symbolic movement through discursive logics is collective, and aims toward the recuperation of conscious collectivity.

The prevailing logic of discourse is realism, whose accomplishment of naturalizing the symbolic process, including the disorderly textuality of the signifier, is so great that we do not recognize it as discourse. This is narrative discourse, the closed text I have alluded to in the extreme, Barthes's encratic language, his readerly rather than writerly text. Nichols (1981:134), following Wollen, indicates attributes of the classical narrative: 'narrative transitivity, identification, transparency, single diegesis, closure, pleasure and fiction . . .' The logic of realism is, of course, symbolically and historically produced. It is a production of contextual conditional movement of signification which is successfully reified by an illusion of live, unmediated 'reality.' In mass culture, this is sustained by unconcious identification with apparatuses of symbolic production. Realism is not only a form of language, however powerful its effectivity. It is a form of life that encourages and encodes a desire that is within and reinforces social relations. The desire of realism is power and authority, that continually re-establishes its own significatory security by the repressive imposi-tion of convention against the flow of indecisive and hetero-geneous meaning. For post-structuralist feminism, realism is phallocentric, the discursive logic of the father and his symbolic order.

Against the world of the fathers, of a collective historical subject whose instrumental success is built on repression and denial, is the children's world: of configurational rather than conventional meaning, gesture and image before worldly speech, and totalizing freedom, both before and after repression. This is the world that film promises, just while it places the refugee from realism into the spectator's chair of identification with the 'real' means of symbolic production. In what Biro (1982) calls 'film-thinking,' there is the 'film's rejection of the tyranny of naturalism' in favor of allusive and evocative 'experience-thought' that is the 'concrete logic' of children's discourse as kaleidoscope. (Biro, 1982:17): 'This kal-eidoscopic liveliness, fragmentation, and crowdedness, the inces-sant restructuring and regrouping of parts are very characteristic of the logic of film as well.' In the concrete logic of children's and films' thought (1982:20), 'through concrete and visual details and their continuous transformation, we gain insight into invisible structures of process in motion.' The images of film thought can grasp what eludes speech (1982:24): 'just like child-thought, the film communicates in dramatized actions, and perhaps this is precisely what facilitates the presentation of the *whole* . . .' The desire of concrete discursive logic is sensuous immediacy, but, importantly, it includes the dynamism that secure realism's desire of power must repress in favor of stabilized conventional meaning. In concrete discursive logic, the film displays *its* potential as a collective subject with the capacity to *compose meaning in motion* (emphasis added, Biro, 1982: 50,52).

> Of course, the cinema itself has had to undergo a certain historical development in order to work out the ways of handling the new modes of time-space relationships. The starting point was the recording and reproduction of movement. In time, the more cinema broke away from more reproduction – description and automatic transmission of

events – the greater its capacity grew for signification, which was due in no small measure to segmenting, to a *conscious articulation of motion*. Thus it was possible for thought to gain superiority over the image. In other words, film produced its rich and multilayered meaning by composing movements made of equally rich and varied elements. The result was not merely a real photograph of single physical movements, but the embodiment of a more abstract, sensory, and intellectual 'semantic' order.

Before the re-composition to a semantic order, there is (Kristeva, 1980:125): 'the crisis or the unsettling process of meaning and subject . . .' This is the linguistically associative thought that escapes the father's named symbolic order to live instead (Kristeva, 1980: 133) the semiotic disposition. The discourse of the semiotic disposition is the text of (1980: 135) 'a questionable *subject-in-process*.' The desire of this subject is to flee the repressive order, but to flee in the figuration of poetic language. Poetic language, unlike the linguistic convention of realism, by fleeing from the powerful repression of the symbolic language of the father, is born in early relation to the mother. Maintaining the energy of the initial maternal relation is poetic language's desire:incest. Kristeva describes the incestuous subject of poetic language (1980:136):

Language as symbolic function constitutes itself at the cost of repressing instinctual drive and continuous relation to the mother. On the contrary, the unsettled and questionable subject of poetic language (for whom the word is never uniquely sign) maintains itself at the cost of reactivating this repressed instinctual maternal element.

Poetic language is part of a discourse of instinctually fueled polysemic freedom. It accepts the significatory heterogeneity of poetry rather than the nominalist decisiveness of repressive narrative realism. It is the discursive logic of poetry, incest, even madness and, in its semiotic dispositional opposition to symbolic paternalism, it is feminine. This is the subject of discourse of whom Derrida observes (1979:55) 'That which will not be pinned down by truth, is in truth feminine.'

If the semiotic disposition is unsettled and undecidable, must it ultimately return to the more predictable collective subject of realism? Are film-thought and poetry recreational or de-naturalizing moments within the symbolic order of realism, as practices of de-reification which only finally serve the commodifications of meaning? An alternative is to develop the discursive logic of relational speech, or responsible dialogic conversation that Baudrillard (1981) sees eradicated by the monologic of the mass media. In a relational discursive logic, the positioning and desire of the subject is contextual, but rational and decidable. Concrete, poetic and realist discourses are accessible, but not coerced or inevitably imposed. This is the discourse of democratic informationalism, where de-naturalization does not lead to expanded commodification, but instead to enriched relationality. The logic of rational social relations depends on social knowledge. But the search for knowledge – like the effort to recoup child-experience through film which leads to spectatorial identification and desensitization – had led, as Dewey (1929) describes, to 'a quest for certainty' and to an objectivization of the historical process of social knowing (Bernstein, 1983).

Hermeneutics is an intellectual movement that intends to redeem the dialogic practical historical character of knowledge, to create in the discursive encounter a continually transformed historical subject and practical action on the world. Bernstein's (1983) commentary on Gadamer (1984) underlines his opposition to both the discourse of objective realism and the individual Romantic subjectivist tendency of purely poetic discourse, or aesthetic language. 'Phronesis' is the Aristotelian term which captures the interest in practical, historical social knowledge (Bernstein, 1983:146):

> Phronesis . . . is not to be identified with the type of 'objective knowledge' that is detached from one's own being and becoming . . . phronesis, the form of reasoning appropriate to praxis, which deals with what is variable and always involves a mediation between the universal and the particular that requires deliberation and choice.

The hermeneutical emphasis speaks to, and against, the objectivism of social knowledge that still characterizes conventional sociology. The 'old' sociology of education is vibrantly sustained by sociological objectivism, during a continuing cultural restoration that prefers positivism in the academy. While hermeneutical orientations that aim to redeem relational discourse can be dismissed as non-scientific, post-modernism challenges the scientific discourses of legitimation on their own terms. Lyotard (1984) writes of a 'postmodern scientific discourse' which moves science from the discursive logic of realism to a relational, dialogic contextual or pragmatic definition of science. 'Simplifying to the extreme,' writes Lyotard (1984:xxiv), 'I define *postmodern* as incredulity toward metanarratives.'

What Lyotard tries to do by this term is to separate the practice of science from the discursive logic of realistic narrative, to surpass (1984:29) 'the recurrence of the narrative in the scientific.' Doing this, he reviews the de-legitimation of the grand nineteenth-century meta-narratives of idealism and emancipation which, he claims, have now eroded, as the legitimation of science. They have taken along with them the meta-view of narrativity itself (Lyotard, 1984:37): 'The grand narrative has lost its credibility, regardless of what mode of unification it uses, regardless of whether it is a speculative narrative or a narrative of emancipation..' On narrativity (1984:xxiv): 'The narrative function is losing its functors, its great hero, its great dangers, its great voyages, its great good. It is being dispersed in clouds of narrative language elements – . . . '

The dispersion of narrative and de-legitimation of narrative science through the erosion of its meta-narratives of legitimation occurs in a condition conducive to the kind of local vernaculars that Luke's (1983) ecologism calls for (Lyotard, 1984:xxiv): 'There are many different language games – a heterogeneity of elements. They only give rise to institutions in patches – local determinism.'

What Lyotard intends is to question the realism of scientific knowledge as the concrete and the poetic have historically questioned the power of realism. He interrogates scientific realism, however, on scientific grounds, by suggesting that the text of science can be grasped pragmatically, within the context of its sustaining discourses. In an altered 'post-modern' context, conventional positivist claims of scientific knowledge give way to a new interdeterminate localism, where science understands itself pragmatically. From there, it changes the meaning of knowledge itself, to represent change, indeterminateness and instability, and less of a 'quest for certainty' than for one of inventive, plural generativity. Lyotard legitimates this post-modern pragmatics of scientific knowledge from within science itself, calling attention to unstable systems theories and a view of determinism according to the 'local state of the process.' Not timeless narrative, but 'morphogenesis,' the generation of series of contextual rules that enable dissensus and destabilization becomes a goal for the postmodern adventurer. 'Postmodern science . . . is changing the meaning of the word *knowledge*, while expressing how such a change can take place . . .' (1984: 60–66).

Hermeneutics and Lyotard's post-modernism join post-structuralism with a pragmatic emphasis, to proclaim the centrality of knowledge processes, language and speech in the formation of social life. But, as we have seen in discussions of cultural restoration and institutional reorganization, of capitalist crisis and corporatism, of mass cultural spectatorism and the ideological character of new sociology, this view is not embedded in the common practice of everyday life, no matter how much we think it may analytically capture the historically local determination of our society. To bring everyday life to modern historical awareness requires a mass practice of transforming the context and textual, or discursive logic, within which collective, though individualized, identities understand and experience their lives. This awareness, as Thompson (1978) observes, is not the first, but the last stage in an historical process of collective formation. That process entails a transformative movement from one discursive logic to another, to paraphrase Kristeva, from one collective subject to another. The process by which the collective subject is transformed is education.

8
Education

Redefinition

The mode of historical transformation from collective subject to collective subject, discourse to discourse, is itself historically variable. The new sociologists of education worked within the discursive logic of realism. They operated there as a left-negation of the binary which constituted a politics of realism. By accepting the meta-framework of realism, they accepted also the hegemonic class's misleading definition of the socially formative power of schooling. New sociology rejected the false promise of the claim, but not the assumption of the school's efficacy. The ruling class though, as Mills (1956) showed, used schools as only one small part of its own process of collective self-formation. The school itself, as Welter (1962) argued, had already become an egalitarian, but de-politicized ideology by the Progressive era; precisely the time when the old sociology of education began to translate school ideologies into scientized imitations of Progressive belief in the form of the new academic social sciences.

The ideology of the school was rightly placed in question by Illich (1971) and Reimer (1972), but probably too late historically. The practical reformation of education that de-schooling aimed at was soon caught by the same political defeat that shaped new sociology of education (Wexler and Whitson, 1982). Liberalism, displaying its hegemonic effectiveness, absorbed radical critiques into its terms of debate, and so insured the continuation of the ideology of school as education. It was, however, finally not the realist, liberal-encoded radical academic sociologies of education, but the rightist collective social movements which placed the school ideology in severest doubt. De-schooling from the right showed the non-equivalence between the school as institution and the educational needs of a social formation.

The school ideology contains and limits the motive force of education as a symbolic movement; as a process of discursive transformation that changes the character of the collective subject by bringing it continually into historical movement. Along with rightist movements that seek cultural restoration and assertion of capitalist interest by intensifying the exploitation of labor, intellectual movements attack the solidity of those institutions which enable continuation of such liberal industrialist ideologies as schooling. These movements are directed less at the social relations of the institutions of the liberal regime that made possible both new sociology style radical social critiques and the ultimate triumph of objectivism masquerading as science. Rather, they are aimed more at the discursive means of institutional production. They are an attack on the metaphysical bases of industrial capitalism, which offer a pragmatic possibility for both the transcendental idealism and positive empiricism by which its university knowledge sector secures the borders of a broad cultural regime. The post-structuralist and Foucauldian language of 'transgression' and 'rupture,' its spatial imagery of discursive 'networks,' its talk of boundaries and border police, are all indirect acknowledgments of the kind of discursive guerilla attack in which they are engaged.

The movements of women and increasingly, the visibility of Third World movements, also lead to a questioning of the assumptions and discursive means of production within which new sociology style criticisms are contained in the regime of liberal capitalism. Together, these movements place the institutions – the social sector of the 'grand narrative' of legitimated realism – into temporal and spatial social doubt. As that happens, the battle over various particular discursive domains, and ultimately, in the semiotic society, over the most powerful means of knowledge production – information, science, signification, image, electronic signal – comes more clearly into the open. Under these conditions of group conflict, the prevailing ideologies among them the historic ideology of the school, lose the spell-binding power that extends even to defining the terms of opposition. Moreover, the agonistic groups realize the extent to which collective self-definition, 'consciousness', is a necessary weapon on their path of struggle. They recognize an immediate vested interest in locating and seizing what is not only society's generative energy, but their own symbolic resources, without which the struggle in meaning cannot be fought.

In this view, there is no single movement that highlights the means by which discursive logics are moved into alignment with anticipations, self-definitions, and perceived immediate needs of their respective collective subjects. Those subjects themselves no longer develop in direct proximate communicative contact, as in the orthodox Marxist imagining of the formation of a revolutionary industrial working class. They are not all in the same spatial location, or even at the same node on a set of controlling grids. Rather, what is necessary is that they seek the same principles of articulation, configuration, and self-defining gestalt formation; that they are, as we say, 'on the same wave length.' Like the discursive apparatus which they need to control, they are debureaucratized, decentralized and dispersed, so that their singularity as collective subject is based not on unitary integration, but on a common processual location, a similar trajectory of motion, within the logic that defines their collective mode of being.

For this reason, it is likely vain to search, as does Touraine – who, more than any other contemporary sociologist provides, I think, the social analytic terms to grasp the new historical pragmatics of action – for a single movement that is central to the formation of the collective subject of historical movement during the symbolic period. Touraine does, of course, recognize the local, contextual ecological vernaculars of action. He writes (1981:77, emphasis added): 'The social movement is the organized collective behavior of a class actor struggling against his class adversary for *the social control of historicity in a concrete community*.' At the same time, however, he expresses his faith in the existence of a unitary, single movement, rather than a dispersed, in tandem movement in simultaneous motion along those same grid-like social networks of controlling information and signification by which all participants and configured elements are defined. (Touraine, 1981:24):

> . . . the practical aim of our research: to discover the social movement which in the programmed society will occupy the central position held by the workers' movement in industrial

society and the civil liberties movement in the market society by
which it was preceded.

It is in the struggle for formation, on the surface, Melucci's
(1980) 'identity politics,' that the social movements themselves
locate the crucial, contextually appropriate motors of their own
historical formation. In the process of movement, and not in its
belated academic paradigmatic routinization, ideologies are revealed and socially effective resources are located. So it is now,
even as an incipient liberal counter-restoration against the
commodified de-schooling that may capitalize education reasserts
the school ideology. The new liberal movements for school reform
do not succeed in diverting attention from schooling as a distracted
channel of distorted (ineffective, irrelevant, scholastic) knowledge. Quite aside from the school reforms, it is becoming clearer
in the struggle over knowledge production that education means
the capacity to control, to generate, refigure, configure and
extrapolate the signifier. In Maoist terms, it is 'the struggle
through language.'

When the literary theorists speak or write about 'discourse
forming the subject,' they are not describing a purely theoretical
discovery, but a real historic change in the mode of production and
education. *The relation between mass discourse and individual
formation and motivation is the emergent educational relation.*
Where the forces of production become informational/com-
municational, semiotic, and the formation of the subject occurs
significantly through mass discourse, then it is that relation which
is the educational one. The mass communications/individual
relation now already better exemplifies the educational relation
than does the school, which as we know it, with all its structural
imitations of industrial and, later, corporate productive organization, is being surpassed, as new modes of education develop.

Both critical new sociology of education, as the left-liberal
binary, and positivist academic social and educational psychologies as the right-liberal binary, observe this shift, and make it more
difficult to rationally re-appropriate the discursive means of
signification, speech, identity and social relations. New sociology
does this by glamorizing working-class culture as resistance to the
school's institutional regimes. When, however, the analysis of
resistance begins to move toward the self-formative role of youth's

cultural action, then new sociology begins to undo its own ideological blockage (Hebdige, 1979; Castleman, 1982).

For its part on the liberal right, academic educational psychology ignores the collective discursive formation of the individual to focus instead on more refined forms of organizational stratification by measuring individual differences. In such recent advances as 'cognitive science,' it does acknowledge changing forces of informational production, but removes them from social relations and mystifies them in a typical naturalizing way, by making them into individual attributes. Complementary, general, academic social psychology of education remains, as I have argued, a rearguard functionalist sociology, with its deployment of ahistorical reification in concepts like socialization, roles, influence, group dynamics, leadership in the classroom, and so on (Wexler, 1983; 1985b).

A similar process of ideologizing and blocking analysis of social change occurs in depth psychology. The unconscious formation of the individual was once described as universal instincts or libido, mechanical energy. Now, the unconscious formation of the individual takes account of, and in turn displaces understanding of, social change by saying that 'the unconscious is structured like a language.' Signification replaces mechanical energy, but in an individualized and universalized form – the double device of capitalist ideology.

The ruling class still cannot understand why school-education does not work, and why, even among the most privileged youths, it is not instrumental rewards that provide a basis for conformity to the social routines of schools. In our study of identity and disaffection among socially diverse youths, we describe how school-education does not engage the energy and attention necessary for the educational labor of identity production (Wexler et al., 1988). One reason for this is that the school's organization of pedagogy, its actual mode of immediate social relations, is modelled on the older mode of production and organization, while youths are already relating to future organizational and productive forms through which they do their collective self-production, for identity-work. To put it in orthodox Marxist terms, the conflict of generations that characterizes these schools is the result of a structural contradiction between the forces and relations of production. Educators are imposing on youths a mode of social relations that is contradictory to forces of interactional technology through which they are doing their work, which is the identity work of becoming somebody.

An accomplishment of successful identification, which is the educational principle that sometimes works inside the school, is to replicate in the individual the tension of symbolic disjunction between labor-power and myth, which enables a continuous activity of the unconscious: interpretation away from production, and the fears and needs it generates, into serialized mythologies of domesticity and sexuality. Identification is rightfully an educational ideal, for its efficacy preserves the appeal and ideological promise of schools. The failures are as important as the successes of identification in schooling. With disaffection, the student moves identity work into the mythological realm, and seeks to blot out the actual conditions of identity production in the school. This is not 'resistance,' but self-mythologizing, facing the student away from the conditions of her/his own self-production. The identifying student becomes like the teacher, torn, always hopeful of self-realization in social production in the schoolplace, yet ready for a more displaced, symbolic expression of self-realization through consumption.

Popular educational practice: culture, movement, criticism

Discursive self-formation as part of collective re-definition, in the process of collective action, is a current active educational principle. This education can sometimes be observed within the social life of schools (Wexler et al., 1988; Crichlow, 1988). But, more often the dynamic struggle *through education* as discursive practice occurs precisely in non-consumption spheres of youth cultural action. Here there is discovery of self and collectivity, of the formative power of symbolic action. Here, it becomes evident the extent to which the institutional apparatus of the state, to which the school belongs, operates in opposition to the popular practice of education. New sociology of education was right to move from the individual meliorist ideology of school as the means of equalizing the conditions of individual competition to a view of school as social class reproduction. But, emplaced within realism, only anticipating a changed society and education by its slogan of 'sociology of knowledge,' new sociology could not yet fully see the dispersed collective formation in symbolic struggle over the means of significatory, self and collective formative production.

The graffiti of the New York subway 'writing gangs' is an icon, an extreme though telling 'ideal type' example of this process in its early stages. This is the process of producing collective self-definition and the sense of symbolic efficacy that is increasingly necessary for the operation of the symbolic control devices of production, consumption and identity formation in the social apparatus. Lacking this educative process, mass discourse really will write the subject; socialization really will be the correct term for totalization through individualized monitoring; and school really will be the central locus of historical collective action; which really will then be social and cultural reproduction. The alternative is communicative, responsible, generative contextual post-modern vernacular sorts of knowledge that avoid familiar totalizing ideologies of legitimation.

The alternative is a social writing that begins from and encourages social reciprocal relation rather than spectatorially incorporative identification. First, a hint of the collective feeling, Durkheim's a 'collective effervescence' (1957), that is the social climate in which knowledge is created. Castleman quotes a writer in the subway train yards (1982:51):

> . . . and you're spraying and you look down the track and you
> see all these brothers working on one goal – to make the train
> beautiful. There's so much peace in that. You got that creative
> feeling, that vibe that comes out of all that work happening . . .
> Everyone's looking out for the man . . . You get close to each
> other . .

Wicked Gary writes his name (Castleman, 1982:76):

> Writing your name identifies who you are. The more you write
> your name, the more you begin to think about and the more
> you begin to be about who you are. Once you start doing that,
> you start to assert your individualism and when you do that, you
> have an identity.

Wicked Gary describes the process of group self-education as collective formation in symbolic production when he tells of traveling up from Brooklyn to write in the Bronx (Castleman, 1982:86–7):

> We knew everything that was happening. That was our
> playground, that was our work and . . . we were involved.
> Schedules of trains, schedules of tunnels, we had information
> on everything. It was a whole other system of communication
> and interaction from the normal system that we dealt with like
> the English language and money and stuff like that. We had our
> own language, our own technology, terminology. The words we
> had meant things to us that nobody else could identify. We had
> our own tools of the trade. We had all this happening for us.

The process of symbolic collective self-definition is transgressive, though formative, because it carves, draws, or writes collective identity on the legitimated 'private property' of institutional cultural space. As Nathan Glazer wrote (quoted in Castleman, 1982:176):

> I have not interviewed the subway riders, but I am one myself,
> and while I do not find myself consciously making the
> connection between the graffiti-makers and the criminals who
> occasionally rob, rape and assault passengers, the sense that all
> are part of one world of uncontrollable predators seems
> acceptable.

Castleman then quotes New York Metropolitan Transit Authority chairman Richard Ravitch (Castleman, 1982:176) who underlines that the issue is one of symbolic control. 'I fully understand that graffiti is not in the same category as murder or robbery. However, it is a symbol that we have lost control.'

Graffiti writing may be only an ideal-typical example of a process of simultaneous self and group conscious collective formation through rationally intended operation of the means of symbolic production – collective, pragmatic social writing. For Baudrillard (1981), this graffiti is the transgressive discourse of the streets that overcomes the commodified positivity of the sign.

As I have argued, textualism, and, less evidently, symbolic economies of identity, are forms of social speech that are historically appropriate to a society where discourse is a central means of social production and where the mobilization of collective energies is mediated through individual identity. These symbolic practices potentially offer a de-reification display of the processes that constitute apparently stable and integral products: cultural meaning and personal identity.

These practices are contradictory because while they denaturalize social life by decomposing it, the same decomposition lends itself to easier incorporation of transparent cultural and personal elements into structured processes of capital. The cultural restoration, the institutional reorganization toward corporatist forms, and the shifts in production, culture and person that outline the contemporary semiotic society do not dislodge the commodification and exploitation of value which defines capitalism as a social system. As I have suggested, what has changed is that pillars of the ideological apparatus – natural culture and personal identity – are now drawn out of reified hiding into the social relations of capital. What has changed also is that symbolic practices, like textualism, that increasingly supplant even the socially critical discourse, do not operate by theoretically containing social contradictions. Instead, they work by *oscillation*, from an illuminating and critical moment of de-reification to an inclusion of newly transparent cultural and social dynamic elements into the cycle of exploitative commodity production.

It is this re-commodification that leads Baudrillard to call for the cultural transgression of the streets; not further de-reification of culture, but the destruction of the sign. The 'symbolic' that he wishes to restore is the 'reciprocity of speech.' But first: 'Only total revolution, theoretical and practical, can restore the symbolic in the demise of the sign and of value. Even signs must burn.'

An alternative is to block the reintegrative commodity phase by an intervening appropriation of de-reified cultural and personal 'things.' Such an appropriation engages the display of the constituent processes of culture and identity in its own process of formation. This intervention uses the transparent moment of the de-reification/commodification dynamic for its own formative empowerment. Concretely, that means the collective production of meaning and identity.

Collective production ruptures the natural-seeming private ownership of value of significatory and identity labor. It is too early in the analysis of our own research (Wexler et al., 1988) on youths' social lives, as it may also be in social history, to know precisely the contextually variable, appropriate practices which transform a private symbolic economy of identity into a social one. We do know that they are practices which persuade the participants in the economy that the identity value of others is being produced at their expense, and that identity is in a social value rather than a private 'thing' or attribute. Under conditions of such awareness, and a balanced mixture of identity-commitments and deprivations, the symbolic apparatus can be intentionally altered. Collective action in a social system that mobilizes energies through the privatization of the economy of identity, is directed toward a socialization of identity value.

The discourse of textualism is now a more familiar discursive movement than that of identity economics. If textualism is now the academic discourse of the semiotic society, criticism is its potentially transformative intervention. If literary theory is the socially sublimated theory of a semiotic society, its conventional practice, literary criticism, is the starting point for a counter-practice. Criticism does not mean either individualist impressionism or scientistic formalism. Criticism reads through the text, using its transparency for the process of social/self formation. Criticism means socially transformative reading, and cultural literacy as the conscious cultural reconstitution that blocks re-commodification.

Active criticism means cultural reappropriation, reversing current mythological translations of everday life into pseudo-concrete, serialized realism. For example, making the unconscious translation of the psychology of labor power into the myths of personal sexual and domestic life a conscious interpretive practice of the organized re-theft of mass communications is 'literacy.' In place of an educational social psychology of identification: the struggle of expression. Expression, in a signified society, does not mean simply writing, or interpretation. It does not mean substituting a positive or utopian hermeneutic for a negative, critical one. It means, rather, changing the mode of individual-discourse relation. Writing is 'writing-over.'

In the semiotized, signified society, self-formation means the ability to write-over, to express the process of group formation, in which criticism is the interpretive moment. This points toward a new literacy and a new meaning of reading and writing. In our brief example, I claim that writing gangs are engaged in the collective 'writing-over' in education. In the semiotic society, criticism means discursive reappropriation through socially formative action. The reciprocal symbol defeats the unilateral sign when writing asserts social relations.

The historical movement of the collective subject and her institutions is not, I think, going to be accomplished by guerilla symbolic action. The current pervasiveness of the knowledge regime of realism does encourage the symbolic transgression of street writing, and even a search within that collective activity for the outlines of an historically appropriate theory of practice. Transgressions can open a necessary way to the concrete and semiotic discursive dispositions. The post-structuralist language of exile (Handelman, 1982:176, 193) can help free social analysts of education from an incorporated academically established, but only putatively critical social theory on the one hand, and a socially inauthentic identification with 'the working class' or with the triadic oppressed groups of 'class, race and gender,' on the other. Social analysis of education, like educational practice in and out of schools, can know its historical exile and the centrality of cultural action as education. But, the symbolic movement of historical practice is not limited to the moment of exile, of de-reification and decomposition. Unlike the modern critic Harold Bloom, of whom Handelman writes (1982:193): 'He, too, prefers to remain faithful to exile, to displacement, to discontinuity; to defer and differ, to assuage his sorrow through rereading – not transcending – the text' a practical social analysis wants the text contexualized. The goal of social practice is messianic – a collective return, and social redemption.

Contextualization of the outlines of this symbolic movement, collective formation, writing view of educational practice, means organized social activity, on the grounds of the ideological institutions themselves. It implies analysis of the collective means of current symbolic criticism. Literary criticism is now moving away from its conventional emphasis in authorized intention to interest in criticism and interpretation as a community action. The communal definition of meaning appropriation parallels the incipient socialization included in the view of scientific knowledge as also a symbolic *communal* product (Bernstein, 1983). The literary critic, Frank Kermode, comments on this movement toward a communal emphasis in literary criticism (1983:9): 'And that is surely enough for anybody to attempt the reconstruction of the Common Reader on a new, historically appropriate plan.' The literary interest in criticism as an expression of collective meaning extends further to Hohendal (1982), who directly analyzes literary critical practice as an aspect of the social institution of criticism.

The same socializing tendency that acknowledges and articulates social processes of the collective production of meaning can be directed toward an institution certainly no more ideological than criticism – school. Application of the academic 'textual turn' to the study of signification in schooling – a further step in the early promise of a sociology of school knowledge – is subject to the same dangers of de-contextualization and ahistoricism as is post-structuralist criticism in social life generally. Re-contextualized study of knowledge production in schools includes the interactional processes of the institution, the professional identity dynamics of teachers, and, most importantly: analysis of political practice and possibility in school, as preface to an educational politics.

New sociology of education unintentionally served the ideology of the school by failing to articulate a contextual, institutional, educational politics. 'Critical pedagogy' was a misdirection from an historical, practical educational politics. Classifying and romanticizing cultural emanations as 'resistances' was a diversion from asking what contemporary forms might replace the clubs, societies, and coffee-houses that once served as the public social places and occasions for education. In discussion of French feminism, and life history studies, and in the New York writing gangs, I offered brief examples of diverse educational sites and movements. French feminism offers a critical anticipation of the symbolic power being flexed by an advanced consumer culture. Unlike the first or even 'second stage' of feminism (Friedan, 1981), post-structuralist feminists already understand the place toward which the cultural sales effort is headed: the appropriation of the subject of desire in language:

> In the twentieth century, after suffering through fascism and revisionism, we should have learned that there can be no socio-political transformation without a transformation of subjects: in other words, in our relation to social constraints, to pleasure and more deeply to language (Kristeva, 1981:141).

This feminism, by its critique of naturalized phallic discourse, underlines awareness of the power of language. Beyond writing, this sector of the feminist movement already sees the re-definition of knowledge. In the social transformation of informationalism, de-centered discourse and subjectivity are cultural ancillaries of a market and technically driven disassembling of the commodity form. Dispersion is not merely a discursive invention of post-structuralism, but also the practice of network management in a post-industrial society. Feminist post-structuralism is not a disinterested spectator to such a transformation.

The life-history movement does not struggle against authoritarian discourse by significatory play. The subject does not have to make itself elusively mobile, to slide away happily from the father's decisive presence. This subject instead has been denied location in history; recognition of the historical identity has been suppressed, ignored or distorted by traditional history writing. The de-legitimation of positivist social science knowledge that has occurred both during the expanded and depressed cycles of the academic industry (Altbach and Berdahl, 1981) opens the door for the voices of history's subjects. As in the struggle for ambiguity and contradiction, authoritatively imposed knowledge that is centrally administered and legitimated is particularly destructive of discursively formed collective subjects.

A mass educational politics implies, if not a single, unitary movement, then a popular articulation that directs attention to the fact that the common practices of these movements are what we now historically mean by education. Any popular educational movement requires collective work to press toward articulation and realization. Not only will new sites of social communication need to develop, but even the goal of universal enlightenment will be historically redefined. The meaning of literacy in an information, semiotic society, is not only that the artefacts (television, microcomputers, telecommunications) are new, but that the social relation to the artefacts also changes. A new enlightenment aim of contemporary popular articulation of educational movements is consciously to appropriate and use various knowledge practices for collective aims.

A new popular educational movement begins from contextual redefinition. The artefacts and practices of education begin to change. Being literate demands the ability to regard mass commmunications in ways that do not force the suppression of the culturally created historical subject. Reading is an ambiguously useful term to describe altered forms of cultural relations and what it means to be literate and empowered in them. The contours of a new education will be determined in the interaction between contemporary structural transformations and social movements. Movements from the periphery will comprise the democratic political education of a new society. I do not know whether they will remain disparate, or if they will become unified in a common social movement. I do not know whether their ideals will languish in the historical vault of intellectualisms, or become a mass practice of enlightenment for a new era. I do not know precisely what re-appropriation, expression, writing-over, literacy and criticism will mean in the emerging society. But I think that they are the questions to guide work toward an historically meaningful educational practice. That work means, I think, giving up backward-looking radical romanticism, overcoming the fear of communications technology, and most importantly, beginning to understand that education is education in the process of creative, active symbolic appropriation, and collective self-formation through active criticism. This work requires, I think, immersion in the collective symbolic text, and a systematic understanding of its relation to both the forces of production and to the individual unconscious as analysis of historical collective subjects. That is just part of the intellectual work that lies ahead after a new sociology of education.

As we look ahead, it may become evident that there was some virtue in defeat of what was once an historically progressive discourse of new sociology of education. The virtue is that the defeat passes the new sociologists back into a wider social life, where they can realize their socially transformative aspirations. The form of this wider social participation may not be as dramatic as that which Marx suggested (Bottomore and Rubel, 1956:186):

> Finally, in times when class struggle nears the decisive hour, the process of dissolution going on within the ruling class, in fact within the whole range of old society, assumes such a violent, glaring character, that a small section of the ruling class cuts itself adrift, and joins the revolutionary class, the class that holds the future in its hands. Just as, therefore, at an earlier

period, a section of the nobility went over to the bourgeoisie, so now a portion of the bourgeoisie goes over to the proletariat, and in particular, a portion of the bourgeois ideologists, who have raised themselves to the level of comprehending theoretically the historical movement as a whole.

Institutional educational practice: knowledge and society again

Instead, the form of social participation that historic defeat encourages is reflexive. Post-new sociology of education returns, under these circumstances, to the original site of its critical analysis and practical political action: the university. This return does not mean insularity from the wider discourses of popular movements and collective cultural actions. But, it does recognize the institutional character of processes of knowledge production, even if those institutional boundaries are diffuse, and it does acknowledge the continuing power of formally coded knowledge. Critique of new sociology of education, through post-structuralism and post-industrialism, leads to the generative question of the discourse: knowledge and society, again. But now, the earlier customary separation between education, its social context, and sociology of education as a study or reflection on these topics and their relation to each other has begun effectively to disappear as part of an historical transformation in social knowledge. The importance of knowledge in social life, the organization of the production and distribution of knowledge, and the relation of professional sociologists and educators to social knowledge are each aspects of the transformation. The relation between knowledge and society, which has always been both historically variable yet culturally made to appear as natural and stable, is changing. The realist form of new sociology of education that saw education, its social context, and sociology of education as separate domains is increasingly less tenable in a semiotic society.

I have already described re-organization of public educational institutions toward a corporatist form. It has meant ultimately the reconstruction of the immediate social relation and institutional organization of education as a commodity market. It is a process that has included the cultural re-definition of education, particularly its detachment from a secular public sphere; the re-definition of relational, interactional knowledge, toward skills as commodities; the adaptation of market practices as the internally regulative principles of school life, and the societal organization of what is still called 'education' as learning products, in privately owned, skill commodity markets.

A limitation of this description of corporatism in education is that it looks primarily at knowledge consumption and distribution. The process of the *production* of knowledge, the specific character of that knowledge, the organization of the site of its production, the relation of that site to the field in which it operates, have all been neglected. I want to reconstitute the 'macrostructural' distinction between the overall societal process of making a fund, base or capital of new knowledge, and its productive, though consumption-oriented, realization in primary and secondary schools. There have been changes in knowledge, at university's relation to society. As we have seen, there is also an important and simultaneous change in the languages and discourse in which knowledge is made and presented, in the university and in society more generally. I have argued that at the center of these changes is the emergence of a post-industrial, informational or 'semiotic society.'

I have used the term 'semiotic society' to indicate an important connection that is usually ignored, the connection between social production and academic discourse between the popularity of new academic languages, the varieties of interpretivism, and the information change in knowledge production. To reiterate Finlay-Pelinski (1982:257):

if at one time, in a certain episteme, the dominant conditions of production were economic, it is possible that in this present context the dominant conditions of production have indeed become discursive or communicational.

This may overemphasize the connection, but it indicates why a textualist study of discourse may at once also be a study of production.

With an increased awareness of a relation between knowledge and social production, the boundary between sites of knowledge production, notably the university, and 'society' is penetrated, begins to recede, and instigates further changes in the internal knowledge apparatus of the university – even to the point of putting in question the organization of knowledge as 'disciplines,' and then, finally, of doubting the natural and inevitable separation of these disciplines from social practice.

Reduced viability of the concept 'context' is an effect of this historical change in knowledge: its increasingly systematic, central, and conscious relations to social production. With a new kind of knowledge that is more directly used in social production, the institutional relation, society/knowledge, can no longer be thought of in the taken-for-granted way of context 'affecting' education and knowledge: the 'text,' knowledge and education, may not only become the 'context,' but its most determinant aspect. There are several avenues by which to approach understanding this changed boundary relation, and also to ask what it may mean for education as an institutional educational practice in relation to an active popular educational practice.

Parsons' (1968:195) view of the American university as in a balanced functional subsystem differentiation, is now challenged, practically as well as theoretically. Compare, for example, Parsons' view with that expressed by modern scholars of knowledge and education in recent monographs of the Carnegie Commission. First, Parsons:

> The academic system is not primarily an 'engine' of change (or reform) in the sense either that government strove to be in the New Deal or, more extremely, that Communist governments attempt to be in undertaking radical restructuring of their societies.

On the other hand, a recent headline in the *Chronicle of Higher Education* (January 29, 1986) reads: 'Strength of U.S. Said to Depend on Universities.' The Newman report (1985:xvi) links higher education to a 'true American resurgence.' 'We believe that the United States is gearing up for an economic renewal. Education at all levels is expected to play a major role . . .' (p. xiv). And, following a description of the economic role of education: 'The most critical demand is to restore to higher education its original purpose of preparing graduates for a life of involved and committed citizenship.' Eurich, in her (1985) Carnegie report, *Corporate Classrooms*, noted: 'The authors of

Global Stakes emphasize that *knowledge* has become a strategic resource as vital as natural resources and physical investments.' Eurich describes how this view drives a variety of aspects of 'the corporate learning enterprise,' each of which reduces the boundaries of subsystem differentiation between knowledge-producing and distributing organizations (formerly, 'schools' and 'society.') The perceived centrality of systematic knowledge in social production for national security in a post-industrial world is altering the society/knowledge boundary. Post-industrialism, in theory and practice, has the effect of de-naturalizing the current compartmentalized organization of knowledge that we take for granted.

Historians' accounts of the origins of our organization of knowledge and its relation to society underline this variability. They reveal how much the current, only apparently natural social organization of knowledge is part of the earlier historical social formation of industrialism. The so-called historical 'revolution in higher education' refers to the fact that (Bender, 1984:84): 'The institutional structure of intellectual life was radically transformed in the United States between the Civil War and World War I.' Bender (1984) relates this development of the current university structure not only to the rise of industrialism, but also as a response to a perceived crisis of urban social life, an historically specific social and cultural transformation.

What is important is not only that the present organization of knowledge be understood as part of the general historical social formation of industrialism, or as a response to a more general societal process of reorganization. But, that, as Bender argues, it was only one of several historic possible responses to a specific social crisis. The particular relation of knowledge to society that the industrial university came to embody, emerged victorious against alternative ways of structuring the knowledge/society relation. In the modern university, organized around 'disciplinary communities,' the compartmentalization of intellectuals won out in a conflict among (Bender, 1984:90) 'three distinct responses to this crisis of the city and of intellectual life.' Personalism and the civic culture of informed citizens were displaced by the professional/disciplinary associations of the modern university.

As we identify and respond to the purported 'crisis' of international economic competition and national commitment that arise in the dawn of society built around a post-industrial technology, there are, again, alternative responses possible. There are different paths of action before us, through which we determine ultimately the meaning of knowledge in relation to educational practice. None of these paths, I believe, leaves intact the traditional view of the relation between knowledge, social institutions and systematic reflection on that relation, upon which rests the appeal of the boundary conveniently marked as 'context,' and which is at the core of the cultural forms of both conventional and new sociologies of education.

Paths

Each of these paths of a reconstituted society/knowledge relation is already being travelled, and each has implications for how we shall understand knowledge and education socially, in the future. Each, therefore, is also a model for different directions after the new sociology of education. I want only to indicate the outlines of three contemporary 'responses' to the present sociohistorical and cultural transformations: the global symbolic movement and the local crisis of capital.

First, there are the post-industrial industrialists. In this model, there is a direct absorption of knowledge into the production process. This erases the claim of a boundary between universities as neutral professional sites of academic disciplines and social production. It is an institutional effect of industrial corporatism and state demands at the site of the 'higher learning.' The social organizational infrastructure of universities and professional associations that operated and legitimated 'basic science' as 'autonomous knowledge' during the industrial era, no longer offers the immediate productivity that a knowledge-energy production apparatus requires. The present arrangements can be seen as transitional, by noting various makeshift school–university and corporate–university–state linkages. Not simply 'corporate classrooms' are at issue, but the conversion in knowledge from science to technology. The translation of research into technology, the application of knowledge, is intensified and recoded so that there is less lagtime in production use. Knowledge is technology.

On this path, the university sells out its subsystem differentiation, as it now begins to sell its fixed capital for operating expenses. Sociology of education will then return to its efficiency-face of Progressivism, as a servant of power, with the end of basic knowledge as fixed capital: from autonomous, basic science to educated technology. The corporatism that I indicated earlier is thus only a preface to this fundamental reorganization in the production and distribution of knowledge.

A second path appears to retain the autonomy of the university, but at some cost. This is what I would call the new science. This is a version of what Rorty has described as 'the rise of textualism,' or of Rabinow and Sullivan's 'interpretive turn' in the social sciences. This is a denial of the view that I argued in this book – that symbolic theory is the high cultural representation of the information/semiotic society, despite that discourse's own denial of representation.

Textualism, in its scholasticism of the text, denies its own social/historicity in the same way that positivist scientism in social science claimed its methodological, historical and political neutrality. To the extent that Geertz and Rorty are right, and variants of interpretivism become the language and metaphor of the social sciences, the knowledge/society relation will remain denied by a socially deracinated approach to the internal relations of knowledge. That is exemplified by 'deconstruction' of the text that occurs without inter-textuality. What this means in sociology of education is a new methodologism to complement, if not replace, multivariate probabilism. This is already evident among the Yale Derrideans, and the literary routinization of the linguistic anti-ontological/metaphysical revolution as 'techniques' of literary method. What has already begun is a diffusion of systematic symbolic, textual interpretivism to social science. Post-structuralism also ends in technique. The result is that sociology of education will become 'textualized,' in the theory and method. But, the denial of the historical and social character of the changing knowledge/society boundary will remain. Textualism is the new scientism, and its potential for critical practice is reduced to assimilate technique.

The third path is a 'post-industrial populism,' which implies a transformation of social knowledge. Bernstein's (1983) summary of the development of a post-empiricist philosophy of science, and the community of inquirers who live, Kuhnian, 'beyond objectivism and relativism' is an idealist fore-shadowing of this change in the social relations of knowledge production.

On this path, knowledge is seen only partly as expert, but also as a means of public cultivation. The current hermeneutical interest in the social sciences, and the corollary emphasis on knowledge-traditions and communities, is, I think, a displaced partial realization of the possibility of public knowledge. Hermeneutical, like post-structuralist, interpretivism reforms sociology and education, as well as sociology of education toward a constructivist interest, yet without thereby examining the concrete social relations of knowledge implied. The sociopolitical implications are ignored.

Yet a post-sociology of education, a social analysis of education could emerge with post-industrialism. It would be one that practices the social boundary deconstruction of knowledge and exercises intelligent discursive reflection on social knowledge. In this way, sociology of education, by taking historical account of the variable institutional production of knowledge, becomes 'balanced' between expert and public, the reflexive moment of post-industrial knowledge. In that role, it makes education as collective discursive practice into a conscious social process.

At the same time, there is, I think, a relatively autonomous moment of expertise and professional difference within post-industrialism, a knowledge practice neither 'in-corporated' nor denied by scholasticism. The university can play a *differentiated*, active role which Latour (1983) ascribes to the social role of the scientific laboratory. By examining the concrete social relations of knowledge working across the knowledge/society boundary, Latour shows how a laboratory operates knowledge as settings for the development of 'inscription devices' (1983:165):

> The specificity of science is not to be found in cognitive, social or psychological qualities, but in the special construction of laboratories in a manner which reverses the scale of phenomena so as to make things *readable* [emphasis added], and then accelerates the frequency of trials, allowing many mistakes to be made and registered.

This view of 'inscription technology' and the particular material conditions of science as enabling unusual kinds of reading, takes the active moment of interpretivism. Against a displaced idealist populism, a material scientific practice of self-reflective reading examines the production, leverage, consumption, and finally the modern politics of knowledge as a new post-sociology of education.

The changed socio-political context of education and sociology of education is one in which education and knowledge are at the heart of the so-called context. The easiest solutions to the crises and possibilities of the present are, I think, to accept corporate education and a fully applied sociology of education on the one side, and, on the other, to laud and imitate the new science of interpretive textualism that insures a specialized, professional disciplinary community in the enclave of the university. The most difficult path, and the most promising, is to actively appropriate the awareness that historical change brings to the surface: awareness of the deeply socio-political concrete character of knowledge, science, and education and the asking of what that now implies for public social practice. In a semiotic even more than an industrial, society, knowledge is power.

Bibliography

Abel, E.K. (1984), *Terminal Degrees*, New York, Praeger.

Altbach, P.G. and Berdahl, R. (eds) (1981), *Higher Education in American Society*, Buffalo, Prometheus Books.

Altbach, P.G. Laufer, R.S. and McVey, S. (eds) (1971), *Academic Supermarkets: A critical Case Study of a Multiversity*, San Francisco, Jossey-Bass.

Althusser, L. (1971), 'Ideology and ideological state apparatuses,' in *Lenin and Philosophy and Other Essays*, New York, Monthly Review Press.

Anderson, P. (1976), *Considerations on Western Marxism*, London, New Left Books.

Anyon, J. (1979), 'Ideology and United States history textbooks,' *Harvard Educational Review*, vol. 49, no. 3, pp.361–86.

Anyon, J. (1981a), 'Social class and school knowledge,' *Curriculum Inquiry*, vol. 11, no. 1, pp. 3–41.

Anyon, J. (1981b), 'Elementary schooling and distinctions of social class,' *Interchange*, vol. 12, nos 2–3, pp. 118–32.

Anyon, J. (1983), 'Intersections of gender and class: accommodation and resistance by working-class and affluent females to contradictory sex ideologies,' in Stephen Walker and Len Barton (eds), *Gender, Class and Education*, Sussex, England, Falmer Press.

Apple, M.W. (1978), 'The new sociology of education: analyzing cultural and economic reproduction', *Harvard Educational Review*, vol. 48, no. 1, pp. 495–503.

Apple, M.W. (1979a), *Ideology and Curriculum*, Boston and London, Routledge & Kegan Paul.

Apple, M.W. (1979b), 'The other side of the hidden curriculum: correspondence theories and the labor process,' *Journal of Education*, vol. 162, no. 1, pp. 47–66.

Apple, M.W. (1981), 'Reproduction, contestation and curriculum: an essay in self-criticism,' *Interchange*, vol. 12, nos 2–3, pp. 27–47.

Apple, M.W. (ed.) (1982a), *Cultural and Economic Reproduction in Education*, Boston and London, Routledge & Kegan Paul.

Apple, M.W. (1982b), *Education and Power*, Boston and London, Routledge & Kegan Paul.

Apple, M.W. (1982c), 'Curricular form and the logic of technical control,' in M.W. Apple (ed.), *Cultural and Economic Reproduction in Education*, Boston and London, Routledge & Kegan Paul.

Apple, M.W. (1984), 'The political economy of text publishing,' *Educational Theory*, vol. 34, no.4, pp. 307–19.

Apple, M.W. and Weis, L. (eds) (1983), *Ideology and Practice in Schooling*, Philadelphia, Temple University Press.

Aronowitz, S. (1973), *False Promises*, New York, McGraw-Hill.

Aronowitz, S. (1978), 'Marx, Braverman, and the logic of capital,' *Insurgent Sociologist*, vol. 8, pp. 126–46.

Aronowitz, S. (1979), 'Film – the art form of late capitalism,' *Social Text*, 1, pp. 110–29.

Banks, O. (1982), 'The sociology of education: 1952–1982,' *British Journal of Educational Studies*, vol. 30, no.1, pp. 18–31.

Barthes, R. (1974), *S/Z*, New York, Hill & Wang.

Barthes, R. (1975), *The Pleasure of the Text*, New York, Hill & Wang.

Barthes, R. (1981), 'Theory of the text,' in R. Young (ed.), *Untying the text: A Post-Structuralist Reader*, Boston and London, Routledge & Kegan Paul.

Baudrillard, J. (1981), *For a Critique of the Political Economy of the Sign*, St Louis, Telos Press.

Bell, D. (1979), 'Communications technology: for better or for worse,' *Harvard Business Review*, vol. 1, no. 1, pp. 20–42.

Ben-David, J. (1978), 'Emergence of national traditions in the sociology of science: the United States and Great Britain,' in Jerry Gaston (ed.), *Sociology of Science*, San Francisco, Jossey-Bass.

Ben-David, J. and Collins, R. (1966), 'Social factors in the origins of a new science: the case of psychology,' *American Sociological Review*, vol. 31, no. 4, pp. 451–65.

Bender, T. (1984), 'The erosion of public culture: cities, discourses and professional disciplines', in Haskell, T., *Authority of Experts*, Bloomington, Indiana University Press.

Benjamin, W. (1969), *Illuminations*, New York, Schocken Books.

Bernstein, B. (1958), 'Some sociological determinants of perception: an enquiry into subcultural differences,' *The British Journal of Socoiology*, vol. IX, no. 2, pp. 159–74.

Bernstein, B. (1975), *Class, Codes, and Control: Towards a Theory of Educational Transmissions*, London, Routledge & Kegan Paul.

Bernstein, B. (1982), 'Codes, modalities and the process of cultural reproductions: a model,' in M.W. Apple (ed.), *Cultural and Economic Reproduction in Education*, Boston and London, Routledge & Kegan Paul.

Bernstein, R.J. (1983), *Beyond Objectivism and Relativism: Science, Hermeneutics, and Praxis*, Philadelphia, University of Pennsylvania Press.

Bertaux, D. (1981), 'From the life-history approach to the transformation of sociological practice,' in D. Bertaux (ed.), *Biography and Society: The Life History Approach in the Social Sciences*, Beverly Hills, Sage.

Biro, Y. (1982), *Profane Mythology*, Bloomington, Indiana University Press.

Black, H. (1967), *The American Schoolbook*, New York, William Morrow.

Bloom, B.S., Davis, A. and Hess, R. (1965), *Compensatory Education for Cultural Deprivation*, New York, Holt, Rinehart & Winston.

Bloom, H. (1975), *A Map of Misreading*, New York, Oxford University Press.

Bloom, H. (1982), *Agon*, New York, Oxford University Press.

Boardman, S.G. and Butler, M.J. (eds) (1981), 'Competency assessment in teacher education: making it work,' American Association of Colleges for Teacher Education, Washington, D.C.

Boocock, Sarane S. (1972), *An Introduction to the Sociology of Learning*, Boston, Houghton Mifflin.

Bottomore, T.B., and Rubel, M. (eds) (1956), *Karl Marx: Selected Writings in Sociology and Social Philosophy*, New York, McGraw-Hill.

Bourdieu, P. (1973), 'Cultural reproduction and social reproduction,' in R. Brown (ed.), *Knowledge, Education, and Cultural Change*, London, Tavistock.

Bourdieu, P. and Passerson, J.C. (1977), *Reproduction: In Education, Society and Culture*, London, Sage.

Bowles, S. and Gintis, H. (1976), *Schooling in Capitalist America*, New York, Basic Books.

Bowles, S. and Gintis, H. (1982), 'The crisis of liberal democratic capitalism: the case of the United States,' *Politics and Society*, vol. II, no. 1, pp. 51–93.

Boyd, W.L. (1978), 'The changing politics of curriculum policy-making for American schools,' *Review of Educational Research*, vol. 48, no. 4, pp. 577–628.

Breines, W. (1982), *Community and Organization in the New Left: 1962–1968*, New York, Praeger.

Brenkman, J. (1979), 'Mass media: from collective experience to the culture of privatization,' *Social Text*, vol. 1, pp. 94–109.

Brodinsky, R. (1982), 'The new right: the movement and its impact,' *Phi Delta Kappan*, vol. 64, no. 2, October.

Brown, R. (ed.) (1973), *Knowledge, Education, and Cultural Change*, London, Tavistock.

Brown, T.M. (1974), 'From mechanism to vitalism in eighteenth-century English physiology,' *Journal of the History of Biology*, vol. 7, no. 2, pp. 179–216.

Brown, T.M. (1979), 'Putting paradigms into history,' unpublished manuscript, Department of History, University of Rochester.

Burris, B.H. (1983), *No Room at the Top: Underemployment and Alienation in the Corporation*, New York, Praeger.

Callahan, R.E. (1962), *Education and the Cult of Efficiency*, Chicago, Chicago University Press.

Canter, L. (1979), 'Taking charge of student behavior,' *The Principal*, vol. 58, no. 4, pp. 33–41.

Card, B.Y. (1959), 'American educational sociology from 1890 to 1950: A sociological analysis,' unpublished Ph.D. dissertation, Stanford University.

Castells, M. (1980), *The Economic Crisis and American Society*, Princeton, New Jersey, Princeton University Press.

Castleman, C. (1982), *Getting Up*, Cambridge, Mass., MIT Press.

Cixous, H. (1981), 'The laugh of the Medusa,' in E. Marks and I. de Courtivron (eds), *New French Feminisms*, New York, Schocken Books.

Clarricoates, K. (1981), 'The experience of patriarchal schooling,' *Interchange*, vol. 12, nos 2–3, pp. 185–205.

Coleman, J.S. et al. (1966), *Equality of Educational Opportunity*, Washington, National Center for Educational Statistics.

Coleman, J.S., Hoffer, T. and Kilgore, S. (1982), 'Cognitive outcomes in public and private schools,' *Sociology of Education*, vol. 55, no. 2/3, pp. 65–76.

Cooper, D. (1971), *The Death of the Family*, New York, Pantheon Books.

Corrigan, P. and Willis, P. (1980), 'Cultural forms and class mediations,' *Media, Culture and Society*, no. 2, pp. 297–312.

Coward, R. and Ellis, J. (1977), *Language and Materialism: Developments in Semiology and the Theory of the Subject*, Boston and London, Routledge & Kegan Paul.

Crichlow, W. (1988), 'Coming to terms: a study of the responses of Afro-American students to processes of education in an urban high school,' Ed.D. dissertation, University of Rochester, in preparation.

Curti, M. (1935), *The Social Ideas of American Educators*, Totowa, New Jersey, Littlefield, Adams & Co.

Dannefer, W.D. (1980), 'Rationality and passion in private experience: modern consciousness and the social world of old cars,' *Social Problems*, vol. 27, no. 4, pp. 392–412.

Deleuze, Gilles and Guattari, F. (1979), *Anti-Oedipus: Capitalism and Schizophrenia*, New York, Viking Press.

Derber, C. (1983), 'Managing professionals,' *Theory and Society*, vol. 12, pp. 309–41.

Derrida, J. (1970), 'Structure, sign, and play in the discourse of the human sciences,' in R. Macksey and E. Donato (eds), *The Language of Criticism and the Sciences of Man: The Structuralist Controversy*, Baltimore, Johns Hopkins University Press.

Derrida, J. (1979), *Spurs*, Chicago, University of Chicago Press.

Derrida, J. (1982), *Margins of Philosophy*, Chicago, University of Chicago Press.

Dewey, J. (1927), *The Public and Its Problems*, Athens, Ohio, Swallow Press.

Dewey, J. (1929), *The Quest for Certainty*, New York, Minton, Balch & Co.

Dizard, W.P. Jr. (1982), *The Coming Information Age*, New York, Longman.

Dreeben, R. (1968), *On What is Learned in School*, Reading, Mass., Addison-Wesley.

Dreyfus, H.L. and Rabinow, P. (1982), *Michel Foucault: Beyond Structuralism and Hermeneutics*, Chicago, University of Chicago Press.

Durkheim, E. (1957), *The Elementary Forms of the Religious Life*, London, Allen & Unwin.

Eagleton, T. (1976a), *Criticism and Ideology: A Study in Marxist Literary Theory*, London, New Left Books.

Eagleton, T. (1976b), *Marxism and Literary Criticism*, Berkeley, University of California.

Eagleton, T. (1983), *Literary Theory*, Oxford, Basil Blackwell.

Eco, U. (1979), *The Role of the Reader: Explorations in the Semiotics of Texts*, Bloomington, Indiana University Press.

Education Week (1982), Education Summary, 'Curriculum,' Nov. 3, p. 5.

Education Week (1982), 'New data indicate lag in state aid to public schools,' Nov. 3, p. 13.

Edwards, R. (1979), *Contested Terrain: The Transformation of Workplace in the Twentieth Century*, New York, Basic Books.

Ehrenreich, B. and Ehrenreich, J. (1977a), 'The professional-managerial class,' *Radical America*, vol. 11, no. 2, pp. 7–31.

Ehrenreich, B. and Ehrenreich, J. (1977b), 'The new left,' *Radical America*, vol. II, no. 3, pp. 7–22.

Ellis, J. (1982), *Visible Fictions*, London, Routledge & Kegan Paul.

Epstein, E.J. (1973), *News from Nowhere: Television and the News*, New York, Random House.

Euchner, C. (1982), 'New tracking systems needed, excellence commission is told,' *Education Week*, Oct. 6, p. 8.

Eurich, Nell P. (1985), *Corporate Classrooms*, New Jersey, Princeton University Press.

Ewen, S. (1976), *Captains of Consciousness*, New York, McGraw-Hill.

Ewen, S. and Ewen, E. (1982), *Channels of Desire*, New York, McGraw-Hill.

Featherman, D.L. and Hauser, R.M. (1978), *Opportunity and Change*, New York, Academic Press.

Federation of Behavioral, Psychological and Cognitive Sciences, Greeno, J.G. (1982) 'Plan for a meeting in research retention education in mathematics, science and technology,' November.

Feldman, K.A. (1971), 'Some methods for assessing college impacts,' *Sociology of Education*, vol. 44, no. 2, pp. 133–50.

Fendrich, J. and Imersheim, A. (1982), 'Economic and political responses to the Reagan fiscal and monetary policies,' presented at the 77th Annual Meeting of the American Sociology Association, San Francisco, September.

Feuer, J. (1983), 'The concept of live television: ontology as ideology,' in E.A. Kaplan (ed.), *Regarding Television*, Frederick, Maryland, University Publications of America.

Feuer, L.S. (ed.) (1959), *Basic Writings on Politics and Philosophy: Karl Marx and Friedrich Engels*, Garden City, New York, Anchor Books.

Finlay-Pelinski, M. (1982), 'Semiotics or history: from content analysis to contextualized discursive praxis,' *Semiotica*, vol. 40, no. 314, pp. 229–66.

Finney, R.L. (1922), *Causes and Cures for the Soviet Unrest: An Appeal to the Middle Class*, New York, Macmillan.

Fitzgerald, F. (1979), *America Revised*, Boston, Little Brown.

Flacks, R. (1967), 'The liberated generation: an exploration of the roots of student protest,' *Journal of Social Issues*, vol. 23, pp. 52–75.

Flacks, R. (1971), *Youth and Social Change*, Chicago, Markham.

Foster, S.G. (1982), 'Service economy and technological change will require new skills, experts predict,' *Education Week*, Nov. 3, p. 6.

Foucault, M. (1970), *The Order of Things: An Archaeology of the Human Sciences*, New York, Random House.

Foucault, M. (1972), *The Archaeology of Knowledge*, New York, Harper, Torchbooks.

Foucault, M. (1978), *The History of Sexuality, vol. I*, New York, Pantheon Books.

Foucault, M. (1979), *Discipline and Punish: The Birth of Prison*, New York, Vintage Books.

Foucault, M. (1981), 'The order of the text,' in R. Young (ed.), *Untying the Text: A Post-Structuralist Reader*, Boston and London, Routledge & Kegan Paul.

Foucault, M. (1982), 'The subject and power,' in H.L. Dreyfus and P. Rabinow, *Michel Foucault: Beyond Structuralism and Hermeneutics*, Chicago, University of Chicago Press.

Fox, R. (1945), *The Novel and the People*, New York, International Publishers.

Frankfurt Institute of Social Research (1956), *Aspects of Sociology*, Boston, Beacon.

Friedan, B. (1981), *The Second Stage*, New York, Summit.

Friedrichs, G. and Schaff, A. (eds) (1983), *Microelectronics and Society: A Report to the Club of Rome*, New York, Pergamon Press.

Gabler, M. and Gabler N. (1982), 'Mind control through textbook,' *Phi Delta Kappan*, vol. 64, no. 2, October, p.96.

Gadamer, H. (1984), *Truth and Method*, New York, Crossroad.

Gauthier, X. (1981), 'Why witches,' in E. Marks and I. de Courtivron (eds), *New French Feminisms*, New York, Schocken Books.

Geertz, C. (1973), *The Interpretation of Cultures*, New York, Basic.

Geertz, C. (1980), 'Blurred genres: The refiguration of social thought,' *American Scholar*, Spring, pp. 115–79.

Giddens, A. (1979), *Central Problems in Social Theory: Actions, Contradictions and Structure in Social Analysis*, London, Macmillan.

Giroux, H.A. (1981), *Ideology, Culture, and the Process of Schooling*, Philadelphia, Temple University Press.

Giroux, H. (1983), *Theory and Resistance in Education*, South Hadley, Massachusetts, Bergin & Garvey Publishers.

Goffman, E. (1962), *Asylums*, Chicago, Aldine.

Golding, P. and Murdock, G. (1979), 'Ideology and the mass media: the question of determination,' in M. Barret, P. Corrigan, A. Kuhn and J. Wolf (eds), *Ideology and Cultural Production*, New York, St Martin's Press, pp. 198–224.

Goldmann, L. (1976), *Cultural Creation in Modern Society*, St Louis, Telos Press.

Gorbutt, D. (1972), 'The new sociology of education,' *Education for Teaching*, pp. 3–11.

Gordon, D. (1980), 'Stages of accumulation and long cycles,' in T. Hopkins and I. Wallerstein (eds), *Processes of the World System*, Beverly Hills, Sage.

Gouldner, A.W. (1970), *The Coming Crisis of Western Sociology*, New York, Avon.

Gouldner, A.W. (1979), *The Future of Intellectuals and the Rise of the New Class*, New York, Seabury Press.

Gramsci, A. (1971), *Selections from the Prison Notebooks*, New York, International.

Graubard, A. (1974), *Free the Childern: Radical Reform and the Free*

School Movement, New York, Vintage.

Greenberg, D.S. (1982), 'Gives slight reason to cheer,' *Education Week*, June 10, p. 19.

Habermas, J. (1981), 'New social movements,' *Telos*, no. 49, pp. 33–7, Fall.

Hall, S. (1981), 'Moving right,' *Socialist Review*, no. 55, pp. 113–37.

Halsey, A.H., Floud, J. and Anderson, C. (eds) (1961), *Education, Economy, and Society*, New York, Free Press.

Hammond, J.L. and Martin, G.T. Jr. (1982), 'The Reagan program: ruling class response to economic crisis,' presented at the Annual American Sociological Association, San Francisco, September.

Handelman, Susan A. (1982), *The Slayers of Moses*, Albany State University of New York Press.

Hargreaves, A. (1982), 'Resistance and relative autonomy theories: problems of distortion and incoherence in recent Marxist analyses of education,' *British Journal of Sociology of Education*, vol. 3, no. 2, pp. 107–126.

Haskell, Thomas L. (1984), *The Authority of Experts*, Bloomington, Indiana University Press.

Hawkes, T. (1977), *Structuralism and Semiotics*, London, Methuen.

Hawley, Ellis W. (1978), 'The discovery and study of "corporate liberalism",' *Business History Review*, vol. 3, no. 3, pp. 309–20.

Heard, A. (1982), 'Private schools' enrollment falls, census reports,' *Education Week*, Oct. 13, p.1.

Heard, A. (1982), 'Colorado district turns to private financing of construction,' *Education Week*, October 20, p. 6.

Hebdige, D. (1979), *Subcultures: The Meaning of Style*, London. Methuen.

Held, D. (1980), *Introduction to Critical Theory*, Berkeley, University of California Press..

Henderson, B. (1976), 'Two types of film theory,' in B. Nichols (ed.), *Movies and Methods: An Anthology*, Berkeley, University of California Press.

Heydebrand, W.V. (1983), 'Technocratic corporatism: toward a theory of occupational and organizational transformation,' in R. Hall and R. Quinn (eds), *Organizational Theory and Public Policy*, Beverly Hills, California, Sage.

Hofstadter, R. (1955), *Social Darwinism in American Thought*, Boston, Beacon.

Hohendal, P.U. (1982), *The Institution of Criticism*, Ithaca, Cornell University Press.

Hollingshead, A.B. (1949), *Elmtown's Youth: The Impact of Social Classes on Adolescents*, New York, Wiley.

Hoover, T. et al. (1982), 'State superintendents respond to Reaganomics,' *Phi Delta Kappan*, vol. 64, no, 2, Oct., pp. 124–5.

Horkheimer, M. (1972), *Critical Theory*, New York, Herder & Herder.

Horkheimer, M. and Adorno, T.W. (1972), *Dialectic of Enlightenment*, New York, Herder & Herder.

Howard, R.J. (1982), *Three Faces of Hermeneutics*, Berkeley, University of California Press.

Huber, Margaret A. (1981), 'The renewal of curriculum theory in the 1970's: An historical study,' *Journal of Curriculum Theorizing*, vol. 3, no. 1, pp. 14–84.

Husen, T. and Postlethwaite, T. Neville (eds) (1985), *The International Encylopedia of Education*, Oxford, Pergamon Press.

Illich, I. (1971), *Deschooling Society*, New York, Harper & Row.

Irigaray, L. (1981), 'This sex which is not one,' in E. Marks and I. de Courtivron (eds), *New French Feminisms*, New York, Schocken Books.

Iser, W. (1978), *The Act of Reading: A Theory of Aesthetic Response*, Baltimore, Johns Hopkins University Press.

Jameson, F. (1972), *The Prison-House of Language: A Critical Account of Structuralism and Russian Formalism*, Princeton, Princeton University Press.

Johnson, K. (1985), 'How does ideology mobilise?' unpublished manuscript.

Kaplan, E.A. (ed.) (1983), *Regarding Television*, Frederick, Maryland, University Publications of America.

Karabel, J. and Halsey, A.H. (1976), 'The new sociology of education,' *Theory and Society*, vol. 3, no. 4, pp. 529–52.

Karabel, J. and Halsey, A.H. (1977), *Power and Ideology in Education*, New York, Oxford University Press.

Karier, C.J., Vidas, P.C. and Spring, J. (eds) (1973), *Roots of Crisis: American Education in the 20th Century*, Chicago, Rand McNally.

Katz, M.B. (1968), *The Irony of Early School Reform: Education Innovation in Mid-Nineteenth Century Massachusetts*, Cambridge, Mass., Harvard University Press.

Katz, M.B. (1971), *Class Bureaucracy and Schools: The Illusion of Educational Change in America*, New York, Praeger.

Kelley, D.R. (1982), *The Beginning of Ideology: Consciousness and Society in the French Reformation*, New York, Cambridge University Press.

Keniston, K. (1968), *Young Radicals*, New York, Harcourt, Brace & World.

Kermode, F. (1983), 'The common reader,' *Daedalus*, vol. 112, no. 1, pp. 1–11.

Kerr, C. and Gade, M. (1981), 'Current and emerging issues facing

American higher education,' in P.A. Altbach and R.O. Berdahl (eds), *Higher Education in American Society*, Buffalo, Prometheus Books.

Kerr, N.D. (1964), 'The school board as an agency of legitimation,' *Sociology of Education*, vol. 38, no. 1, pp. 34–59.

King, A. (1983), 'Introduction: a new industrial revolution or just another technology?,' in G. Friedrichs and A. Schaff (eds), *Microelectronics and Society: A Report to the Club of Rome*, New York, A Mentor Book.

Kirst, M.W. (1981), 'Loss of support of public secondary schools: some causes and solutions,' *Daedalus*, vol. 110, no. 3, pp. 45–68.

Knorr-Cetina, K.D. and Michael Mulkay (1983), *Science Observed*, Beverly Hills, Sage.

Kristeva, J. (1980), *Desire in Language: A Semiotic Approach to Literature and Art*, New York, Columbia University Press.

Lasch, C. (1984), *The Minimal Self*, New York, W.W. Norton.

Latour, B. (1983), 'Give me a laboratory and I will raise The World,' in Knorr-Cetina, K.D. and Mulkay, M., *Science Observed*, Beverly Hills, Sage.

LaVorgna, J.P. (1982), 'Schools in the workplace,' *Phi Delta Kappan*, vol. 64, no. 2, October, pp. 128–9.

Lazerson, M. (1971), *Origins of the Urban School: Public Education in Massachusetts 1870–1915*, Cambridge, Mass., Harvard University Press.

Lemert, C.C. and Gillan, G. (1982), *Michel Foucault: Social Theory as Transgression*, New York, Columbia University Press.

Lenk, K. (1983), 'Information technology and society,' in G. Friedrichs and A. Schaff (eds), *Microelectronics and Society: A Report to the Club of Rome*, New York, Mentor.

Lentricchia, F. (1980), *After the New Criticism*, Chicago, University of Chicago Press.

Lifton, R.J. (1961), *Thought Reform and the Psychology of Totalism*, New York, W.W. Norton.

Livant, B. (1975), 'The "Communications" commodity,' unpublished manuscript.

Livant, B. (1982), 'Working at watching: to reply a Sut Jhally,' *Canadian Journal of Political and Social Theory*, vol. 6, nos 1–2, pp. 211–15.

Livingstone, David (1987), *Critical Pedagogy and Cultural Power*, Massachusetts, Bergin & Garvey.

Lukács, G. (1971), *History and Class Consciousness: Studies in Marxist Dialectics*, Cambridge, Mass., MIT Press.

Luke, T. (1983), 'Informationalism and ecology,' *Telos*, vol. 54, summer, pp. 59–73.

Lyotard, J. (1984), *The Postmodern Condition: A Report on Knowledge*, Minneapolis, University of Minnesota Press.

MacCannell, D. and MacCannell, J.F. (1982), *The Time of the Sign*, Bloomington, Indiana University Press.

MacDonald, M. (1980), 'Socio-cultural reproduction and women's education,' in Rosemary Deem (ed.), *Schooling for Women's Work*, London, Routledge & Kegan Paul.

McNeil, L.M. (1981), Response to Henry Giroux's 'Pedagogy, Pessimism, and the Politics of Conformity,' *Curriculum Inquiry*, vol. 11, no. 4, Winter, pp. 393–4.

MacPherson, C.B. (1962), *The Political Theory of Possessive Individualism: Hobbes to Locke*, London, Oxford University Press.

Mannheim, K. (1936), *Ideology and Utopia: An Introduction to the Sociology of Knowledge*, New York, Harcourt, Brace & World.

Marable, M. (1980), 'Black nationalism in the 1970's: through the prism of race and class,' *Socialist Review*, nos 50–51, summer, pp. 57–108.

Marable, M. (1981), *Blackwater: Historical Studies in Race, Class Consciousness and Revolution*, Dayton, Ohio, Black Praxis Press.

Marcuse, H. (1955), *Eros and Civilization*, Boston, Beacon Press.

Marcuse, H. (1968), 'The affirmative character of culture,' *Negations*, Boston, Beacon.

Marx, K. (1959), *Selections*, Moscow, Foreign Languages Publishing House.

Marx, Karl (1971), *Capital: Volume One*, New York, International.

Melucci, A. (1980), 'The new social movements: a theoretical approach,' *Social Science Information*, vol. 19, no. 2, pp. 199–226.

Miles, M.W. (1971), *The Radical Probe*, New York, Atheneum.

Mills, C.W. (1956), *The Power Elite*, New York, Oxford University Press.

Mirga, T. and White, E. (1982), 'Poll finds rising concern about school finance,' *Education Week*, Sep. 1, p. 1.

Mosco, V. (1982), *Pushbutton Fantasies*, Norwood, New Jersey, Ablex.

Newman, F. (1985), *Higher Education and the American Resurgence*, New York, Carnegie.

Nichols, B. (1981), *Ideology and the Image*, Bloomington, Indiana University Press.

Noble, D. (1982), 'The selling of the university,' *The Nation*, February 6, pp. 143–8.

Ogbu, J.U. (1981), 'School ethnography: a multilevel approach,' *Anthropology and Education Quarterly*, vol. 12, no. 1, pp. 3–29.

Olsen, P. (1981), 'Theme issue: rethinking social reproduction,' *Interchange*, vol. 12, nos 2–3.

Palmer, R.E. (1969), *Hermeneutics*, Evanston, Illinois, Northwestern University Press.

Panitch, L. (1977), 'The development of corporatism in Liberal democracies,' *Comparative Political Studies*, vol. 10, no. 1, 61–90.

Parenti, M. (1980), 'Political bigotry in academe,' *Chronicle of Higher Education*, vol. 19, no. 18, p. 56.

Parsons, T. (1959), 'The school class as a social system: some of its functions in American society,' *Harvard Educational Review*, vol. 29, no. 4, pp. 292–318.

Parsons, T. (1968), 'The Academic System: a sociologist's view', *The Public Interest*, 13, 173–97.

Perkinson, H.J. (1968), *The Imperfect Panacea: American Faith in Education, 1865–1965*, New York, Random House.

Persell, C.H. (1977), *Education and Inequality*, New York, Free Press.

Peters, C.C. (1924), *Foundations of Educational Sociology*, New York, Macmillan.

Phillips, K. (1982), 'Post conservative America,' *N.Y. Review*, May 13, pp. 27–32.

Picou, J.S. (1979), 'Research patterns in the sociology of education: 1963–1978,' presented at Sociology of Education, ASA Meetings, Boston, Massachusetts.

Pinar, W.F. (1979), 'The abstract and the concrete in curriculum theorizing,' unpublished manuscript, Graduate School of Education and Human Development, University of Rochester.

Piven, F.F. and Cloward, R.A. (1982), *The New Class War*, New York, Pantheon Books.

Przeworski, A. (1977), 'Proletariat into a class: the process of class formation from Karl Kautsky's "The Class Struggle" to recent controversies,' *Politics and Society*, no. 4, pp. 343–401.

Rabinow, P. (ed.) (1984), *The Foucault Reader*, New York, Pantheon Books.

Rabinow, P. and Sullivan, W.M. (eds) (1979), *Interpretive Social Science*, Berkeley, University of California Press.

Rada, J. (1980), *The Impact of Micro-Electronics*, Geneva, International Labour Organisation.

Ranbom, S. (1982), 'Americans view college as path to better life,' *Education Week*, Oct. 20, p. 11.

Reimer, E. (1972), *School is Dead: Alternatives in Education*, Garden City, New York, Anchor.

Richards, R.R. (1970), 'Perspectives on sociological inquiry in education 1917–1940,' unpublished Ph.D. dissertation, The University of Wisconsin.

Ricoeur, P. (1981), *Hermeneutics and the Human Sciences*, New York, Cambridge University Press.

Roberts, D.F. and Bachen, C.M. (1981), 'Mass communication effects,' *Annual Reviews of Psychology*, vol. 32, pp. 307–56.

Roberts, J. (1982), 'Classes in chaos,' *Wall Street Journal*, May 13, p. 1.

Rohatyn, F. (1981), 'Reconstructing America,' *N.Y. Review*, Mar. 5, pp. 16–20.

Rohatyn, F. (1982), 'The state of the banks,' *N.Y. Review*, Nov. 4, pp. 3–8.

Rorty, R. (1979), *Philosophy and the Mirror of Nature*, Princeton, New Jersey, Princeton University Press.

Rorty, R. (1982), *Consequences of Pragmatism*, Sussex, England, Harvester Press.

Rosen, B.C. (1961), 'Family structure and achievement motivation,' *American Sociological Review*, vol. 26, no. 4, pp. 574–85.

Rothman, S. and Lichter, S.R. (1982), *Roots of Radicalism: Jews, Christians, and the New Left*, New York, Oxford University Press.

Ruby, J. (ed.) (1982), *A Crack in the Mirror: Reflective Perspectives in Anthropology*, Philadelphia, University of Philadelphia Press.

Rude, G. (1980), *Ideology and Popular Protest*, New York, Pantheon.

Salganik, L.H. (1981), 'The fall and rise of vouchers,' *Teachers College Record*, vol. 83, no. 2, pp. 263–83.

Schiller, H.I. (1981), *Who Knows: Information in the Age of the Fortune 500*, Norwood, New Jersey, Ablex.

Schiller, H.I. (1984), *Information and the Crisis Economy*, Norwood, New Jersey, Ablex.

Schlechty, P. and Vance, V.S. (1982), 'Recruitment, selection and retention: the shape of the teaching force,' *National Institute of Education*, Washington, D.C.

Scholes, R. (1982), *Semiotics and Interpretation*, New Haven, Yale University Press.

Sewell, W.H. (1981), 'Inequality of opportunity for higher education,' *American Sociological Review*, vol. 36, no. 5, pp. 793–809.

Shapin, S. (1980), 'Social uses of science,' in G.S. Rouseau and R. Porter (eds), *The Ferment of Knowledge*, New York, Cambridge University Press.

Sharp, R. (1980), *Knowledge, Ideology and the Politics of Schooling: Towards a Marxist Analysis of Education*, Boston, Routledge & Kegan Paul.

Silver, H. (1965), *The Concept of Popular Education*, London, Mac-Gibbon & Kee.

Simon, R.I. (1985), 'Critical pedagogy,' in T. Husen and N. Postlewaite (eds), *The International Encyclopedia of Education*, Oxford Pergamon.

Spring, J.H. (1972), *Education and the Rise of the Corporate State*, Boston, Beacon.

Spring, J.H. (1976), *The Sorting Machine*, New York, McKay.

Stadtman, V.A. (1981), 'Happenings on the way to the 1980s,' in P.A. Altbach and R.O. Berdahl (eds), *Higher Education in American Society*, Buffalo, Prometheus Books.

Stam, R. (1983), 'Television news and its spectator,' in E.A. Kaplan (ed.), *Regarding Television*, Frederick, Maryland, University Publications of America.

Stearns, P.N. (1980), 'Toward a wider vision: trends in social history,' in Michael Kammen (ed.), *The Past Before Us: Contemporary Historical Writing in the United States*, Ithaca, Cornell University Press.

Sutton, F.X. et al. (1956), *The American Business Creed*, Cambridge, Mass., Harvard University Press.

Szreter, R. (1980), 'Institutionalising a new specialism: early years of the Journal of Educational Sociology,' *British Journal of Sociology of Education*, vol. 1, no. 2, pp. 173–82.

Taxel, J. (1980), 'The depiction of the American revolution in children's fiction: A study in the sociology of school knowledge,' Ph.D. dissertation, University of Wisconsin.

Thompson, E.P. (1978), 'Eighteenth-century English society: class struggle without class?' *Social History*, vol. 3, no. 2, pp. 133–65.

Thompson, P. (1978), *The Voice of the Past: Oral History*, Oxford, Oxford University Press.

Toch, T. (1982), 'New activism marks corporate role in schools,' *Education Week*, Nov. 10, p. 1.

Toffler, A. (1971), *Future Shock*, New York, Bantam.

Touraine, A. (1981), *The Voice and the Eye*, New York, Cambridge University Press.

Trotsky, L. (1975), *Literature and Revolution*, Ann Arbor, University of Michigan Press.

Turner, R.H. (1976), 'The real self: from institution to impulse,' *American Journal of Sociology*, vol. 82, pp. 989–1014.

Tyack, D. and Hansot, E. (1982), *Managers of Virtue, Public School Leadership in America, 1820–1980*, New York, Basic Books.

van den Berg, A. (1980), 'Critical theory: is there still hope?,' *American Journal of Sociology*, vol. 86, no. 3, pp. 449–78.

Walker, P. (ed.) (1979), *Between Labor and Capital*, Boston, South End Press.

Wallace, A.F.C. (1978), 'Paradigmatic processes in culture change,' in *Rockdale: The Growth of an American Village in the Early Industrial Revolution*, New York, Knopf.

Walton, S. (1982), 'A.F.T. Businesses to explore problems in science education,' *Education Week*, Nov. 17.

Weber, M. (1963), *The Sociology of Religion*, Boston, Beacon.

Weisskopf, T. (1981), 'The current economic crisis in historical perspective,' *Socialist Review*, vol. 57, pp. 9–53.

Wells, R.H. and Picou, J.S. (1981), *American Sociology: Theoretical and Methodological Structure*, Washington, D.C., University Press of America, Inc.

Welter, R. (1962), *Popular Education and Democratic Thought in America*, New York, Columbia University Press.

Wexler, P. (1976), *The Sociology of Education: Beyond Equality*, Indianapolis, Bobbs-Merrill.

Wexler, P. (1977), 'Comment on Ralph Turner's "The Real Self: From Institution to Impulse" ' *American Journal of Sociology*, vol. 83, no. 1, pp. 178–85.

Wexler, P. (1978), 'Ideology and utopia in American sociology of education,' in A. Kloskowska and G. Martinotti (eds), *Education in a Changing Society*, Beverly Hills, California, Sage.

Wexler, P. (1981), 'Body and soul: sources of social change and strategies of education,' *British Journal of Sociology of Education*, vol. 2, no. 3, pp. 247–63.

Wexler, P. (1982), 'Ideology and education: from critique to class action,' *Interchange*, vol. 13, no. 3, pp. 53–78.

Wexler, P. (1983), *Critical Social Psychology*, Boston and London, Routledge & Kegan Paul.

Wexler, P. (1985a), 'Social change and practice of social education,' *Social Education*, vol. 49, no. 5, pp. 390–4.

Wexler, P. (1985b), 'After social psychology,' in H. Stam and T. Rogers (eds), *Metapsychology and Psychological Theory*, New York, Hemisphere.

Wexler, P. and Grabiner, G. (1985), 'The education question: America during the crisis,' in R. Sharp (ed.), *Capitalist Crisis, Education and the State: A Comparative Politics of Education*, Melbourne, Macmillan.

Wexler, P. and Whitson, T. (1982), 'Hegemony and education,' *Psychology and Social Theory*, no. 3, Fall, pp. 31–42.

Wexler, P., Whitson, T. and Moskowitz, E.J. (1981), 'Deschooling by default: the changing social functions of public schools,' *Interchange*, vol. 12, nos 2–3, pp. 133–50.

Wexler, P. et al. (1988), *Becoming Somebody: Studies in High School*, in preparation.

Wexler, P. Martusewicz, R. and Kern J. (1987), 'Popular Educational Politics' in D. Livingstone (ed.), *Critical Pedagogy and Cultural Power*, South Hadley, Bergin & Garvey.

Whitley, R.D. (1977), *Social Processes of Scientific Development*, London, Routledge & Kegan Paul.

Whitson, J.A. (1985), 'Socializing influences and "the freedom of speech": textual approaches to interdisciplinary interpretation in education, law, and social sciences,' unpublished Ph.D. dissertation, University of Rochester.

Whitty, G. and Young, M. (eds) (1976), *Explorations in the Politics of School Knowledge*, Nafferton, Driffield, England, Nafferton Books.

Williams, G.A. (1969), *Artisans and Sans-Culottes: Popular Movements in France and Britain During the French Revolution*, New York, W.W. Norton.

Williams, R. (1977), *Marxism and Literature*, New York, Oxford University Press.

Willis, P. (1977), *Learning to Labour: How Working Class Kids get Working Class Jobs*, Westmead, England, Saxon House.

Willis, P. and P. Corrigan (1983), 'Orders of experience: the differences of working class cultural forms', *Social Text*, vol. 7, Spring/Summer, pp. 5–105.

Wirt, F.M. and Kirst, M.W. (1982), *Schools in Conflict*, Berkeley, McCutchan.

Wolin, S. (1980), 'Paradigms and political theories,' in G. Gutting (ed.), *Paradigms and Revolutions: Appraisals and Applications of Thomas Kuhn's Philosophy of Science*, London, Notre Dame.

Wright, W. (1977), *Six Guns and Society: A Structural Study of the Western*, Berkeley, University of California Press.

Wrigley, J. (1980), 'Class politics and school reform in Chicago,' in Zeitlin, M. (ed.), *Classes, Class Conflict, and The State: Empirical Studies in Class Analysis*, Cambridge, Mass., Winthrop.

Wrigley, J. (1982), *Class Politics and Public Schools*, New Brunswick, New Jersey, Rutgers University Press.

Yale French Studies (1982), *The Pedagogical Imperative: Teaching as a Literary Genre*, no. 63, New Haven, Yale University Press.

Young, M.F.D. (ed.) (1971), *Knowledge and Control: New Directions for the Sociology of Education*, London, Collier-Macmillan.

Young, M. and Whitty, G. (1977), *Society, State and Schooling*, Sussex, England, Falmer Press.

Young, R. (1973), 'The historiographic and ideological contents of the nineteenth century debate on man's place in nature,' in M. Teich and R. Young (eds.), *Changing Perspectives in the History of Science: Esssays in Honour of Joseph Needham*, London, Heinemann.

Young, R. (1981), *Untying the Text: A Post-Structuralist Reader*, Boston and London, Routledge & Kegan Paul.

Index